GRADING IN THE POST-PROCESS CLASSROOM

From Theory to Practice

EDITED BY

LIBBY ALLISON
LIZBETH BRYANT
MAUREEN HOURIGAN

CrossCurrents

New Perspectives in Rhetoric and Composition

CHARLES I. SCHUSTER, SERIES EDITOR

BOYNTON/COOK PUBLISHERS
HEINEMANN
PORTSMOUTH, NH

Boynton/Cook Publishers, Inc.
A subsidiary of Reed Elsevier, Inc.
361 Hanover Street
Portsmouth, NH 03801-3912

Offices and agents throughout the world

Library of Congress Cataloging-in-Publication Data
Grading in the post-process classroom : from theory to practice /
edited by Libby Allison, Lizbeth Bryant, and Maureen Hourigan.
    p.   cm.
    Includes bibliographical references.
    ISBN 0-86709-437-0
    1. Grading and marking (Students)—United States. I. Allison,
Libby. II. Bryant, Lizbeth. III. Hourigan, Maureen M., 1942–
LB3051.G66683   1997
371.27'2—dc21
                                                   97-28934
                                                       CIP

Series Editor: Charles Schuster
Production: Elizabeth Valway
Cover Design: Joanne Tranchemontagne
Manufacturing: Louise Richardson

Printed in the United States of America on acid-free paper

01 00 99 98 97 DA 1 2 3 4 5

To the Jims and Joe in Our Lives,
and to Our Students, Past, Present, and Future

Contents

Foreword
Two Stories Absent Their Morals

Story One

Years ago, a student arrived at my office door midsemester to talk, not about writing, revising, or next week's assignment. Nor about literature, life, the Vietnam War, the structure of the university, or any one of innumerable subjects about which we could have had a meaningful dialogue.

She came to talk about her grade. "Why did you give me a C+ on this essay?" she asked, not with hostility, not belligerently, but with steady and unswerving insistence. "Well," I said, trying to deflect her inquiry like any good pedagogue, "Let's talk about what you can do to improve it." That talk, not surprisingly, consisted largely of a monologue in which I told her what was wrong, what could be changed, and how she might restructure her ideas. She listened, but not really (nor at this late remove can I blame her). Every few minutes, as I paused or turned a page, she asked a variation of the same question: "If I do what you say, will I earn an A?" "If I make these changes, will you raise my grade to an A?" After I had gone on for about 35 minutes, she said, "I see what you are saying, but what I really want to know is—will that earn me an A???"

"An A!?" I finally exploded. "You think the only thing that is important is the grade!" I nearly shrieked. "Here," I went on, "you don't like the C+ I gave you, I'll raise it to a B. How's that?" And as she sat staring at the paper, I crossed out the old grade and replaced it with a B. "No," I said, "I can see that you are still not satisfied. You want an A? Here it is." And I crossed out the B and in its place marked a three-inch high A.

The student stared at me in disbelief. "Are you really going to change it to an A?" she asked. "YES!" I said, opening my grade book and putting a big, inky A next to her name. "See," I said, "there it is. I'll bet just an A isn't good enough for you," I continued, feeling myself on a roll. "Here, I'll give you an A+; does that make you feel better about your work? How about an A+++++++?" I marked seven pluses after the A. "Now are you satisfied? Since all you want is the grade, here it is, in ink, right in my grade book. Now you have gotten what you came for. We have nothing more to talk about."

She left a few minutes later in dubious triumph, taking with her the essay on top of which I had marked an A+++++++. She knew that the A was not real, no matter how exorbitantly it stood atop her work. I sat there half fuming, half pleased with my hyperbolic gesture.

The student continued to attend class regularly and to participate in discussions. She wrote the rest of the required essays, but we never communicated our different interests, never bridged that gap between my wanting her to care about what I was teaching and her wanting me to care about giving out A's. She never came to see me again.

Some Observations

One: Ultimately, the student earned a B in my course. I think she really deserved a B, but who can say? Frankly, grading was totally up to me; maybe I gave her a lower grade out of perversity. Was it because I thought she so exclusively wanted an A that I knew she did not deserve one?

Two: I think she knew that I would find some way not to give her a final grade of A, no matter what she did, how hard she tried, how many inky A's I marked on top of her essays or in my grade book. I think she may have been right.

Three: Part of what I wanted to do was teach her a lesson about learning. I failed.

Four: Another of my motivations, whether she realized it or not, was to humiliate her.

Five: My student's motive was less complicated: she wanted a 4.0, for whatever reasons. She taught me a lesson that I only slowly learned—namely, that grades matter. To many students, they matter more than learning. And unless we can somehow resolve satisfactorily the issue of grading with our students, a wide range of possibilities gets shut down.

Six: When I think of this student now—and of the many others who have tried to bridge that gulf between the A and the B or the C (between, to paraphrase Mark Twain, lightning and the lightning bug)—I am reminded that I cannot tell students how to earn an A. I can, however, tell them how to earn F's, D's, C's, and B's. Those grades, in my personal philosophy of evaluation, are earnable and achievable through sheer hard work and steady application. The A, however, descends upon a student through a kind of rhetorical grace: the writer makes a discovery that changes her writing and thinking; the student simply provides a series of miraculous insights into the subject at hand; the first essay is stunning in both style and substance, even before I offer any commentary. There is no map for how to get there; it happens through a kind of transubstantiation.

Seven: I am not at all sure that I believe Observation Six.

Story Two

It is 1967. I am a first-year graduate student in the M.A. program at Hunter College in New York City. Part of CUNY, Hunter has offered me a scholarship presumably as a consequence of my undergraduate accomplishments at Ohio State. An Honors student at OSU, I achieved virtually all A's and B's, with mostly the former in my major, English. Clearly, I was a student who sought and often attained high grades.

Hunter, however, disabled me. The classes were primarily lecture; even in the seminars the professor spoke most of the time, with us students sitting in stunned and scriptural silence. The college had no campus, only a building on 69th Street filled with armed guards whose only apparent responsibility was to stride the hallways in order to protect us against the ravages of the frequent Vietnam War protests that coursed through the veins of the city like radioactive microbes. I felt placeless, nomadic, an intellectual derelict. I did not like most of my fellow graduate students, nor did I like most of my professors. Not surprisingly, no one seemed to care whether I flourished or floundered. No matter how hard I worked, for the first and only time in my life I could not earn A's in English. In one course, I barely scraped by with a B, coming within a decimal of failing the course.

Out of ten courses, I remember earning only two A's, one of which was a clear gift. Was it because I was a Master's student? Did the faculty reserve their A's exclusively for Ph.D. candidates? Did I get dumber when I moved from Columbus to New York City? (Many New Yorkers might respond in the affirmative.) Was Hunter College more rigorous than Ohio State? Was I so distracted by the pleasures of the city, its films and bookstores and restaurants, that I failed to apply myself? Did Hunter discover my true inner self, that soft and flabby pseudointellectual buried inside, my true secret sharer? To invoke Mike Rose, was my name really "ruse"?

Some Observations

One: Even now, thirty years later, the experience puzzles me. It took me four years to finish that degree, working full-time in private industry for the last three. When I moved on to the more rigorous Ph.D., accepted by the University of Iowa in large part through the intervention of a generous professor at Hunter, I do not think I ever earned less than an A. Maybe it was being back in the Midwest; like Atlas, I guess I needed to have my feet planted on the soil of home in order to marshal my strength.

Two: My personal history makes me ask: which student am I? Am I the studious scholar who earned almost exclusively A's, or the mediocre dolt who could barely maintain his B? Do those grades really bear any correspondence to my ability and achievement? Which of the contrasting experiences represents my true potential and ability? Both? Neither?

Three: While peripatetically drifting through the halls of Hunter, looking futilely for safe harbor, should I have gathered resolve, gone to see my professors, and asked them, "What do I need to do to earn an A?" Should I have blazed the path followed years later by my own student?

I offer these experiences as two of the many perspectives from which I think about grades. I might have told others: my battle with grade inflation in the writing program when I served as Director of Composition at the University of Wisconsin-Milwaukee; my experiments with contract grading; the professor who awarded an A to a student whom he had never met; my son, who seems so self-directed as to be largely oblivious to the grades he receives, although he is pleased when he earns an A from a professor he admires.

All these stories circle around the same perplexing subject that motivated editors Libby Allison, Lizbeth Bryant, and Maureen Hourigan to create this volume: the relation between grading and teaching, evaluation and accomplishment. As teachers, we struggle to find ways to convert our students' maniacal concern for grades into a desire to learn. We struggle to assign grades fairly, not as rewards or punishments, but as reasonable and meaningful indices of achievement. Many of us see the relationship between grades and teaching as tenuous at best, yet those free-floating signifiers are unavoidable. No matter whether I teach well or poorly, whether my students learn anything, I must post those inky marks over to the Registrar. Given their durability and their power, a great deal can and must be said about grades and about their relationship to teaching and learning. This volume offers us a series of thoughtful, rigorous, and useful provocations to renew that discussion.

And renewed it should be. Although the desire to ban grades from the classroom derives from a philosophy of education that I admire (see Chapter 1 in this volume), most of us will almost certainly have to find ways to tame the power of grades rather than expect to see them disappear. Grades really are ubiquitous, transcending the school experience. We get the movie critics' top ten, the best and worst cars of 1995, the Morningstar rankings of mutual funds. My hometown restaurant reviewer awards restaurants one to four stars, while the sports editor assigns one to five footballs to every aspect of the Green Bay Packers' on-field performance, from offensive line to special teams. If sports is a metaphor for life, we can see in the westernized version of it an obsession with ranking, with making the grade, receiving that number-one ranking.

My students want their version of recognition: an A in my class. Somehow, some way, I must find a way to mediate between my desire to teach and my obligation to grade. I have no illusions about how impossible this is; in a deeply commodified world, everything has its price and its value. The assumption is that the commodity itself is fixed, that it has a static and stable nature, something that is not at all true of learning, particularly learning to think, write, and read. Yet fifteen weeks after classes have begun, I must sit in the quiet of my study and rank my students, taking into account their effort, improvement, progress, ability, citizenship, alacrity, eagerness, content, style, correctness, originality . . . the list extends indefinitely.

The essays in this volume have helped me to think harder and better about issues of grading. At the same time, they remind me of how deeply my experience has taught me to mistrust not just grades but the process of grading. For that alone, I stand in their debt. Come to think of it, were I grading this book on its influence and achievement, I would have to give it a grade of . . . well, maybe it is best if I defer evaluation and leave that judgment up to the reader.

Charles Schuster
University of Wisconsin-Milwaukee

Acknowledgments

We would like to acknowledge the suppport and efforts of the numerous people who helped make this project a success: the administrators at Texas A&M University261 Corpus Christi who provided a home for the book and course release time for Libby Allison and Lizbeth Bryant; Kent State, Trumbull, for its in-kind help for Maureen Hourigan; the expert secretarial support of Janie Lara and Nelda Walker-Sanford; and the editorial assistance of Sue Willman. Special recognition goes to Chuck Schuster, Series Editor for Cross-Currents, for his guidance, encouragement, and advice throughout the entire process of compiling this collection. Finally, we would like to thank our colleagues and students for sharing their stories of grading with us. We would be glad for your comments about the subject of grading. You can reach us at lallison@tamucc.edu, lbryant@tamucc.edu, or hourigam@trumbull.kent.edu.

Introduction

Grading in the Post-Process Classroom
When Theory and Practice Collide

> The great variety of methods of evaluation from the seventeenth century until recent years indicates a growing dissatisfaction with the efficiency of these methods. The demands of evaluation became increasingly more insistent and more difficult to satisfy. One method after another was tried, each change was motivated by some external social, political, or economic variation in the world.
>
> —Mary Lovett Smallwood (1935)

> RESOLVED, that the National Council of Teachers of English encourage teachers to refrain as much as possible from using grades to evaluate and respond to student writing, using instead such techniques as narrative evaluations, written comments, dialogue journals, and conferences.
>
> —NCTE (1994)

Mary Lovett Smallwood's (1935) report of "dissatisfaction with the efficiency" of evaluation methods rings no less true for composition teachers at the close of the twentieth century than it did for educators some sixty years before. Just as changing social, political, or economic conditions brought about development of "new ways of examining and grading" from the seventeenth century until the 1930s (115), vast sociodemographic changes in access to higher education in the last sixty years call for new ways of evaluating and responding to student writing. The 1993 NCTE Resolution on Grading (NCTE 1994, 3), which recommends that writing teachers "refrain as much as possible from using grades," is one such response. But curiously, the NCTE's call for de-emphasizing grading appears at a time when grades have become ever more present in all teachers' lives. Students, faculty, parents, administrators, and legislators are constantly asking us to give them, average them, raise them, lower them, and justify them. Everyone, both within the university and without, has an opinion about grades and is quick to tell us what we should do about them. Even popular newspaper advice-giver Ann Landers (1996) has entered the arena. In a response to a letter writer who suggests teachers "dispense with grading the papers altogether and just teach the subject matter," she counsels: "Some teachers have been doing that for quite some time—no grades, just 'pass' or 'fail.' I prefer the old-fashioned way. It motivates those who strive for excellence, and I'm all for that" (C–2).

Writing teachers, whether new teaching assistants or experienced writing program administrators, thus find ourselves in a double bind. Exhorted by NCTE not to use grades to evaluate our students' papers, we find ourselves pressured by our institutions (largely shaped by objective, scientific notions of reality) to give more exacting ones. Consider, for example, Duke University's proposal to initiate an "achievement index" to curb grade inflation in its push "for a more intellectual campus environment" (Gose 1997, A40). The index is to be calculated with the aid of an algorithm that compares a student with his or her classmates in a multitude of ways, penalizing those who do well in "easy" classes (classes without a distribution of grades from A to F) with a lower-than-earned grade point average. Despite students' opposition to its implementation and the inability of all but statisticians to understand how it would work, the administration is urging its faculty to approve the proposal. Student opponents of the proposal argue that the new index "may create a perverse incentive to help your classmates fail"; an art history professor charges that Duke teachers incapable of eliciting excellent work from Duke's excellent students ought themselves be regarded as failures. The index's inventor, however, dismisses such criticisms as motivated by selfishness (A40).

As the Duke situation illustrates, grading is an inescapable factor in the construction of all teachers' pedagogies and the definition of their positions of power in the classroom, their departments, the institutions in which they teach, and even the larger communities in which they live. In short, despite the NCTE Resolution, grading will not leave us alone. For writing teachers, in particular, grading has become a nemesis.

Perhaps surprisingly, hierarchical grading schemes are a comparatively new phenomenon in American postsecondary institutions, as Smallwood's *An Historical Study of Examinations and Grading Systems in Early American Universities: A Critical Study of the Original Records of Harvard, William and Mary, Yale, Mount Holyoke, and Michigan from Their Founding to 1900* (1935) shows. Very early in American higher education history, students did not get grades; rather, they were given exams—usually oral—primarily for conferring baccalaureate degrees. Prior to the 1800s, writes Smallwood, various methods of ranking and sorting students were tried, including attempts to sort students based on the "social position of their families" (41). After 1775, "the idea of a definite scale began to appear," particularly in the assignment of Commencement roles to graduates (107). The first real marking system was implemented at Yale in 1783, but hierarchical grading, as it is applied in most colleges and universities today, did not begin until after 1800. Smallwood points out that leaders in educational institutions "came to an acute realization that evaluation is a necessary and desirable part of academic procedure. As a result a variety of scales came into existence" (42).

In 1813, Yale initiated the first numerical scale, using the numbers one to four, with decimals (108). A few years later, Harvard, too, implemented a numerical scale, first based on twenty and then 100 (multiples of four) to provide exactness of measurement. Importantly, the university attempted to include individual differences in its marking system as well. Using aggregate scales that paid particular attention to a student's record in his senior year, Harvard attempted to account for possible differences in natural ability by comparing a student not only with other students, but also with himself (109). Smallwood points out the significance of Harvard's marking system:

> It is interesting to turn back to Harvard in 1825 and find that one of the foremost uses of the grading system has continued down to the present day. That is the attempt to arrange the members of a class according to their measurable ability—a method tried over and over again with apparent lack of success. (59)

Duke's proposed attainment scale, described earlier, seems yet another instance of Smallwood's astute observation.

By the 1860s, American scholars, influenced by visits to the growing universities of Europe, began to view grades as largely quantitative measures. At times they shared "an almost fanatical belief that minute distinctions could be made" (110). By the turn of the century, however, universities returned to placing students in four scholastic groups (not unlike homogeneous groupings employed today). Retrospectively observing the pendulum swing from one grading scale to another, Smallwood remarks:

> The point of view held by the faculty was one which demanded an exact conception of a student's ability, which it was really impossible to obtain with complete accuracy. This being true, all the numerical system of grading accomplished was to *involve faculty in further difficulties.* (110) *(emphasis added)*

All in all, however, grading practices seemed to change gradually, and while their universities tried first one grading system then another, few educators questioned whether grades ought be given at all.

The first real grading controversy coincided with the rise of the scientific measurement movement and was sparked by the publication of Starch and Elliot's landmark study, "Reliability of the Grading of High-School Work in English," in 1912. When the authors distributed two English papers written by two high school students to English teachers in 142 different high schools and asked them to grade them, discrepancies in marks were widespread. One paper's scores ranged from sixty to ninety-seven points and the other from fifty to ninety-eight points on a 100-point scale (451–52). As evidence of the subjectivity of grading moved educators away from reliance on a 100-point marking scale, many turned to "grading on a curve," in which the majority of students in any group would get average grades, to insure a fairer grade distribution (Kirschenbaum, Napier, and Simon 1971, 57). To account for classrooms that did not contain a cross section of the population (thereby negating a normal distribution curve), proponents recommended the use of intelligence tests. Standardized testing was in great vogue, for as Nicholas Lemann (1995) points out, psychometricians thought that they had discovered a means of measuring "the one essential human ability—what the British psychometrician Charles Spearman, in a famous 1904 article, called 'the general factor,' or g" (http://www.The Atlantic.com.Atlantic/issues/95Sep/ets/grtsort.2htm). Intelligence, they believed, was an inherited, biologically grounded trait.

Intelligence tests were used for purposes other than identifying school aptitude. By 1917, Lewis Terman of Stanford attributed "enormous" increases in the rates of societal "troubles" to biologically grounded "feeble-mindedness": "Only recently have we begun to recognize how serious a menace [feeble-mindedness] is to the social, economic, and moral welfare of the state. . . . It is responsible . . . for the majority of cases of chronic and semi-chronic pauperism" (Kamin 1995, 476–77). Immigrants, especially the most recently arrived, fared poorly on intelligence tests and were judged far less capable than native-born Americans. Curiously, Lemann notes, the highest-scoring group on intelligence tests today is Jews, but in 1923, when Jews were among the most recent and lowest-scoring immigrant populations, one psychometrician wrote, "Our figures . . . would rather tend to disprove the popular belief that the Jew is highly intelligent . . ." (Lemann 1995). In all, the scientific measurement movement "went a long way toward destroying the idea that any child could learn as well as any other child if he tried hard enough" (Smith and Dobbin 1960, 784). In fact, the concept of scientifically measurable differences in mass testing underscored the need for individualized education.

Within a few years of the inception of intelligence testing, a widespread critique was in place. By the early 1920s, even Spearman no longer believed that any single g factor existed. Increasingly, IQ tests were regarded as more a measure of a test taker's education and fluency in English than his or her innate ability (Lemann 1995). With the 1930s and the Great Depression came dramatic changes in the way Americans viewed their political, economic, and social lives and the roles of American institutions. Almost a third of all Americans lived in poverty. Since the difficulties of so many could not logically be blamed on lack of intelligence, issues surrounding the use of intelligence testing faded for a time (Lemann 1995). At this time, too, some educators with philosophical ties to John Dewey countered the practice of the scientific measurement of students by focusing on individual learning through social interaction, and "learning by doing."[1] Similarly, Edna Lamson, in her 1940 study of the literature on grading in colleges, declared that teachers should not rigidly apply a normal distribution curve to their classes. Instead, she recommended that teachers formulate a philosophy of their own grading practices and establish clear-cut standards to be shared with students (Smith and Dobbin 1960, 786). Her recommendations characterized how grading was to be practiced by many academicians for years, even today.

Throughout the 1940s and 1950s research interest in the mechanical aspects of marking decreased (Smith and Dobbin 1960, 787). As in the preceding century, mechanical systems of marking were replaced with more descriptive ones and those in turn were displaced by objective examinations and normal distribution curves (Kirschenbaum, Napier, and Simon 1971, 63–64). Arguments against the widespread use of intelligence testing, especially as a predictor of school performance, appeared. Critics charged that the use of school performance to validate IQ was "circular," for the validation was too similar to the test itself [Lemann 1995]). In 1948, *The Scientific Monthly* published the widely read "The Measurement of Mental Systems (Can Intelligence Be Measured?)," which branded IQ tests a fraud—"a way of wrapping the fortunate children of the middle and upper-middle classes in a mantle of scientifically demonstrated superiority," an argument that lingers today (Lemann 1995). Following the GI Bill of 1944, unprecedented numbers of nontraditional-aged white males enrolled in colleges and universities. Motivated and mature, their grade point averages soared to record highs, despite the use of conventional grading practices. In fact, during the veterans' first year at Stanford University, "Nonveterans called veterans 'DAR's,' for 'Damn Average Raisers'" (Olson 1974, 51).

The rise of the Civil Rights movement and student protests against the Vietnam conflict in the 1960s and early 1970s brought long lasting and seemingly revolutionary changes to American postsecondary institutions. On the one hand, there emerged the use of nontraditional grading methods (such as pass/fail for elective courses, contract and/or narrative grading) found in some mainstream American universities and in well-known alternative educational colleges today (Kirschenbaum, Napier, and Simon 1971, 69–70; 292–307; http://hampshire.edu/html/cs/ahen/ahen.html). On the other came charges of grade inflation, an issue that has periodically bedeviled American universities since the introduction of electives into the universities in the 1880s (Smallwood 1935, 110). J. E. Stone in "Inflated Grades, Inflated Enrollment, and Inflated Budgets: An Analysis and Call for Review of State Laws" (1996), outlines the argument that holds the social and political forces prominent in the 1960s responsible for grade inflation in the 1990s:

> A number of researchers and commentators collectively implicate the rise of radical egalitarianism. . . . They seem to believe that such forces undermined respect for achievement-based distinctions and with it the intellectual and moral authority of faculty—an authority based on achievement. . . . [Academic success] came to be viewed as a source invidious comparisons and, as such, contrary to egalitarian ideals.

Further, Stone notes, whether or not one accepts the common wisdom summarized above, grade inflation continues "to be linked to the sixties in the sense of serving to maintain educational institutions that critics claim are a microcosm of the sixties era, i.e., microcosms more congenial to equality than merit based distinctions" (http://olam.ed.asu.edu/epaa/v3n11.html).

While Stone defends and welcomes higher grades that represent better learning on the part of students, many faculty and students consider those higher grades as evidence of undeserving students getting better grades. Those who see higher grades as signs of "inflation" charge that students today are overly ambitious, yet unmotivated; that the "opening" up of the curriculum in the 1960s dropped standards (Cole 1993, B1); and that administrators and untenured faculty are more concerned with student retention than standards (Savitt 1994, B3). Critics of the "inflation" interpretation, however, believe reasons for the higher GPAs include more effective teaching methods, the increased number of returning, more motivated students to the classroom, and more concern for individual learning differences (Hettinger 1994, B3). Interestingly, despite public and scholarly reception of the phenomena of grade inflation, data are conspicuously absent. No studies of grade inflation have been published by state education committees, nor are they forthcoming from regional accrediting agencies or from such organizations as the Southern Region Education Board or National Center for Higher Education (http://olam.ed.asu.edu/epaa/v3n11.html). Suggestions for improving the present grading system range from Duke's proposed "attainment scale," to Dartmouth's inclusion of the average grade for all students in a first-year course on a student's transcript (Cole 1993, B1), to all-out abolition of the "meaningless mean" GPA (Milton, Pollio, and Eison 1986, 218).

It is in the context of renewed attention to grading, particularly "inflated" grading, that *Grading in the Post-Process Classroom: From Theory to Practice* appears. Writing teachers ourselves, we editors asked, "What can we do?" Caught between the NCTE's call for alternative grading schemes and administrators' calls for more stringent ones, caught between poststructural theories of language use, which question the potential for hierarchies, and administrators who demand even more finely tuned ones, caught between liberatory approaches that seek to teach students to become resistant, critical thinkers and the consumer approach some students bring to education, what are writing instructors at millenium's end to do? No simple answer exists. For those of us who would choose not to give grades, consider Kathleen Yancey's postings on RHETNT-L as evidence of the complexity of grading issues. She points out that "it is only because of *grades* that girls get some kind of fair shot in school . . . When we take grades away, we take away the one means currently available for girls and women to show what they do know" (1996). Moreover, for those of us who abhor the consequences of ranking our students, consider the remarks of editor Maureen Hourigan's daughter Karen about grading. About to sit for her first examinations in law school, she remarked: "If I don't do well, it doesn't mean I'm not a good person; it just means I won't get a good job." Whether we like it or not, grades are the currency of the worlds in which our students live.

When the theories that drive our practices clash with the common wisdom of our departments or universities, we teachers face difficult ethical, professional, and personal choices. The pressure of grade roll politics, for example, has cost more than one professor his position. Consider this cautionary tale from *The George-Anne*, the student newspaper of Georgia Southern University. Despite being chosen by students as Gamma Beta Phi's Professor of the Year for 1996, Abasi Malik's contract was not renewed. He was fired, he believes, because his grades did not fit the English department's bell curve (Miller 1996, May 7, 1). While the pressure of grade roll politics cost Malik his position, a colleague at a local community college in Texas recounts an experience that ends, perhaps, more happily. Like many teachers, she would contact the students who were failing or were in danger of failing her course or who had stopped attending altogether to suggest they drop the course. This policy removed F's and many D's from her grades sheets (and her students' transcripts as well). When the administration confronted her with the fact that her grades were not conforming to the bell curve, she made an "intelligent choice": she stopped contacting those students who were in danger of failing. Their D's and F's balance out the higher grades, and she remains in her position. But at what cost to both herself and her students?

Problems with grading involve more than administrators and teachers. In 1996, *The Chronicle of Higher Education* reported that twenty-eight students were "suing their universities this year for breach of contract, fraud, misrepresentation, or negligence. . . . Those filing the lawsuits claimed to be exposing shoddy educational programs" (May 1996, A29). One student, James M. Houston, who earned a Ph.D. with distinction in educational leadership at Northern Arizona University in 1995, claims that the "faculty has a 'diploma mill' mind set and poor teaching skills." He "hardly studied, spent little time on his class work, but still managed to earn a 4.0 grade point average" (May 1996, A29).

Moreover, writing teachers who wish to employ a liberatory pedagogy by turning the responsibility for establishing criteria and assigning grades to their students often find students reluctant to accept the task. Liz Bryant recalls her experience in an introductory graduate composition theory course, where she attempted to give her students the responsibility and power to develop the course syllabus. The assessment, evaluation, and grades committee came back with a very specific proposal outlining the breakdown of the final grade, but failed to mention any process for assessment and evaluation. Liz asked who would assign grades to these areas. They informed Liz that she would be giving the grade. The group then explained that one member had suggested that the students grade themselves. The class responded to this suggestion with a resounding, "No, we have to take classes with each other. We would make enemies." Who wants this responsibility of placing students in a lettered hierarchy? These students didn't.

Maureen Hourigan's experience in her first-semester, first-year writing classes was just as disappointing. She asked her students to compose a journal entry, describing if or how grades would fit into their conceptions of an ideal university. She had expected them to choose pass/fail grading. Instead, Maureen's students wanted traditional grades, or perhaps more accurately, wanted A's. An anonymous student who had graduated from basic writing courses proposed that "students that seem to want to stick in there and try hard get a better grade." Another anonymous classmate argued for the strictest grading policy of all: standardized tests that would erase any consideration of "effort" in determining a grade's final calculation. "It is important that grading remain stringent," she wrote. "The only way you can tell who is really ready after high school graduation is by uniform entrance exams." Her stringent standardized entrance examinations policy would have denied entrance to the university to almost all of her fellow classmates. Maureen interprets the situation this way: so caught up in late twentieth-century values of competition, individualism, and authoritarianism were her students that they could not imagine an academy devoid of hierarchies. Thus, underprepared students who had once been satisfied with merely getting through now wanted to be on top of the heap; traditional A students, however, were reluctant to share the heap-top with "lesser" others.

Charles Schuster's stories in the Foreword and this one told by Liz Bryant poignantly illustrate that grading impacts teachers' personal as well as professional lives. Liz's daughter Amy went off to Southwest Texas State University, a midsized Texas state school, in the fall of 1996. After three weeks in her first-semester writing class, Amy came home with a grade on her first composition—F. The left margin was full of red editorial marks— "dic," "x," "sp"—with two sheets telling her what these marks meant. She received no response to the ideas in the essay from her class peers or instructor. Amy slapped the essay on Liz's desk and proclaimed, "I can't write. Why am I so stupid? I thought writing in college was supposed to be fun. You said it would be better than high school."

Writing teachers responding to Amy's "Why?" might be tempted to respond with a "Why" of our own: Why, when the NCTE resolution on grading clearly states that we should develop "alternatives to giving students grades in writing courses, alternatives that would evaluate progress in ways sensitive to the needs of both students and individual universities, colleges, and school districts" (NCTE 1994, 3) are we still giving grades? The stories about grades recounted above provide one answer: Grading is deeply embedded in our culture. Chapters in *Grading in the Post-Process Classroom*, written both by prominent scholars and newer voices in the field of rhetoric and composition, provide additional responses to the NCTE directive. The collection is titled "Post-Process" because contributors move beyond the process writing movement's focus on a scientific, cognitivistic, and universalistic approach to writing expertise toward a focus on such social factors as race, class, ethnicity, and gender in constructing which writing is considered "expert" and who is authorized to produce it. In their look at the grading debate that has surfaced periodically throughout the history of the American academy, authors in this collection use new lenses to examine the historical and ideological underpinnings of grading practices and offer interventionist strategies to help teachers and students cope with the inevitable problems of grading. Interspersed among essays in more typically academic voices are short personal essays from writers situated in such diverse contexts as New York's Hudson Valley, San Francisco, and Corpus Christi, Texas. They paint a sometimes grave, sometimes gratified face on the issues of grading raised in the collection.

We have chosen to divide the collection into two parts. Like a collective Penelope, we would weave the threads of the chapters together, here tying student-generated grading criteria to new methods of portfolio evaluation, there binding collaborative grading practices to new writing technologies; here beginning with one voice, there substituting another. In truth, our tapestry unraveled every night. While the collection begins with the voice of David Bleich, it could have begun just as appropriately with the voice of James Sosnoski. On one hand, it was Bleich's scholarship and humanistic approach to teaching, an approach that privileges a less coercive method of assessment and evaluation, that provided the starting point for the editors' collective feelings about hierarchical grading practices. On the other, it was Sosnoski's observation that most articles on the subject of grading end with the impractical suggestion that teachers should not give grades (Harkin and Schilb 1991, 216) that prompted us to offer alternative grading schemes in this collection. Victor Villanueva's "Afterword" is in many ways a Foreword, for his overview of the unspoken things authors in this volume collectively take for granted is something new teachers of writing may want to read first rather than last. Ultimately, we realized that choosing not to place all portfolio chapters, for instance, in a separate, smaller section underscored our

belief that to place the essays in neat compartments created the kind of hierarchy we are arguing against. That said, we believe enough conceptual similarities underlie the various practices outlined in this collection that teachers
interested in reconfiguring positions of power within their classrooms will
find something to work on while, in contributor Betty Shiffman's words,
"waiting for the revolution."

Essays in Part I, The Ideology of Grading, address the politics of grading in the traditional academy and the authoritarian and competitive ideolo-
gies that underpin hierarchical grading schemes. In order to avoid what
Henry Giroux (1988) terms "historical amnesia" (4), Bleich presents a historical account of grading practices, tracing the bureaucratic ideology that under-
lies them back three thousand years (Chapter 1). Eleanor Agnew analyzes the
politics of "higher standards" campaigns, pointing out that the institutional
accountability movement has reduced academic standards to mere sets of
numbers (Chapter 2). John Sandman and Michael Weiser's personal narrative provides a cautionary tale about the constraints that colleagues, depart-,
ments, and institutions place on grading (Chapter 3). Part I ends with Betty
Shiffman's examination of supposedly liberating alternative grading practices, uncovering the rejected but pervasive values of competition and individualism in them (Chapter 4).

Most of the chapters in Part II, The Post-Process Classroom: Theory into
Practice, offer interventionist, theoretically informed and context-specific
alternative grading strategies that take into account and value the different
literacies that so many of today's nontraditional students bring with them to
the traditional academy. To one degree or another, they call for a redefini-
tion of expertise and authority in order to begin to change traditional, and
often oppressive, teacher-student relationships in the classroom. Several
essays in Part II offer new ways to configure portfolios for classroom rather
than assessment purposes, and several describe student-generated grading
criteria as means of reconfiguring positions of power within the classroom,
if not within the academy. Xin Liu Gale (Chapter 5) maintains that the
teacher's deferred authority in a portfolio classroom creates only the illusion
of a democratic classroom; new reading assignments, integrated writing
assignments, and conferences with students enabled her to fulfill her responsibilities as a teacher and to wean her students from grades as motivators for
revision. Peeples and Hart-Davidson (Chapter 6) perceive grading as a technology that defines who possesses expertise in the classroom. Student-
experts in their portfolio classroom not only generate criteria for assignments
but are also given the opportunity to revise the criteria during the semester.
Juan Flores (Chapter 8) responds by emphasizing that grading criteria must
be couched in consideration of students' culture, class, and gender and that
grading on a bell curve marginalizes students and undermines learning.

Several authors propose collaborative practices that redefine relationships of power in the classroom. Anne Righton Malone and Barbara Tindall

exchange letters with their students to make grading less an absolute statement of authority and more a collaborative act of interpretation (Chapter 9). Kathleen Strickland and James Strickland demystify grading by working with students to create student-owned criteria for individual assignments that meet the outcomes that administrators prescribe for the course (Chapter 10). Making the construction of a collaboratively written grading policy an inescapable first task for his first-semester writing students brought unexpected success to William Dolphin's multicultural classroom in San Francisco (Chapter 7). And students in Sosnoski's virtual classroom publish an on-line electronic almanac written for persons interested in their university locale and neighborhoods. While the course employs pass/fail grading, students may petition the faculty to grant them an A on the basis of the virtual audience's responses to their work (Chapter 11).

Headnotes situate each writer within a context, both within his or her university and within his or her classroom. We editors invite you to find a starting place of your own, choosing threads to weave into interventionist alternative grading strategies that will empower your students in your classrooms and your academies.

Notes

1. Black Mountain College in North Carolina was one of the alternative educational colleges that began during the 1930s. For an interesting history of the college, see *The Arts of Black Mountain College* by Mary Emma Harris, published by MIT Press in 1986. See also *Writing Instruction in Nineteenth-Century American Colleges*, where renowned compositionist James A. Berlin cites John Dewey's early work as influencing Fred Newton Scott, an early twentieth century rhetorician, whose work Berlin laments as having been defeated by current-traditional rhetoric.

References

Alternative Higher Education Network. http://hampshire.edu/html/cs/ahen/ahen.html [cited 1 November 1996].

Cole, W. 1993. "The Perils of Grade Inflation." Opinion. *The Chronicle of Higher Education* 6 January, B1.

Giroux, H. A. 1988. *Schooling and the Struggle for Public Life: Critical Pedagogy in the Modern Age*. American Culture Series. Minneapolis: University of Minnesota Press.

Gose, B. 1997. "Duke May Shift Grading System to Reward Students Who Take Challenging Classes." *The Chronicle of Higher Education* 14 February, A40.

Harkin, P. and J. Schilb, eds. 1991. *Contending with Words: Composition and Rhetoric in a Postmodern Age*. New York: MLA.

Hettinger, J. 1994. "The Causes and Consequences of Grade Inflation." Letter to the Editor. *The Chronicle of Higher Education* 9 February, B3.

Kirschenbaum, H., R. Napier, and S. B. Simon. 1971. *Wad-ja-get?: The Grading Game in American Education.* New York: Hart.

Landers, Ann. 1996. "Spell-Checker No Substitute for English Skills." *Corpus Christi Caller-Times* 17 October, C–2.

Lemann, N. 1995. "The Great Sorting." http://www.the Atlantic.com.atlantic/issues/95Sep/ets/grtsort.2htm [cited 2 January 1997].

May, H. 1996. "Ex-Students Sue Universities over Quality of Education," *The Chronicle of Higher Education* 16 August, A29, 32.

Miller, J. 1996. "Professor of the Year's Contract Not Renewed." *The George-Anne* 7 May, 1, 10.

Milton, O., H. R. Pollio, and J. A. Eison. 1986. *Making Sense of College Grades: Why the Grading System Does Not Work and What Can Be Done About It.* San Francisco: Jossey-Bass.

NCTE. 1994. "NCTE Members Pass Resolutions on Grading and Teaching Tolerance." *The Council Chronicle* 3 February.

Olson, K. W. 1974. *The G.I. Bill, the Veterans, and the Colleges.* Lexington, KY: University of Kentucky Press.

Savitt, R. 1994. "The Causes and Consequences of Grade Inflation." Letter to the Editor. *The Chronicle of Higher Education* 9 February, B3.

Smallwood, M. L. 1935. *An Historical Study of Examinations and Grading Systems in Early American Universities: A Critical Study of the Original Records of Harvard, William and Mary, Yale, Mount Holyoke, and Michigan from Their Founding to 1900.* London: Oxford University Press.

Smith A. Z. and J. E. Dobbin. 1960. "Marks and Marking Systems." In *Encyclopedia of Educational Research* ed. C. W. Harris, 783–91. New York: Macmillian.

Starch, D. and E. C. Elliott. 1912. "Reliability of the Grading of High-School Work in English." *The School Review* XX (January-December): 442–57.

Stone, J. E. "Inflated Grades, Inflated Enrollment, and Inflated Budgets: An Analysis and Call for Review of State Laws." http://olam.ed.asu.edu/epaa/v3n11.html [cited 15 September 1996].

Yancey, K. 1996. "Re: Grades." RHETNT-L@missou1.missouri.edu. 26 August.

Part One

The Ideology of Grading

Chapter One

What Can Be Done
About Grading?

David Bleich

David Bleich teaches English, Women's Studies, and Jewish Studies at the University of Rochester, a private research university. There are about thirty-four hundred undergraduates and four thousand graduate students. Teachers of graduate courses may grade on a satisfactory/fail basis; undergraduate students must get grades. Bleich's graduate courses are graded on a satisfactory/fail basis; his undergraduate courses are graded on a portfolio basis, with only one grade given at the end of the semester. Bleich has been trying for many years to persuade university officials that a reduction or elimination of testing and grading practices would result in greater student motivation and success. In this essay, Bleich considers the history of testing and grading as bureaucratic tools and then suggests how forms of narrative evaluation, used in appropriate and continuing ways by both students and teachers to help each other, should replace the present system of testing and grading.

A Psychology of Grading

The history of testing and grading suggests that these practices are a tradition of civilization rather than common local phenomena. Periodically the practices recede in prominence, but because the tradition goes beyond local practices, new versions of testing and grading return sooner or later. Today we are in one of those returning periods. After a long trend, starting in the 60s, of reduced emphasis on grades characterized by new methods of evaluation and by "grade inflation," grades are currently being revived as the keepers of "standards" and the enemies of "slackers."

Because of changing historical circumstances, the rationality of each return to grades is different. Today's return may be characterized by the "My Turn" essay by physics professor Kurt Wiesenfeld of Georgia Tech (1996). Wiesenfeld's essay exemplifies the way in which teachers—through the process of grading—are blamed for corporate greed. He reports that 10 percent (twelve) of his class of 120 physics students asked that their final grade be raised. He characterizes the students' requests as the "disgruntled consumer" approach. Here is the nub of his point:

> What alarms me is their indifference toward grades as an indication of personal effort and performance. Many, when pressed about why they think they deserve a better grade, admit they don't deserve one but would like one anyway. Having been raised on gold stars for effort and smiley faces for self-esteem, they've learned that they can get by without hard work and real talent if they can talk the professor into giving them a break. This attitude is beyond cynicism. There's a weird innocence to the assumption that one expects (even deserves) a better grade simply by begging for it.
>
> . . . Perhaps these students see me as a commodities broker with something they want—a grade. Though intrinsically worthless, grades, if properly manipulated, can be traded for what has value: a degree, which means a job, which means money. The one thing college actually offers—a chance to learn—is considered irrelevant, even less than worthless, because of the long hours and hard work required.
>
> In a society saturated with surface values, love of knowledge for its own sake does sound eccentric. The benefits of fame and wealth are more obvious. So is it right to blame students for reflecting the superficial values saturating our society? Yes, of course it's right. (16)

And this is what this column tries to do: demonstrate why such an attitude on the part of "students"—even though it was 10 percent of his sample—can lead to serious harm, such as accidental death on construction sites due to slipshod calculation of stresses and forces. The accidents Wiesenfeld refers to occurred recently on Olympic Games construction sites. Wiesenfeld's reasoning goes like this: "grade-grousing students" are good at getting "partial credit" for their work, but not learning the material leads to incompetence, which potentially leads to broken bridges and the collapse of a light tower that killed a worker. He does not consider that these accidents might also have been caused by delays in building, corner-cutting by contractors, hurry-up work policies—circumstances resulting from the scramble for the enormous profits generated by the Games. Why, however, are schools and students being blamed (by implication) for the negligence of those actually overseeing the construction sites? Perhaps unwittingly, Wiesenfeld became a propagandist for corporate interests: if we had better students, the greed of those who already have enough would not be so apparent. The return of grades today results from the return of corporate bullying, the disempowerment of unions, and the victory of individualism over other ways of thinking. The students Wiesenfeld complains about are emulating their role models in Western economies. Students, much like pawns in a bureaucracy, bargain for a grade. He mentions the 10 percent, "the grade-grousing 10 percent," who are offensive and concludes that something is wrong with students and teachers. However, when in the history of education would one find less than 10 percent of a classroom in violation of accepted ethical standards?

A bureaucratic mentality permeates the psychology of grading. The grade-givers evaluate students' work by comparing it to other students, arriving at a grade through the assumption of a ranking grid. For the grade-getter, the psychology is the learning of material only as it relates to the instruments of evaluation: tests and the teachers' grading psychology in response to essays. The relation of the material to the work is cordoned off from the relation of material to the student's ability to mold it to the needs of the course. The administrator expects that each student's performance can be reduced to a single parameter, that is, "the C student," disclosed to anyone who wants to know. Society is reassured by this psychology of grades that each individual's performance is predictable. As a result, the process of grading becomes so enmeshed with the academic bureaucracy that the process of teaching and learning is lost.

Like Wiesenfeld, I have had to take steps to proscribe the attitudes he describes with a minority of students. Even though I teach English and not physics; even though I give no exams and record only one grade at the end of the semester; even though I do not give pluses or minuses and use a modified contract approach; even though I do not have students grade themselves, I do not believe I have succeeded in "overcoming" the psychology of grading to any significant extent. Students adapt to my policy by making sure of the difference between an A and a B. That most succeed honestly does not mean that some are not "fooling" my system. But unlike Wiesenfeld I am not concerned with these few, since they exist in any grading system, including teaching contexts having no grades at all. Rather, I am concerned about those I consider to have succeeded in my class—to have benefitted regardless of their grade—but who will be surprised when the same level of effort in another class will be criticized and perhaps penalized.[1] Regardless of what we teachers can do on our own about grading, in any grading system we still penalize students merely by *holding different standards*. Without a grading system, different faculty standards of achievement can coexist. Different standards do function now, but because of the grading system, their differences are obscured by the classification of students into achievement tracks that are identically coded in every subject for every teacher in every school. Now, let us allow that many students with less than the highest GPAs do go to professional schools or succeed in other ways; the grading system is not preventing *everyone* from working toward fulfilling lives. The question we need to entertain, however, concerns the psychological and ideological effects of becoming acculturated into a grading system, of not facing these effects for the rest of our lives, and pretending that no harm was done. What harm is this system doing and how can it be changed? The contributors to this volume try to answer these questions with regard to the seemingly narrow questions of grading in the *writing* classrooms. Let me reflect on the question of grading in historical and social contexts.

Testing and Grading in Bureaucracies

The grading system seems to be ingrained in the "DNA" of society; level upon level of contexts and situations exist for testing, grading, and ranking. As I discuss in another essay,[2] F. Allan Hanson (1993), an anthropologist, examines grading behavior—testing, ranking, admission-to-privilege, and exclusion-from-privilege—in the Chou dynasty about three thousand years ago. Testing was done to sustain the emperor's bureaucracy. The tests were themselves products of a bureaucracy, bureaucratically administered, designed to keep the bureaucracy in power. In this way, bureaucrats affect the social psychology of the majority: "They are the mechanisms for defining or producing the concept of the person in contemporary society and that they maintain the person under surveillance and domination" (3). One of Hanson's main ideas is "surveillance."[3] In mid-twentieth century France, the bureaucracy was especially effective, since it ran the country during and after World War II while the government changed every few months. Bureaucracies in modern times are not much different than what they were in ancient China: instruments for maintaining civil order and peace, allowing life to "go on" in what seems to be an "as usual" style. Bureaucracies aren't responsive to changes in society, but respond very well to orders given from above. Because social change is a potential threat to order, the bureaucracy becomes one way to slow or stop change. Bureaucracies are especially useful to the privileged, whose way of life always needs to be preserved, while the rest of society always needs to improve its lot.

Hanson's study is a response to today's industrialized societies having brought testing to overwhelming levels. Increased testing is a response in part to the diversification of the population brought on by the reduction of colonialism and the gradual emancipation of nonwhite populations and women. In postcolonial societies, bureaucratic behavior serves both the former imperialists and the local privileged populations who were closest to the colonial power. In industrialized societies, the bureaucracy serves the "ruling class" by administering to collective needs, maintaining an accepted level of legality. In each case the bureaucracy does not have the "best interests of the majority" at heart; rather, it keeps a stable balance among conflicting interests and privileges. Hanson's study shows how testing in every phase of society is meant to bring the popular majorities under greater control. Testing practices are, in turn, supported by the "scientific" status of the statistical techniques of sorting to which testing lends itself. Testing combines with statistical analysis to supply "proof" of how efficacious certain forms of exclusion are.

The testing that takes place in school educates the students as to their place in society: as individuals in competition with every other individual for jobs and other valuable items. Testing and grading teaches students to view others as rivals and to view their own potential for achievement as a result of these rituals.

The responses to testing and grading we frequently hear are similar to responses to bureaucracies: "you can't live with them; you can't live without them." This form of paradoxical justification is often given by those in power trying to appear ethically and politically responsible. Many bureaucratic managers know and feel its injustice, but they cannot oppose it without endangering their jobs. Because they are pulled in opposite directions by practical and moral values, they describe their situation as paradoxical. There is reason to understand bureaucracies in society as well as academic bureaucracies as behaving according to the same social psychology, as discussed by Kathleen E. Ferguson in her book, *The Feminist Case Against Bureaucracy* (1984). She characterizes bureaucracies as dispensable or at least changeable; neither testing and grading nor bureaucracies, in themselves, can be understood as isolated culpable practices or institutions that besmirch otherwise innocent societies. Rather, because feminism views society in general as androcentric, from a feminist perspective, bureaucracies appear to be apparatuses that serve men's interests more than women's. Testing and grading, being principal bureaucratic functions in the academy, can be characterized as androcentric practices: devices for a few people (usually men) to sort, control, and order the total student body in schools where the grading system obtains—the vast majority of schools.

Here is Ferguson's description of a bureaucracy:

> Following [Max] Weber, the modern bureaucracy is usually described as an organization having the following traits: a complex rational division of labor, with fixed duties and jurisdictions; stable, rule-governed authority channels and universally applied performance guidelines; a horizontal division of graded authority, or hierarchy, entailing supervision from above; a complex system of written record-keeping, based on scientific procedures that standardize communications and increase control; objective recruitment based on impersonal standards of expertise; predictable, standardized management procedures following general rules; and a tendency to require total loyalty from its members toward the way of life the organization requires. (7)

Ferguson claims that contemporary mass society is more saturated by bureaucratic traits than ever before in history, even allowing for the thousands of years of their existence, a claim consistent with Hanson's regarding the contemporary proliferation of testing. The foregoing description suggests that postsecondary schools function according to bureaucratic, rather than scholarly or pedagogical, principles. Classrooms vary, however. Some teachers run their classes in bureaucratic style, but many do not; when the door is closed, in many cases the bureaucracy stops. Except for this: even teachers who "close the door" must open it again for grades to enter the bureaucracy.

The Academic Bureaucracy

Here is how Ferguson's (1984) description of bureaucracies applies to universities and postsecondary academic institutions.

1. *Rational division of labor, with fixed duties and jurisdictions.* There are departments, courses, and curricula administered by groups of experts who are careful not to "step out of" their discipline or subject matter. They teach their subjects autonomously, as they see fit.

2. *Rule-governed authority channels and universally applied performance guidelines.* Teachers are supervised by Chairs, Chairs by Deans, Deans by Provosts, and so on. Teachers must teach and evaluate their students, reporting student performance to chairs and deans on grade-sheets. Universal performance guidelines exist in the traditional grading system's for students, and, recently, in the students' "course opinion questionnaire," which is the same for every course and virtually the same from school to school.

3. *Horizontal division of graded authority.* All departments resemble one another. All schools have a similar hierarchy of faculty and deans; tenure is determined more or less the same way in most schools: deans following faculty committees' recommendations, with veto power residing in Provosts and Presidents.

4. *Complex record keeping, with standardized communications and increased control.* Most teachers' grade books are black with small marks recording absences, grades for in-class work, grades for out-of-class work, for class participation, lateness, or any other factor declared to be germane to a final evaluation. Most classroom "policies" designate the percentage contribution of any one activity to the final grade; i.e., "the final exam counts for 30 percent of your final grade." This is the most common gesture toward "scientific procedures" in most classrooms. For the evaluation of faculty, a similar situation exists, except most of a faculty member's records are "confidential," or secret.[4]

5. *Objective recruitment and impersonal standards.* I have sat on several hiring committees. The illusion of objective recruitment is created in part by practices such as weighted votes by, say, five committee members, so that the candidate with the highest "score" gets

the offer. This candidate can be the second choice of every committee member, but he/she will still get the first offer. Few challenge
this result. It is considered fair because the system is "impersonal."
The hard work of hammering out a consensus based on principle, on
departmental needs, or on interpersonal considerations is eschewed
in favor of the imaginary scientific justice achieved through the
weighted vote.[5]

6. *Predictable, standardized management procedures.* This means that
bureaucratically recognized classes of people are assumed to be
comprised of like individuals—teachers, students, seniors, untenured assistants, and so on. Even though each person departs in
important ways from any conception of a standard or norm, this fact
is ignored as "personnel cases" emerge. A certain number of
absences results in "failure." An insufficient number of publications
results in tenure denial. And so on. In today's schools, teachers and
administrators fear erring on the side of generosity toward students
and untenured faculty members because bureaucratic ideology is the
accepted perspective.

The bureaucratic style, an aspect of society on which the "corporate"
mentality is increasing its influence, is pervasive in schools. Bureaucratic
functioning is growing into bureaucratic domination, as suggested in the
recent economic study by David Gordon (1996) that opposes the currently
popular corporate practice of "downsizing." This book suggests how and
why bureaucracies are instruments of the authoritarian policies of corporations. Well-paid by corporate directorates, bureaucracies have become the
overt servants of power-centers rather than of the populations that the power-
centers are supposed to be serving. While this is not always necessarily the
case, the shifts of public power into fewer hands renders the bureaucracies
more powerful, creating an independent class of bureaucrats, or as they are
more usually known, "managers." Gordon explains why downsizing—
reducing the labor force in corporations—has widened the gap between rich
and poor while increasing the fear and anxiety in those holding non-
executive jobs. Increased financial health of corporations has been achieved
at the expense of job loss and job anxiety in the salaried work force in general. Gordon considers why there aren't other secure, appealing jobs created
in other parts of the economy if there has been a *general* improvement in
corporate profitability. The answer is that wealth has been redistributed
within corporations: taken from the salaried work force and given to execu-
tives and *to the larger bureaucracies needed for surveillance and domination
of their own workers.*

> . . . stagnant or falling wages create the need for intensive managerial super-
> vision of frontline employees. If workers do not share in the fruits of the

enterprise, if they are not provided a promise of job security and steady wage growth, what incentive do they have to work as hard as their bosses would like? So the corporations need to monitor the workers' effort and be able to threaten credibly to punish them if they do not perform. The corporations must wield the Stick. Eventually the Stick requires millions of Stick-wielders. (5)

It is a simple situation: wealth has been transferred from those who are barely making ends meet to those already having more than enough. To enforce this policy of corporate government by fear, more "police" are needed, and these are called by Gordon the corporation's "bureaucratic burden." Gordon describes this movement as the "stick strategy," as contrasted with the "carrot" strategy he endorses and whose practical forms he outlines in the last chapter of his book.[6]

Gordon's (1996) use of the term "bureaucratic burden" puts a contemporary twist on an old idea; the constituencies that complained about the excessive regulations of "big government" are now using the same bureaucratic principle to redistribute the wealth among ever fewer people. The weight gain in corporate bureaucracies has been matched by the increasing emulation of corporations by universities,[7] and the resulting license to demand "standards," "grade deflation," and "quality products": students who will fit into the bureaucracies.

Testing and grading teaches people how to be bureaucrats and managers, well-paid servants of society's power centers. It also teaches that some get through the sieve of evaluative barriers to move into higher social/economic classes, but most don't. The bureaucratic ideal slows and stops change. The history of grading over the last three decades suggests that those thinking about it believe that, ultimately, testing and grading are inevitable in one form or another. While this acceptance may be pragmatic, the fact that changing approaches to grades are connected with wider social changes implies that there is no reason to assume the inevitability of grading; rather than grades being necessary for teaching and learning, they are necessary to preserve social and economic hierarchies. Recent conclusions in grading research point to cracks in previous assumptions that academic grading is inevitable or necessarily desirable.

Conventional Approaches to Grading:
The Harm of Denial

One British study of interest is Henry Latham's *On the Action of Examinations Considered as a Means of Selection,* published in 1877. As he describes testing and grading over a century ago, they seem similar to today's practices. "Cramming" was how examinations were passed, and British faculty faced this fact readily by hiring special teachers called "crammers" to "cram" knowledge into students' heads. While competitive examinations and cramming were clearly assumed, Latham's discussion shows awareness of the *inutility* of this technique with regard to certifying a job candidate's potential motivation:

> Competitive Examinations leave us most in the dark about those qualities which find their sphere in active life, but they also fail us in one important point when we want to select men[8] to fill posts intended for the "endowment of research." It is most important to know whether persons have a *taste* for their study, and about this Examinations hardly tell us anything. We meet with cases of hard-headed men who obtain high degrees in a course which they select as offering them the most favourable field, but who never care to open a book in their branch of study afterwards. Their object has been to win a place in the front, and they have done so, as one of the conditions for future getting on: the Examination was one of the hurdles in their race, and they cleared it, but they may care nothing whatever for classics or mathematics or whatever science they have taken. . . .
>
> It must be remarked that if we get wrong results by trusting to Examinations it is usually because we use them to the exclusion of all other modes of judging—much as an invalid who pins his faith on a new nostrum will sometimes give up taking ordinary precautions. We have all the means of forming an opinion that we had before Examinations were introduced, and if these were used with care and method we might get near the truth about some of the moral and personal qualities of candidates. (302, 303)

Here, Latham, in perhaps indirect terms, says that tests don't accomplish two very important things: indicate what a person will do in the "active" life or what taste a person may have for the subject in which the test is given. These two factors are related, perhaps inseparable; taste for a subject—liking it —motivates work in it, in the "active" life, and is certain motivation for success.

Latham (1877) also says that discerning these salient factors is subjective —"the means of forming an opinion"—that is, not reducible to the formalities of testing and grading. Teachers and employers observe students and applicants as people and form opinions and judgments based on a wide variety of factors not always obvious. Values such as "care and method" actually do "bring us nearer to the truth" about a person's abilities and motivation.

Judges of students have long understood how authoritative subjective judgments really are in assessing performance. Those who give grades and who rely on grading systems acknowledge how even the grades themselves are "subjective," but that whether to give them is not a choice consistent with keeping one's job. Latham's formulations above represent the traditional approach to the issue of grading: denial that actual or accurate bases of judgment can be implemented as a regular part of teaching. These bases are holistic views about how a person functions in the real world as emerging from the person's manifestations of taste for the knowledge or understandings developed in school.

A work frequently cited in Milton, Pollio, and Eison's 1986 *Making Sense of College Grades* is Mary Lovett Smallwood's *An Historical Study of Examinations and Grading Systems in Early American Universities* (1935), which discusses developments in five major universities from their founding in the eighteenth century to the beginning of the twentieth. Smallwood's data comes from a period before Latham's, is more comprehensive in that it is taken from five different universities, and suggests how widespread, and thus how ideological, is the conventional approach to grades. Her work discloses materials that, as in Latham's, show the patterns of denial of the harm done by grading.

Smallwood (1935) reviews the history of grading in the United States by noting how at the end of the eighteenth century at Yale the four (Latin) categories of best, good, inferior, and bad were used to classify both students and their work. In various contexts, attempts were made to reduce the subjectivity of these judgments by introducing more detailed scaling,[9] often on a scale of sixty-five to 100. Smallwood observes:

> All these attempts to estimate the student as an individual as well as only one of a group, had desirable results but accomplished almost nothing in obviating the teacher's subjective bias along various lines, particularly in the weighting of various sorts of exercises and subjects on the basis of his view of their value to the student. (109)

The term *bias* suggests that the teacher's judgment pejoratively offsets the effects of the detailed scalar ratings. The more schools tried to eliminate such bias through numerical grading, the more difficulties they created. Different scales were introduced, gradually evolving into a Byzantine set of quantitative evaluative procedures, each with its own signficance. None, either individually or in concert with other measures, overcame the effects of teachers' "subjective" judgments. Therefore, in the early university periods in the United States, there is evidence of awareness of the strong effects of teachers' personal judgments, but also of the persistent but failed attempts to eliminate subjectivity—the same situation that exists today.

Another way in which ambivalence has emerged historically (in this case in the late nineteenth century) is in the contrast between the ways Harvard and Michigan distinguished between "passed" and "not passed" when they each experimented with the abolition of the marking system:

> At the University of Michigan a student simply "passed," but if he failed there were different degrees of failure, such as "conditioned" and "incomplete." At Harvard the reverse was true, variations were on the side of

passing.... Harvard was always more interested in encouraging and rewarding the good student; Michigan felt that emphasis on the superior attainments and merits of one student over another was neither desirable nor democratic. (83)

As Smallwood presents it, there is an "either-or" connotation when Harvard and Michigan are compared. Both wanted to find ways to reestablish distinctions among students, as it must have been obvious that each student is different from every other, and, in order to help all students, their situations should be recognized both individually and categorically. Both the students who passed and those who failed did need to be understood as having done their work in some identifiable qualitative way. And so new categories emerged on either side of the pass/fail line. Conversely, both the Harvard and Michigan nineteenth century pass/fail systems succeeded in solving some problems brought about by scalar grading. The Harvard system transformed a "good grade" into a living accomplishment; the Michigan system taught that qualitative differences in performance were not to be measured against one another nor to compete with one another, and that the categorical distinctions among groups of students did not reflect the relative merit of individuals' inner beings.

Because students need to be recognized for their actual accomplishments, and because abolishing hierarchical evaluation makes such recognition possible, the implied choice of "either Harvard or Michigan" expresses ambivalence about grades without solving the problem. The best solution would be "both Harvard and Michigan": no grading system *and* recognition of each student's accomplishment (or lack thereof) in a qualitative way. However, now, as then, this solution rarely exists.

In the 1960s, almost a century after the foregoing experiments, university grading once again came under scrutiny and changes were proposed. From this period resulted the small percentage of elective courses that students may take pass/fail and the now-ubiquitous student course evaluation forms, where students are "grading" the course and the teacher as part of a policy of recognizing student input. Since their introduction, however, these practices have contributed little to the humanization of grading, and, in most cases, have been harmful to the process of evaluation of students and teachers. In pass/fail electives, the teacher is not told that the student has chosen this path. An element of deception has been institutionalized in order to give the appearance of student control of their performance standards. As a result, the relationship between teacher and student is not founded on trust and honesty; the teacher's contributions are treated as a tap, which can be turned on and off, rather than as elements in a living relationship. Teaching has been diluted and trivialized rather than enriched and intensified. Because the pass/fail choice is worked into a traditional grading psychology, learning in new subjects has been converted to GPA enhancement. If pass/fail were the rule in all three zones of work—the major, the distribution requirements, and the electives—it would then have had its desired effect of substituting attention to the material for attention to the GPA.

Similarly, the student course/teacher evaluation practices have derogated teaching because administrators now use the accumulation of these forms over several semesters as measures of teacher accountability. Low scores can help end a faculty member's appointment; but even high scores can easily be discredited should it serve other administrative policies—reducing faculty size, for example.[10] Because the forms of student evaluations are similar to the forms of grades—some kind of single-factor average—the complicated truths about teaching and learning are buried and cannot be disclosed for the purposes of either crediting or helping either student or teacher.

Solution: Narrative Evaluation

My response to the title question regarding the solution to the problem of grading is the relatively common practice of narrative evaluation, a practice that has existed as long as grading has in the form of the comment, remark, letter, or conversation of recommendation. In a system of scalar grading, a narrative evaluation usually plays a secondary role, as it does today on the report cards of some primary school systems. As students move further along in school, narrative evaluation plays an increasingly important part. To get into college, recommendations are secondary to standardized test scores and to high school grade averages, but recommendations can determine a student's fate if the other materials don't yield a clear decision. In high school and in college, narrative evaluation usually appears on all essays students write, sometimes to justify a letter grade, sometimes alone. Increasingly, portfolios are given narrative evaluations. As email proliferates, *informal* narrative evaluations are frequently passed along by teachers and responded to by students resulting in *conversations* between students and teachers about the work. In graduate school, some faculty members give students long commentaries on their work. Often these commentaries justify grades. But just as often, since the grades themselves do not vary that much, the commentary/ evaluation process assumes a more important role. In some programs, there are files of faculty comments on students' work. Finally, as graduate students seek employment, the salient element (after the students' dissertations) is the dossier file with the student's letters of recommendation. Businesses also use narrative evaluation for their employees' and their own performance; in addition, they often display evaluative notices given by customers—testimonials —in order to promote the business. As this brief review suggests, narrative evaluation has always been considered an important part of teaching, certification, and public accountability processes, and offering such evaluations is not new or revolutionary.

Ideological Functions of Grading

If, as we can see, the role of narrative evaluation increases as a person grows older, why are grades important *at the times they are*, namely, from about the third grade to graduation from college, between ages eight and twenty-one? The answer to this question helps to demonstrate the ideological function of grades. In the early grades, the relation between students and teachers is still considered (in androcentric societies, the only kind there is) a relation between mothers and dependent children. Teachers in the elementary school are mostly women. As the child becomes literate in the third grade and thus potentially autonomous in the finding of information and understanding, a more hierarchical pedagogical style begins to grow in our school systems, so that by the seventh grade, subjects and students are highly segregated from one another according to a variety of criteria. While both men and women are teachers in the seventh grade and beyond, the pedagogical style is increasingly androcentric; school system administrators are mostly men. Through school systems, the values of an already gender-unbalanced society are promulgated through the compartmentalization of subjects and the tracking of students according to their ability to serve the *society as it is,* as opposed to society as the less privileged might prefer it.

A *bureaucratic mentality* is tacitly developed by the grading system. The way a child may achieve in school, as guided by the constant use of tests and grades—starting with the standardized tests of literacy and numeracy in the early grades, their annual use, the use of tests and grades in individual classrooms—is always governed by these bureaucratic styles, leading to the production of the "good student." The "good student" is the one who gets good grades and is tracked "high." This is the same student who knows how to do well on tests, who can discern the special psychology of the test question—what it "wants," so to speak—who can master reading comprehension exercises, word analogy exercises, and similar specialized tasks characteristic of standardized tests. The narrowness of these skills, while definitely a problem, does not by itself represent the problem of the "good student." Rather, all of the skills a student needs to acquire to do well on examinations are skills of compliance and adaptability. They are not skills of creativity, imagination, and resourcefulness. The latter abilities are not usually used or practiced in short class periods; they appear in a more measured or leisurely way in the ordinary experiences of daily life. Sometimes quick thinking is needed, and it can be useful to be able to parry situations with the speed of thought required by examinations, standardized or local. Yet in learning for the long run, for learning how to think in the great variety of contexts of different time lengths and locations, bureaucratic skills are not particularly useful.

The situation is urgent, however, because if the majority of students emerge from the school years with mainly bureaucratic ability, and if a minority of students who don't have this ability but have a variety of other talents and skills are tracked in "lower" groups, this means that existing pedagogical processes and styles are creating a managerial or bureaucratic majority: those who are ready to serve the power-centers of society. If grade-oriented pedagogies diminish in value, influence, status, and power, those people who have something other than bureaucratic ways of thinking enter society and pose a challenge to bureaucratic values.

If you object to grades and tests in schools, the common response is "Why? You are being graded and tested all the time! How can you object?" This is true, as Hanson has described. Grading and testing have an *ideological* authority. *Testing and grading have such great inertia in society because they are the pedagogical means by which an unfairly structured society is perpetuated.*

To propose *any* alternative to testing and grading is thus not simply to oppose a practice that *happens to be* widespread. It is to oppose a practice that perpetuates conditions favorable to the few who govern society. It is to take a *political* position that will cause trouble to those who benefit from training the "best" into bureaucratic functionaries.

In fact, narrative evaluation is a form of *disclosure*, personal and political. It is kept in a secondary position *because* it is a form of disclosure. In a sense, narrative evaluation is *dominated* as groups of people are dominated—locked in certain roles and not permitted to grow. The conflict between grade, or quantitative, evaluation and narrative evaluation is not unlike the "battle of the sexes": easy to joke about, to become amused about, but, underneath, reflecting a profound unfairness in society that requires correction. Of late, practices of disclosure have ameliorated other zones of academic work and society. Curriculums have changed in the last generation to include previously censored works and bodies of literature, to include political critiques of science, intellectual life, and society. One of the foundations of these changes has been the steady, disciplined disclosure of facts previously censored, such as the extent of the history of slavery, the routine use of sadistic violence and local terror, the domination of women and children, the domination of nontechnological societies by those with wealth and material, and so on.

The Value of Nongraded Narrative Evaluation

Narrative evaluation is a way of telling much more of the truths about teaching and learning, more of what really happens in classrooms, much more of what students really think and hope for, than the present systems of mutual grading.[11] To admit narrative evaluation into the mainstream of mutual evaluation is to transform evaluation itself into a conversational style, to transform binding judgments into opinions to be considered, to transform even acceptable categories such as passing and failing into gateways for negotiation and change, and especially, into processes for allowing more people to work toward fulfilling lives. As most of us would admit, almost every kind of narrative evaluation is itself part of teaching, because it provides information and opinion together in a single context, providing assessment and evaluation simultaneously. This combination enhances the usefulness of both the opinion and the information: the opinion is grounded; the information is contextualized. The result is the removal of fear from the context of evaluation. One can reason with it, so to speak. Fear is an internalized representation of the power held by society over its young and unprivileged majorities.[12] Historically, fear of more powerful elements of society has kept the less powerful from enhancing their lives. This is no less true in school. What is revolutionary about the advocacy of narrative evaluation is its ability to remove this fear, its ability to teach people not to fear to begin with, or, conversely, to inform accurately and early just what it is that needs to be feared in school and society. Tests and grades in school are what weapons are in the world at large—instruments of control, domination, and in many worst cases, exclusion and suppression. They are means to substitute coercion for negotiation, judgment for discussion, inertia for change.

In the 1960s, when contemporary forms of grading discussions began, they had a clear political foundation: opposition to the war in Vietnam, which was considered to be a flagrant resurgence of imperial ruthlessness, cruelty, and unchecked violence and murder. There were constant reminders that this was the case: bombings, massacres, and the corruption of our own soldiers. The objections to power that then surfaced on campuses were rooted in the objections to the exercise of military power. The destructiveness of *our own* military power was disclosed to a generation that had previously understood our military power in more acceptable senses—its victories over Germany and Japan. On campus, it was understood that universities collaborated with government and military institutions.[13] The students' own lives were jeopardized by the prospect of being drafted to fight the unjust war. "Student power" mattered in an immediate sense—preserving their lives as individuals, as well as restoring America's good name. The 1960s critique of grading appeared in such circumstances. The advocacy of narrative evaluation at that time had an immediate purpose as well as a traditional purpose.

Descriptive Evaluation

Because of the political circumstances of the 60s critique, Max Marshall's *Teaching Without Grades* (1968)[14] is conspicuous since it does not mention these circumstances, and because Marshall taught biology rather than English or other humanities subjects. That this book should appear without reference to its political context suggests that there was a temporary breach in the traditional school ideology. Marshall could credibly argue formally a perspective he had been enacting behind the closed doors of his classrooms for many years. His book, however, is buried, rarely cited in other studies of grades.[15] Here are his main proposals:

> The principles established are substantially two. First, the grading system, including most suggested substitutes because they also use symbols or words which rank students relative to one another, can be replaced only by attaining a clean break, a genuine nongrading concept. Second, it is possible during most days with classes to ignore relative appraisal altogether and, when called upon to do so, to replace it with pertinent description based on salient or outstanding features. (132–33)

This is a brief statement in a brief book, but it identifies fundamental aspects of the issue of grading: a "genuine nongrading concept" can be accepted if, on a daily basis in classrooms the habits of hierarchical evaluation (ranking) are abandoned and the habits of description are used. Marshall observes, "Description is subjective. Grades are more so" (142). The advantage of description over grades is that description identifies biases and perspectives as well as aspects of both students' and teachers' work. Description can disclose elements that are censored in a grading system, and its use encourages mutuality in the relationships of teachers with students. Description is harder than grading, but it is a part of teaching and not of administration.

Description as a feature of responses to teaching and learning leads to comprehensive summaries of students' work after a course, a year, or other period, as discussed by James Battersby (1973), who proposes:

> an evaluation system based on written reports for each student in each class. These reports would form the substance of the students' academic records and would be the principal resource of reviewers responsible for making probability judgments. (35)

Battersby's report system is accompanied by a credit/no record choice for each course taken. In large lectures, the reports are written by the teaching assistants who have contact with the students, rather than by lecturers who don't. Battersby is an English teacher, but his proposals are identical to Marshall's, as are his justifications:

> Although written reports do not guarantee the emergence of valid types [of performance by students], they at least make real confusion accessible and provide information infinitely more valuable than grades, national test scores, letters of recommendation, and so forth, since they disclose what criteria of evaluation are being applied to what material. Rejuvenated interest in academic subjects, emotional problems, financial shortages, new insights, etc., can all subvert established and characteristic tendencies and instigate the development of new performance possibilities, but the detailed accounts of realized academic achievement, for all their inherent shortcomings, are best equipped to handle the complex problems involved in the process of evaluation. (39–40)

Every teacher knows the variety of reasons that account for students' achievements in school. Part of the continuing frustration with grading is teachers' feelings that the truth about students cannot be recorded; students can not be recognized accurately by their records, nor can the next teachers they get discern from grades what help students may need. The fact remains: only narrative evaluation, per assignment, per course, or per year-long performance of students, teachers, and administrators has a chance of contributing to the growth processes of teaching and learning in schools. The processes of grading as we now know them contribute to the destructive hegemony of administrations, school systems, boards of trustees, and corporate moguls over the processes of teaching and learning.

In this volume, several contributors have mentioned that in response to today's "grade inflation,"[16] administrations have demanded from faculty grade sheets that look like the bell curve—taught to me in graduate school as the 10-20-40-20-10 curve, A through F (no E). Threats are being made to faculty members' jobs if their grade sheets don't mirror this particular response to grade inflation. As we know from the Wiesenfeld commentary cited at the beginning of my essay, the tendency of some, perhaps many, is to crack down—sanctimoniously as Wiesenfeld does—on both student and teacher "slackers"—the supposed beneficiaries of grade inflation. However, in the 60s, as now, grade inflation is a subversive response to runaway corporate power, greed, and ruthlessness. Because of excessive pressure building up for an ever-more compliant bureaucratic managerial class of employees, more and more "good students" are needed; that is, those that will "ace" the grading system. If the grading system becomes more demanding, the "aces" will be more to the liking of those who need strong bureaucracies. In any event, the good students will only be the compliant ones—a situation increasingly the case today. The imaginative, creative, and resourceful students will not fit well into the bureaucracy, unless their special energies are consciously dedicated to enhancing corporate fortunes.

The grading system has been, even since the Chou dynasty, an instrument meant to preserve the traditional hierarchical arrangements in society. To try to change it requires change to be on the professional agendas of a large number of teachers. But obviously it must be part of a wider program for change in how schools are run. I will mention three items that I think should be on our professional agendas as teachers and as teachers of teachers. Two items are for all schools; one item is for postsecondary schools alone.

A Key for Change

Key to changing the grading system is the lowering of the student-to-faculty ratio. Schools attended by the children of the wealthy have classrooms with maximums of fifteen students. As most of us have experienced, a small number of students in a class, with an optimum number between eight and eighteen, usually takes the bite out of the existing grading system; it is easier for evaluations to include narratives—oral and/or written—along with grades. It also shows how unnecessary for teaching grades are, since the salient information and opinion are given in the narrative. However, for public schools and many private ones to have such classroom conditions, twice as many teachers are needed in schools as there are now. If all schools were as seriously expected to support society as are elite secondary and postsecondary schools, the "luxury" of fewer students would be common and would not be a luxury at all but an ordinary feature of school. At the national level, because schooling is narrowly viewed, at best, in terms of upward mobility instead of terms of vocational enfranchisement, the urgency for viewing schools more seriously is not widely appreciated. This failure of perception comes in the refusal to pay higher school taxes; yet it would be surprising if most communities would not continue to prosper if school taxes were doubled. Without such fundamental change in the approach to schools, it will remain difficult to advocate noncompetitive, nonhierarchical styles of teaching and learning.

At research universities, the undergraduate grading system protects the research time for the faculty. Because teachers get tenure mostly for research, the faculty must have the least time-consuming technique of certifying undergraduates, which is the grading system. Most faculty members would not be ready to commit themselves to tenure-through-teaching unless the system itself were different. At universities where one does win tenure through teaching, faculty members are usually responsible for one hundred or more students per semester, and the semiannual student plebiscite becomes an important means of evaluating teaching, though research universities would do well to learn from teaching universities just how much is already done to cultivate committed teaching.

A great deal can be done about grading by simply not doing it. I dispute the attitude toward grading recently proposed by Lad Tobin (1993):

> Making the messiness of grading public is almost always healthy in a writing class. There is never a danger that grades will lose all meaning, because they are so deeply embedded in our culture and consciousness, but we can make them a little less threatening—to our students and ourselves—by exposing the process. (69)

I dispute it because of efforts made long ago and cited in my essay and other places in this volume to hold a principled position about grading that advocates its removal. I read Tobin's remarks much as I read Wiesenfeld's (1996) in the recent *Newsweek*—with the sense of disappointment about how they fail to understand that the deeply embedded grading process derives from social governance that is finally harmful to most people who are not already privileged.

I fear that potential leaders in this profession, even those who have opposed grading in the past like Peter Elbow, refuse to admit that grading serves mostly traditional bureaucratic, elitist, and androcentric interests throughout school and university systems. While an end to grading will not itself change society, viewing grading in this light suggests a new vision of teaching and learning, one that can be advocated, promoted, and even incrementally enacted. This view of teaching and learning discloses the political character of education regardless of which politics is part of what teaching. Finally, the clear consensus in the many discussions of grading that I and other contributors to this volume have read is that most of us who do it don't like or want it. It is about time that we stop wringing our hands about grading and, instead, commit ourselves—teachers and students—to the principles of teaching without competitiveness, hierarchy, and authoritarian value, to teaching through cooperation, interaction, mutual respect, and communication.

Notes

1. Several contributors to this volume have reflected the harm done to students as they move from teacher to teacher, each having different scales of evaluation. Everyone knows that this happens all the time. It is not confronted because one either has to adopt a completely rigid standard, or one has to abandon the letter grade system. Since few want either of these alternatives, the system continues on in hypocrisy.

2. Essay cited in note 14.

3. The introduction of this term is credited by many to Michel Foucault, possibly as an abstraction of what had gone on in France in the mid-twentieth century. "Surveillance" refers to how a central bureaucracy keeps track of citizens. The process of keeping track can vary greatly: for example, very little in the United States to a great deal in Soviet Russia and Nazi Germany.

4. We all know how regularly records are discarded, as teachers grade on how the actual classroom relationships progressed during the semester. The "scientific" policy announcements are meant as hedges against possible lawsuits from disgruntled students and their families who spent many thousands on college. Faculty reports of their own work and progress are also not used, as recently announced at a faculty meeting by a department chair I know. There is little connection between the announced formula for faculty evaluation and the actual formula, which is usually kept secret.

5. The precedence of rules over human needs is discussed at length in Carol Gilligan's *In a Different Voice* (1982), as characteristic of men's prosecution of ethical principles.

6. I and others thinking about teaching will want to reject the reduction of choices to "the carrot and the stick." This formulation can describe the psychology of grading, the practice contested by this discussion. In both this discussion and Gordon's, however, it is essential to emphasize that whatever the "carrot" may mean, the meaning of the "stick" is much less ambiguous: it is related to the use of force to intimidate those who don't have or use "sticks." Sometimes the intimidation is used

to hoard and steal resources; other times it is used to teach others that the "stick" is the prevailing way of life in the rest of society.

7. The January/February 1989 issue of *Academe* has several essays that discuss how universities are increasingly behaving like corporations. I cite and comment on these essays in "Academic Ideology and the New Attention to Teaching" (1995). By 1995, and by the time this essay reaches print, that 1989 trend will have intensified even further, as suggested by the increasing number of reports in *The Chronicle of Higher Education* that tell of trustee interference in the running of universities. These trustees, who are all members of corporate boards, are attempting to micro-manage universities. Of particular concern are the noises they are making to oppose faculty members' tenure.

8. Throughout his study Latham refers exclusively to men as university students and test takers. On the one hand, it seems somewhat surprising to see this assumption used so fluently; but on the other it is just as clear that the complaints about the exams will apply just as well to women as to men. Today's take on this situation could be that men are more willing than women are to pay the price outlined in this passage.

9. These attempts are commonly repeated in today's universities by faculty councils that declare pluses and minuses mandatory in grading. I discuss this matter in *The Double Perspective* (1988 Chapter Six).

10. In my essay, "Academic Ideology and the New Attention to Teaching" (1995, 584 ff), I discuss Victoria Moessner's account of how administrations have abused relatively high ratings by invoking a statistically derived norm for adverse comparison of the teacher's actual ratings.

11. In "Evaluation, Self-Evaluation, and Individualism" (1992), I describe a process of continuing, mutual evaluation, represented in a narrative form.

12. In Judith Fetterley's book *The Resisting Reader* (1978), she notes in her preface, "the fear, the fear, the fear" that has prevented women in the past from even beginning to seize political initiatives.

13. In the 1960s, I was at Indiana University, and it was quite a surprise to learn that faculty members were actually paid by the Central Intelligence Agency to do various tasks.

14. In "Academic Ideology and The New Attention to Teaching" (1995 note 12), I cite several other sources written about the same time. Many who have studied grades conducted elaborate surveys and showed many tables and details. The upshot of the many studies has been, consistently, that college admissions, professional school admissions, and most other situations do not need the administrative boost of a grade point average for each student: discursive documentation makes the case helpfully.

15. It has a similar status to Edward Pauly's *The Classroom Crucible* (1990) today: it speaks from the practical experience of teaching, announcing facts about classrooms and schools that, if taken seriously, would demonstrate the emptiness of how schools are now treated by federal and state agencies.

16. A factor mentioned in 1973 by Battersby as grounds for instituting a system of narrative evaluation.

References

Battersby, J. L. 1973. *Typical Folly: Evaluating Student Performance in Higher Education*. Urbana, IL: NCTE.

Bleich, D. 1988. *The Double Perspective: Language, Literacy and Social Relations*. New York: Oxford University Press

———. 1992. "Evaluation, Self-Evaluation, and Individualism." *ADE Bulletin* 101 (Summer): 9–14.

———. 1995. "Academic Ideology and the New Attention to Teaching." *New Literary History*, 26 (3) Summer: 565–90.

Ferguson, K. E. 1984. *The Feminist Case Against Bureaucracy*. Philadelphia: Temple University Press.

Fetterley, J. 1978. *The Resisting Reader: A Feminist Approach to American Fiction*. Bloomington, IL: Indiana University Press.

Gilligan, C. 1982. *In a Different Voice: Psychological Theory and Women's Development*. Cambridge, MA: Harvard University Press.

Gordon, D. H. 1996. *Fat and Mean: The Corporate Squeeze of Working Americans and the Myth of Managerial "Downsizing."* New York: The Free Press.

Hanson, F. A. 1993. *Testing, Testing: Social Consequences of the Examined Life*. Berkeley: University of California Press.

Latham, H. 1877. *On the Action of Examinations Considered as a Means of Selection*. Cambridge, England: Deighton, Bell and Company.

Marshall, M. S. 1968. *Teaching Without Grades*. Corvallis, OR: Oregon State University Press.

Milton, O., H. R. Pollio, and J. A. Eison. 1986. *Making Sense of College Grades: Why the Grading System Does Not Work and What Can Be Done About It*. San Francisco: Jossey-Bass Publishers.

Pauly, E. 1990. *The Classroom Crucible: What Really Works, What Doesn't, and Why*. New York: Basic Books.

Smallwood, M. L. 1935. *An Historical Study of Examinations and Grading Systems in Early American Universities: A Critical Study of the Original Records of Harvard, William and Mary, Yale, Mount Holyoke, and Michigan from Their Founding to 1900*. London: Oxford University Press.

Tobin, L. 1993. *Writing Relationships: What Really Happens in the Composition Class*. Portsmouth, NH: Boynton/Cook.

Wiesenfeld, K. 1996. "Making the Grade." *Newsweek* 17 June, 16.

Chapter Two

Cross Purposes
Grade Deflation, Classroom Practices

Eleanor Agnew

Eleanor Agnew teaches undergraduate and graduate courses in writing and composition theory at Georgia Southern University, a public institution which serves about fourteen thousand students, primarily from Georgia and Florida. About 25 percent of the entering students are placed in developmental writing classes. Eleanor Agnew examines how the current grade deflation movement and classroom practices long-supported by composition theory are at cross purposes. She argues that academia must shift its focus away from grade distribution back to standards.

The Politics of Grade Distributions

Many new writing instructors join the academy eager to teach freshman composition, only to discover that if they teach it effectively, they face a delicate political problem when it comes time to hand in final grades.

Because of a national paranoia about grade inflation, many English departments are quietly pressuring their writing instructors to grade more stringently, to be cautious about awarding too many A's or B's, in order to help revive flagging academic standards. In particular, teachers need to demonstrate stringency on the final grade rolls, which become public record and are often printed out for all to see. Final grade distributions are thought to be as useful for monitoring the health of department standards as an electrocardiogram is for monitoring heart disease. The primary difference is that cardiologists are usually *pleased* to see a good electrocardiogram reading; English departments, on the other hand, tend to be suspicious of good grades.

Furthermore, cardiologists who suspect heart disease order an echocardiogram so they can observe the heart firsthand, but academicians usually make their diagnosis—grade inflation—without so much as glancing at any of the student papers (let alone the syllabus, texts, assignments, or other components of the course) that generated the grades.

Ekstrom and Villegas (1994), who did a study of how the grading practices at fourteen institutions changed between 1980 and 1990, confirm that

> There appears to be considerable pressure on institutions of higher education and their faculties to reduce what the public perceives as lax standards resulting in ever rising GPA's. Institutions seem to be taking steps to respond to this, primarily by introducing curriculum requirements. At the department level, slightly more than half of the responding faculty reported efforts to raise standards. There also appears to be informal pressure for faculty to meet certain expected department grading standards [which] might be expected to lead to lower overall GPA's. (36)

Sometimes new writing instructors do not "get it" right away. Often, the message is subtle. However, the awareness begins to dawn when they receive the annual faculty grade distributions with an attached memo reminding everyone to "keep grades in line with the department average" because "we do not want to mislead students into thinking that they are better than they are." The message begins to penetrate even more deeply when they notice senior faculty members routinely thumbing through department grade printouts to see if anyone's grades are "too high." But the message truly hits the mark when the chair or a senior colleague talks to them about their "elevated" grade distributions. One teacher received a blunt letter from a concerned administrator at Rutgers University, chiding him for his grades: "I have been concerned for some time about the grading in your classes," the letter reads. "I feel the need to speak out about maintaining department standards. In my view the grades are too high on average. . . . Many students do not merit the excellent grades they are getting from you" (Farley 1995, Exhibit 4).

The problem: writing instructors who have been trained in composition theory know that creating an encouraging, nonpunitive classroom atmosphere and using a process, multiple-drafting pedagogy is at the heart of teaching writing effectively and that under those circumstances even the weakest writers can often achieve some measure of success and produce better written products than they might have in a more traditional writing course. But if the students do "too well," administrators may simply assume that the grades are inflated and that the teacher must be slack, an assumption that can lead to trouble, even job loss.

How did our discipline reach the point where it is afraid of good grades?

History of the Grade Deflation Movement

The push for grade deflation comes in response to reports of grade inflation. Inflated grades are attributed to lightweight teaching and weak students. In *English Journal,* Cosgrove (1995) explains: "The concept [of grade inflation] posits that teachers, facing classes filled with increasingly unresponsive dullards, have progressively eased their evaluation criteria and thus abandoned a once fixed standard of academic accomplishment" (15). Teachers shy away from higher grades and administrators push for lower grades because higher grades signify weakness in the course material, students, and teacher. However, we must acknowledge that grade-conscious English departments have the best of intentions. They want only to ensure that all writing teachers grade student work according to department guidelines and that they do not give high grades for slipshod, mediocre student work. We would all agree on that. (Some readers might even be surprised to know that this writer has stood her ground many times over the years against tearful student pleas for "just five more points" so a grade could be raised to the one the student "needed.") Wiesenfeld (1996) contends that in recent years, more students than ever have demonstrated "a disgruntled consumer approach. If they don't like their grade, they go to the 'return' counter to trade it in for something better" (16).

It is true that grade point averages at the college level began to creep up in the 1960s. By the mid-1970s, there had been a significant rise in college GPAs (Birnbaum 1977, 520). Outcries about slack grading standards at the university level have been resounding through the popular and academic press for several decades (Geisinger 1980; Goldman 1980; Grieves 1982; Iyasere 1984; McDaniel 1984; Wilhide 1982). Even now, hardly a day goes by without some politician, academician, or newspaper columnist publicly bemoaning the sad state of American education while pointing the finger at grade inflation (Cole 1993; Leo 1993; Will 1995).

Simultaneously, the institutional accountability movement has spread swiftly across the nation. According to Hutchings and Marchese (1990), the number of states that promoted institutional assessment increased from just a few in the mid-1980s to about forty by 1990. By 1990, 82 percent of all colleges reported that they were undergoing assessment, which, according to Hutchings and Marchese "has now moved assessment across the threshold from 'another interesting idea' to 'a condition for doing business'" (14, 16). Krueger and Heisserer (1987) state that "assessment is the driving force within any realistic, systematic plan for institutional progress and development" (45). Because accrediting agencies are required by federal law to examine evidence of institutions' learning outcomes, standardized testing has flourished (Hutchings & Marchese 1990, 23). More and more, academic standards have been reduced to sets of numbers.

Fallacies Driving the Grade Deflation Movement

Grade distributions, when isolated from the situation that generated them, are virtually meaningless as a reflection of academic standards, because grades do not give one iota of information about the amount, type, or frequency of coursework; the caliber of student performance or progress over the semester; the effectiveness of the teacher; or the quality of the institution. Grades, writes Elbow (1993), with "no more information or clues about the criteria behind these noises," tell absolutely nothing about what has occurred in the classroom (189–90). Milton (1992) agrees that "it is assumed incorrectly by administrators, students, and society . . . that the letter symbols or grades that ensue [from course tests] are accurate measures of that learning. Nothing could be further from the truth in far too many instances" (20). Milton, Pollio, and Eison (1986) state that colleges and universities are misguided in thinking that "grade emphasis assures high standards" (43). "Educational standards," points out Agnew (1995), "cannot be instantaneously bolstered up with a mere restructuring of the final numbers anymore [sic] than a decaying house can be repaired with a fresh coat of paint" (93).

Not only do grades in isolation say little about a teacher's or an institution's standards, they are notoriously unreliable ranking instruments. Unfortunately, many administrators, politicians, parents, students, as well as educators, believe that grades are infallible symbols, which always represent material of equal value. Not at all. Numerous variables enter into the grading process; identical grades do not necessarily represent equal quality of work, any more than different grades necessarily represent unequal quality. The unreliability of grading has been aptly demonstrated (Diedrich 1974; Lloyd-Jones 1987; White 1994). The same grader may even give a different grade on a different day to the exact same material (Branthwaite, Trueman, and Berrisford 1981). Milton, Pollio, and Eison (1986) state, "An attempt to equate a B from one instructor given during one academic year with a B from another instructor given during some other (or even the same) year is likely to yield an erroneous impression of equality" (45).

In short, as much as teachers may *try* to grade reliably, they almost always bring some individual social, rhetorical, and linguistic priorities to the grading process (Dickson 1991; White 1994). Don't we all know colleagues who are particularly swayed by a paper's colorful style and others who swoon over error-free work?

Imagine, then, the unreliability of grades in typical English departments, where numerous teachers, with wide-ranging backgrounds, ages, and agendas, are assigning different topics, for different purposes, on different days, under different time frames, to different students, and then grading them alone. Even if an entire English department collectively produced perfectly bell curved grade rolls, these grades would not reflect identical quality of student work.

Merely pounding the grade distributions into the proper shape does little to address any problems with the *standards* behind the grades.

Composition Theory and the Grade Deflation Movement

Probably the worst outcome of the grade deflation movement is that it works at cross purposes with composition theory, the very pedagogical approach that could help unskilled or inexperienced writers far more than merely grading more rigorously.

Writing instructors who follow pedagogical models based on composition theory set their students up for success. Student writers who are respected and encouraged as writers, who are given time to think about their topics before writing, who are allowed to consult with teachers and peers during the writing process, who write several drafts *before* they hand in the final copy to be graded, who even come to enjoy writing, are more likely to produce better written texts—and receive better grades—than the students across the hall who write papers for a more traditional teacher who gives them one class period to produce a final draft. (For a thorough discussion about the pedagogical applications of composition theory, see Lindemann 1995.) Unfortunately, many administrators and faculty members are not familiar with composition theory, and because they do not know it or understand it, they are not aware that this model of teaching may enable students to write better than they might have under more traditional models. Looking only at grade printouts in isolation, they quickly assume that grades are inflated. John Sandman and Michael Weiser, whose essay appears in this collection, confirm that they have worked in departments where chairs have circulated grade distributions "to encourage teachers whose grades strayed from the departmental mean to rethink their grading." (See Chapter 3 in this volume.) The authors refer to a departmental memo in which "the chair said that he felt that the composition grades in general were too high, and that he could not accept as reliable the student evaluations of any teachers whose grades were above 3.0."

Effects of Grading Politics on Writing Teachers' Pedagogy

Although grade-conscious English departments may believe they are strengthening their standards by lowering their grades, they are not only failing to address the real issue of standards but also limiting teachers' freedom to teach writing effectively. First, the pressure to conform to expected grade roll distributions forces teachers to put their own professional survival ahead of pedagogy, attitude, and even ethics. Knowing that they must serve up the numbers that administrators want to see, they find themselves insidiously adopting a mind set of self-preservation that works at cross-purposes with effective teaching and ethical evaluation. At first, this punitive mind set may emerge only at the end of the semester when final grades are being calculated. New teachers may shock even themselves when they discover that they feel *thankful* as they calculate a couple of legitimate D's or F's for the final grade roll. These will balance the ledger! Every C brings a sigh of relief. But when there are simply not enough C's, D's, and F's on a grade roll, teachers face a dilemma. Should they risk their jobs? Or should they find a legitimate way of fudging the grades downward just a tad, perhaps by shifting percentages so that the timed final exam essay counts 25 percent instead of 20 percent?

Eventually this numbers game evolves into a higher form of job protection consciousness. The guilt and anguish of those long, end-of-semester afternoons with the calculator and a throbbing conscience ultimately metamorphose from a twice yearly crisis into a more permanent mind set that pervades the curriculum and pedagogy of future semesters. Contributor John Sandman (see Chapter 3 in this volume) writes about a time years ago when he had been warned about "high" grades. Therefore, the next semester, he consciously worked at lowering them. After all, he recalls, "This particular department chair held the simplistic but widespread idea that low grades equal high standards and therefore good teaching."

What other choice did he have?

Thus, when under pressure to prove that they are upholding high standards through mediocre grades, writing instructors begin, consciously or otherwise, to teach towards grade outcomes by creating syllabi that are a little less writer-friendly, with more timed or impromptu activities that are more likely to result in lower grades. Teaching towards grade outcomes can manifest itself in attitude as well as syllabus. Composition theory advocates a positive, encouraging, nonpunitive writing context to bring out the best in student abilities. By contrast, the pedagogical climate created by the grade deflation movement is a negative one. Milton, Pollio, and Eison (1986) recognize the punitive undercurrent that drives the grade deflation movement:

> When faculty and society in general talk about grade inflation, they are describing their own attitudes toward a perceived leniency in evaluation, something that might accurately be rendered as: "Those kids are getting away with murder. The professors are too easy on them—not like when I was a student. How are those kids ever going to grow up and take their place in the real world where everything is not so lenient?" (32–33)

Teachers who fear "inflated" grades may find themselves segueing into more of a gatekeeping mind set during the course and making a more conscious effort to grade individual papers more critically. Contributor John Sandman (Chapter 3) refers to it as "Saving ones' neck by sacrificing one's values, or 'Okay, I'll lower my grades.'" During a time in his career when his job was at stake because of "elevated" grades, he began to grade down in order to please the administrators. He would "read a paper and think, 'This student deserves a B, but I better give it a C+ if I want to keep my job.'"

Cosgrove (1995) agrees:

> Justifying a low paper grade is easy enough when a student's writing is incoherent, careless, or both. Such justifications are not so easy, however, when students are in obvious possession of both intelligence and academic savvy. Even the supposed dregs within a high-level class will neither expect nor easily accept low grades. In other words, if teachers expect to strike a blow for grade deflation, standards, and bell-shaped distributions, they must be prepared to defend their judgements, occasionally at length. (15)

In other words, part of teaching towards the bell curve includes reading student papers with negative expectations and with the intention of sniffing out any possible weaknesses that might provide "evidence" to justify the grades needed to meet the quotas. As contributor Juan Flores (see Chapter 8 in this volume) states in his essay, "Customarily, grading of writing is done with picky-preciseness, as if our students are on trial, guilty before proven innocent. We carefully build our case against them, proving beyond any shadow of doubt that C's, D's, or F's have been objectively assigned and justice dispatched."

Basic Writers as the Victims of Grade Roll Politics

Today, approximately one out of three freshmen who enters college will be placed in a developmental writing course. Most college English teachers will teach basic writers at some time during their careers. Basic writers are the ones most likely to be the sacrificial lambs of the grade deflation movement. Teachers who are under pressure to keep the grades bell curved and to Guard the Gates more closely than ever may find the weaker writers to be the easiest lambs to sacrifice on the altar of grade deflation. Everyone expects them to do poorly anyway! In fact, some critics blame the alleged decline in standards on the democratization of the university that began in the 1960s: in other words, on the new "strangers in academia" (Shaugnessy 1977, 3), the basic writers of yesterday. In 1981, Spinelli reported:

> Many [educators] assert that the state and federal governments are largely responsible for the deterioration in academic standards which have resulted in the decline in student performance and attitudes in higher education. Mandates are issued regularly instructing educators to embrace affirmative action programs . . . all these procedures are designed to accommodate and facilitate a higher education to anyone who desires it, regardless of aptitude, ability or motivation. (2)

This attitude has not died out. In a 1995 column, George Will sneers, "At some colleges remedial courses are now called ESD courses—English as a Second Dialect."

Mina Shaughnessy (1977), who dubbed basic writers "strangers in academia" (3), was the first to acknowledge that inexperienced writers *can* learn to write better in an atmosphere of patience, encouragement, and tolerance. Since then, a large body of literature on basic writers has sprung up, recognizing that inexperience and context, rather than cognitive deficiency (as was once believed), are frequently the cause of weak writing skills. Not only is it difficult for basic writers to conform to the often unfamiliar rhetorical and linguistic conventions dictated by academia, they face the added problem of being social "outsiders." Contributor Juan Flores (see Chapter 8), describes his typical writing student as a Latina whose "defeatist images of racial inferiority borrowed from former teachers and other mainstream cultural icons repress her." It is known that the social, cognitive, rhetorical, and psychological contexts of a writing situation play a very important role in basic writers' ability—or inability—to write (Bizzell 1982; Brand and Powell 1986; Rose 1980; Wolcott and Buhr 1987). However, teachers who feel pressured to anticipate class grade distributions may find themselves striving to be more critical and fault-finding towards the work of basic writers during the course, which is the very thing basic writers need the least. Most important, they may be depriving their weaker writers of the chance to learn the real meaning of writing and the chance to achieve some hard-won measure of success.

Fighting Grade Roll Politics on a Large Scale

We should not overlook the ethical implications of this issue. For many students, going to college is a huge financial sacrifice. Many have had to borrow perhaps hundreds or thousands of dollars to pay for it. Others may be on scholarships, which they will lose if they do not earn a particular GPA. Teachers who succumb to the pressure to grade down just for the sake of the grade roll appearance must think carefully about the impact cosmetically lowered grades have on every student's life.

Departmental grade roll politics is an offshoot of the current national tendency to confuse true *standards* with reams of *numbers*, usually standardized test scores. From kindergarten through college, student achievement is continuously measured through an endless stream of standardized or timed tests. Headlines in the newspapers resound regularly with despair or joy about losses or gains in test points. Television news stories compare states' and countries' rankings of student achievement. Politicians hop on the bandwagon of the "education crisis" and suggest more testing, more hoops, more accountability. Then teachers from K through college, responsible for producing strong test scores from their students, feel even more pressured to teach towards tests. English teachers as a group, through NCTE or other organizations, should engage in a media campaign to inform the public about how the testing industry drives much of our instruction and causes us to be "looking for value in all the wrong places" (White 1994, 7). We need to inform the public that numbers in isolation, whether test scores, international rankings, or grades, not only say very little about standards but also distract us from closely examining some real alternatives to improving standards. With the endorsement of NCTE, English teachers nationwide should write informative letters to the editor or guest columns for their local newspapers, in addition to addressing school boards and parent groups.

Furthermore, because composition theory itself is still widely misunderstood or dismissed as frivolous, many automatically assume that higher grades in writing courses are the result of inflation and low standards rather than good teaching. Will (1995), for example, suggests that the process approach to teaching writing is one of several "academic fads" responsible for the declining literacy in this country. He clearly envisions practitioners of the process approach as some spaced-out breed of New Age flower children for whom anything goes in the classroom, who have no judgment or standards, who are not teaching any grammar or style. Many people who do not know or understand composition theory harbor similar misconceptions about it. Unfortunately, this includes some of our own colleagues in the academy. English teachers, as a group, need to make a public effort to inform their colleagues about what composition theory really entails and to debunk the myths about it. On an individual basis, writing instructors who know comp theory should keep an open dialogue with colleagues who misunderstand and distrust it. For one thing, comp theorists can respectfully disagree with their colleagues who dub the process approach as "that touchy-feely English" or "the type of English where you don't teach them about thesis statements" or "the English where you pass everybody because you don't want to hurt anyone's feelings." These are just a few of the misconceptions I have heard over the years.

Not only should English teachers as a group embark upon a campaign to elevate the status of composition theory in places where it is not known or trusted, they also need, as a group, to work towards discrediting the grade deflation movement and its manifestation in department grade roll politics. One important way of bringing about change would be for more people to do research and scholarship specifically examining the grade deflation movement and its effects. The more published scholarship there is, the more likely that change will take place.

Fighting Grade Roll Politics on a Small Scale

Changes in public attitude take time. Meanwhile, what can average, unempowered writing teachers do? What choices do they have if they want to remain in good standing with their employers? Often, they are the ones with the least clout in the department. They are the graduate assistants, the temporary, the part-time, or the still-untenured instructors, the ones least likely to be in a position to raise questions, to challenge the status quo, to effect a change in attitude within the department. Many feel they have no choice but to go along with the pressure to play grade roll politics. They are the ones who, in effect, have been silenced. In his essay, contributor John Sandman (see Chapter 3) admits that as a first-year lecturer whose job was in question, he felt coerced into providing his department chair with the grade range that was expected. At the other extreme, an occasional instructor will opt for a more heroic course of action, loudly challenge the status quo, flamboyantly give all A's and B's, and end up being fired. However, another alternative exists. Writing teachers can refuse to allow departmental politics to inhibit their good teaching by taking steps to protect themselves and their good standing from any questions that might arise from either colleagues or students. The first step, of course, is to be absolutely confident that they are *not* in any way inflating grades. In addition to the routine procedures—being familiar with department evaluation criteria, attending any recalibration sessions, and reading any model papers that illustrate grade levels—writing teachers should also do the following:

Create a Course Booklet Before Each Course Begins

A course booklet, bound by the campus print shop for students to purchase, is a collection of all the handouts students will need from the first to the last day of the course. It includes all day-to-day instructions, writing assignments, study questions, model papers, peer evaluation sheets, and exercises, as well as any generic handouts.

This booklet serves two purposes.

First, compiling a course booklet *before* the class begins not only forces teachers to define for themselves the specific purpose of the course, but to have a plan in advance for exactly how to get there. This planning prevents them from proceeding along too casually with only day-by-day or week-by-week minigoals, which may not be cohesive in the long run. Not only do teachers who plan as they go along run the risk of finding themselves too tired and overwhelmed five Sundays later to even remember their original goals for the course (let alone stay focused on them during the following week), they may also find themselves resorting to busy work or filler assignments that do not contribute much to student learning but must still be factored in with the final grade.

Making a course booklet will also help instructors decide in advance just how much each course activity should be weighted into the grade. Writing instructors who want to hand in their grades with a clean conscience should be confident that they are really grading what they are supposed to be grading.

Giving too much or even any grade-weight for incidental activities not related to the important course goals may indeed inflate the grades. For example, if the purpose of the course is primarily writing argument, then instructors should be wary of giving too much weight to the fun and easy supplementary activities, such as oral reports or class participation. Offering students extra motivational points for behaviors unrelated to course goals, such as coming to class, attending extra curricular events, or typing papers instead of handwriting them may boost the class morale *during* the course, but will only compound final-grade anxiety at the end of the course when the promise of extra points comes home to roost.

A second purpose is served by course booklets.

They can be routinely submitted to mentors, chairs, or administrators during annual reviews as evidence of a well-planned, challenging course. The myth persists, states Sheridan (1990), that high grades must be the result of lightweight teaching (171). A course booklet will demonstrate otherwise.

Create a Very Clear Grading Policy

This may seem to be an odd suggestion for writing instructors who already feel suffocated by too much institutional grading consciousness; however, a clearly stated policy can be a protection and justification for assigned grades. The course grading policy, with a specific breakdown of the percentage each class activity counts towards the grade and a description of exactly how the grades will be calculated, should be included in the course booklet described above. Carefully planning a grading policy will go a long way towards eliminating any guilt or anguish when final grades are being calculated. Teachers should have no qualms about handing in final grades, no matter how high or low, when there is no haziness in a grading policy that is consistent with department standards.

Elbow (1983) describes the importance of explaining his "gatekeeper functions" at the beginning of a course: "The more I can make it clear to myself and to my students that I do have a commitment to knowledge and institutions, and the more I can make it specifically clear how I am going to fulfill that commitment, the easier it is for me to turn around and make a dialectical change of role into being an extreme ally to students" (335). Farley (1995) agrees that "each professor, at the beginning of the course, will need to make his or her course requirements absolutely clear and unequivocal" (18).

Compile Teaching Portfolios

Teaching portfolios are now being widely used to measure teacher accountability from kindergarten through college. Writing instructors should create their own teaching portfolios—even if they are not required by their institutions—and include these portfolios, along with course booklets, in any packet submitted as part of an annual review. A teacher portfolio might include such items as "samples of student work, teacher-developed plans and materials, videotaped teaching episodes and the teacher's reflections on his or her own teaching" (Wolf 1991, 130). Urbach (1992) suggests photographs or audio recordings as well. Adams (1995) suggests an annotated bibliography of journal articles related to instructional methodology. Writing instructors who voluntarily create teacher portfolios can capture the essence of who they are as teachers in a packet that also contains samples of their graded papers. I particularly suggest that these portfolios include *prewriting* and *all drafts*, as well as the final copy, of four or five different student papers so that anyone who reads these can see the progression of each paper.

Require and Keep Student Portfolios

Because portfolio assessment combines the best of teaching and the best of assessment, it has been officially sanctioned by some institutions as a replacement for departmentally regulated final exams (Belanoff and Elbow 1986; Elbow and Belanoff 1991; Smit 1990; Weiser 1992). Guidelines vary, but typically students are allowed to select what they consider to be the best three or four papers they have written during the semester and to revise them. Next, they write a cover letter summarizing what they have learned about writing, add it to the portfolio, and hand the whole packet in at the end of the semester. Either their whole final grade or a large part of it is based on the material in the portfolio.

Weiser (1992) concludes that portfolio evaluation reduced grade inflation at Purdue. Student portfolios help raise department standards by improving the validity of assessment because portfolios contain a range of student works written under what Smit (1990) calls "'normal' or 'naturalistic' conditions" (51). As Elbow and Belanoff (1991) point out, "We cannot get a trustworthy picture of a student's writing proficiency unless we look at several samples produced on several days in several modes or genres" (5). In addition, the portfolio submissions have been revised to the best of the student's ability, thus giving a clearer impression of the capabilities of each student. They can also provide valuable information about what each student is *not* capable of (Agnew and McLaughlin 1994; Roemer, Schultz, and Durst 1991).

Even if their English departments have not officially embraced portfolio assessment, writing instructors might consider using them on their own. They will not only feel more confident about the validity of their final grades, but they can use the portfolios for a more functional purpose: job protection. If an instructor's grades are ever questioned, the student material that generated those grades will be available as justification. Portfolios can, in other words, be used as a backup for newer, less empowered teachers who fear that they may be called into the Chair's office for a few words.

It is unfortunate that high grades have come to be associated with low standards, particularly in freshman composition. Writing teachers might even be tempted to feel insulted: what is implied about them when it is a foregone assumption that their students will not be able to attain a level of skill higher than average after spending fifteen weeks in a writing class? Chances are, however, the administration's attitude about how grades should turn out is based on a lack of familiarity with composition theory and its pedagogical offshoots. English teachers as a group need to collaborate on a widespread media campaign to reverse this tarnished image. Meanwhile, writing instructors who know how to bring out the best in their students in the classroom owe it to themselves and to their students to do so, without worrying about grade outcomes. To do otherwise is unethical. They should merely be prepared to justify their grades with as much paper trail as possible.

References

Adams, T. 1995. "A Paradigm for Portfolio Assessment in Teacher Education." *Education* 115 (4): 568–70, 528.

Agnew, E. 1995. "Rigorous Grading Does Not Raise Standards: It Only Lowers Grades." *Assessing Writing* 2 (1): 91–103.

Agnew, E. and M. McLaughlin. 1994. "Problems with Portfolio Assessment in the Developmental Writing Classroom." *Notes on Teaching English* 22 (2): 9–14.

Belanoff, P. and P. Elbow. 1986. "Using Portfolios to Increase Collaboration and Community in a Writing Program." *WPA: Writing Program Administration* 9 (1–2): 27–40.

Birnbaum, R. 1977. "Factors Related to University Grade Inflation." *The Journal of Higher Education* 48 (5): 519–39.

Bizzell, P. 1982. "Cognition, Convention and Certainty: What We Need to Know About Writing." *Pre/Text* 3 (2): 213–43.

Brand, A. and J. L. Powell. 1986. "Emotions and the Writing Process: A Description of Apprentice Writers." *The Journal of Educational Research* 79 (5): 280–85.

Branthwaite, A., M. Trueman, and T. Berrisford. 1981. "Unreliability of Marking: Further Evidence and a Possible Explanation." *Educational Review* 33 (1): 41–46.

Cole, W. 1993. "By Rewarding Mediocrity, Professors Are Discouraging Excellence." *The Chronicle of Higher Education* 6 January, B1–2.

Cosgrove, C. 1995. "How to Deflate Writing Grades: Doing unto Our Students What We Do unto Ourselves." *English Journal* 84 (3): 15–17.

Dickson, M. 1991. "The WPA, the Portfolio System, and Academic Freedom." In *Portfolios: Process and Product*, ed. P. Belanoff and M. Dickson, 270–78. Portsmouth, NH: Boynton/Cook.

Diedrich, P. 1974. *Measuring Growth in English*. Urbana, IL: NCTE.

Ekstrom, R. and A. Villegas. 1994. *College Grades: An Exploratory Study of Policies and Practices*. Princeton: Educational Testing Service, Report No. ETS-RR-94-23. ERIC ED 380 492.

Elbow, P. 1983. "Embracing Contraries in the Teaching Process." *College English* 45 (4): 327–39.

——. 1993. "Ranking, Evaluating and Liking: Sorting Out Three Forms of Judgment." *College English* 55 (2): 187–206.

Elbow, P. and P. Belanoff. 1991. "State University of New York at Stony Brook Portfolio-based Evaluation Program." In *Portfolios: Process and Product*, ed. P. Belanoff and M. Dickson, 3–16. Portsmouth, NH: Boynton/Cook.

Farley, B. (1995). "'A' is for Average: The Grading Crisis in Today's Colleges." Issues of Education at Community Colleges: Essays by Fellows in the Mid-Career Fellowship Program at Princeton University. ERIC ED 384.

Geisinger, K. 1980. "Who Are Giving All Those A's?" *Journal of Teacher Education* 31 (2): 11–15.

Goldman, I. 1980. "Please or Perish." *National Review* 3 October, 1196–97.

Grieves, R. 1982. "A Policy Proposal Regarding Grade Inflation." *Educational Research Quarterly* 7 (2): 2–4.

Hutchings, P. and T. Marchese. 1990. "Watching Assessment: Questions, Stories, Prospects." *Change* September/October, 13–38.

Iyasere, M. 1984. "Setting Standards in Multiple-section Courses." *Improving College and University Teaching* 32 (4): 173–79.

Krueger, D. and M. Heisserer. 1987. "Assessment and Involvement: Investments to Enhance Learning." In *Student Outcomes Assessment: What Institutions Stand to Gain*, ed. D. Halpern, 45–56. San Francisco: Jossey-Bass.

Leo, J. 1993. "'A' for Effort. Or for Showing up." *U.S. News & World Report*, 18 October, 22.

Lindemann, E. 1995. *A Rhetoric for Writing Teachers*, 3rd ed. New York: Oxford University Press.

Lloyd-Jones, R. 1987. "Tests of Writing Ability." In *Teaching Composition: Twelve Bibliographical Essays*, ed. G. Tate, 155–76. Fort Worth: Texas Christian University Press.

McDaniel, T. R. 1984. "Grade Inflation Reconsidered." *The Clearing House* 57: 388.

Milton, O. 1992. "We Must Think Anew." *Journal on Excellence in College Teaching* 3:19–32.

Milton, O., H. Pollio, and J. Eison. 1986. *Making Sense of College Grades: Why the Grading System Does Not Work and What Can Be Done About It*. San Francisco: Jossey-Bass.

——. 1988. "GPA Tyranny." *Phi Kappa Phi Journal: National Forum* 68 (3): 43–45.

Roemer, M., L. Schultz, and R. Durst. 1991. "Portfolios and the Process of Change." *CCC* 42 (4): 455–68.

Rose, M. 1980. "Rigid Rules, Inflexible Plans and the Stifling of Language: A Cognitivist Analysis of Writer's Block." *CCC* 31 (4): 389–401.

Shaughnessy, M. 1977. *Errors and Expectations: A Guide for the Teacher of Basic Writing.* New York: Oxford University Press.

Sheridan, H. 1990. "Ichabod Crane Dies Hard: Renewing Professional Commitments to Teaching." In *How Administrators Can Improve Teaching*, ed. P. Seldin and Associates, 165–80. San Francisco: Jossey-Bass.

Smit, D. 1990. "Evaluating a Portfolio System." *WPA: Writing Program Administration* 14 (1–2): 51–62.

Spinelli, T. 1981. "Declining Undergraduate Student Performance in Higher Education." ERIC ED 225 509.

Urbach, F. 1992. "Developing a Teaching Portfolio." *College Teaching* 40 (2): 71–74.

Weiser, I. 1992. "Portfolio Practice and Assessment for Collegiate Basic Writers." In *Portfolios in the Writing Classroom: An Introduction*, ed. K. Yancey, 89–101. Urbana, IL: NCTE.

White, E. 1994. *Teaching and Assessing Writing: Recent Advances in Understanding, Evaluating, and Improving Student Performance.* San Francisco: Jossey-Bass.

Wiesenfeld, K. 1996. "Making the Grade." *Newsweek* 17 June, 16.

Wilhide, D. 1982. "In the Battle Against Grade Inflation, the Winners Are Often the Losers." *Chronicle of Higher Education,* 1 September, 40–45.

Will, G. 1995. "Teach Johnny to Write." *The Washington Post* 2 July, C-7.

Wolcott, W. and D. Buhr. 1987. "Attitude as It Affects Developmental Writers' Essays." *Journal of Basic Writing* 6 (2): 3–15.

Wolf, K. 1991. "The Schoolteacher's Portfolio: Issues in Design, Implementation, and Evaluation." *Phi Delta Kappan* 73 (2): 129–36.

Chapter Three

Departmental and Institutional Influences on Grading
Conflicts of Accountability

John Sandman and Michael Weiser

Eleanor Agnew's "Cross Purposes: Grade Deflation, Classroom Practices" (Chapter 2) unpacks many institutional political issues related to grading. Here John Sandman and Michael Weiser respond with personal testimonies about the impact of these pressures. They contend that questions of how grading can be made more fair and equitable cannot be effectively addressed, let alone answered, unless one takes these pressures into account. John Sandman teaches at State University College of Technology at Delhi, where Michael Weiser also taught from 1990 to 1995. SUNY Delhi is two-year residential college of about two thousand students.

Many of us teach in departments that, due to increasingly limited funding, often combined with obliviousness to or distrust of developments in composition theory and/or writing assessment, have no formal, department-wide grading methods or standards. This situation presents us with certain hitherto ill-defined pressures when grading student writing. How do we negotiate between our often conflicting obligations to give our students the grades we believe they deserve and yet prepare them to meet our colleagues' expectations? And how do we fulfill these obligations while defending ourselves against institutional and departmental pressures to make our grades conform to a mean?

Is There a Test in This Department?

Teachers who are in departments with exit exam requirements for students, which we have both experienced, at least have a clearer idea of the criteria and standards according to which their students' skills—and by implication, their own teaching methods and grading standards—will be judged. It may seem that in a department with no formal assessment program grading student writing is a simple task, since not having to make our grades conform to certain standards seemingly allows us to assign the grades we believe our students deserve without having to answer to anyone. This, however, is not the case. A 1994 study of fourteen colleges and universities found that while none of the departments surveyed had specific grading policies, two-thirds of the faculty members believed that they were expected to grade according to specific standards (Ekstrom and Villegas 1994).

These "tests" for faculty emerge from many different sources. As contributor Eleanor Agnew notes, many department chairs and institutional administrators are committed to fighting grade inflation, largely in response to a public outcry against lax standards. These tests also include colleagues who, upon having one of one's ex-students perform poorly on the writing in their courses, raise complaints about one's liberal grading. And, finally, but most importantly, there are those former students of ours who complain to us about our having failed to prepare them to perform up to a colleague's standards. As Lad Tobin (1993) says in *Writing Relationships*, "While our colleagues are not literally present in our classrooms, we are almost always aware of how our attitude, our approach, our goals and our grades compare with theirs" (141).

Saving One's Neck by Sacrificing One's Values; or, Okay, I'll Lower My Grades

Between us, we have taught in eight different English departments, and in half of those departments the chairs have circulated lists of the average grades given by each teacher in Freshman Composition. The purpose of these lists, sometimes implicit and more often explicit, has been to encourage teachers whose grades strayed from the departmental mean to rethink their grading.[1]

The pressure to rethink one's grades can be enormous for the teacher who is an adjunct or on a yearly contract. Fifteen years ago, when John was a first-year lecturer in composition, the department chair put out one of those lists. In the message attached to the list, the chair said that he felt that the composition grades in general were too high and that he could not accept as reliable the student evaluations of any teachers whose grades were above 3.0. John topped the list, with a 3.32. In the next semester, in order to keep his job, and because he was made to believe that "he was too soft," John lowered his average grade almost a full point, to 2.4. How did he do it? He would read a paper and think, "This student deserves a B, but I better give it a C+ if I want to keep my job." He remembers having to do a lot of circling back to add negative comments that would justify the low grades he was giving. In this case, the change in grading was also a change in teaching; because of the pressure John experienced, he went against his own pedagogical philosophy and the vast amount of research on responding to student writing (Daiker 1989) by giving his students more negative feedback. Because this particular department chair held the simplistic but widespread idea that low grades equal high standards and therefore good teaching, John's contract was renewed.

Dancing in the Dark; or, What Are Our Colleagues Looking for?

In Delhi's department, the average grades given by fifteen composition instructors in 1993–1994 ranged all the way from 1.6 to 3.2. We don't have a clear idea why there is such a wide range, because we have never held a session where all the department members read one or more sample essays and compared their grades, let alone discussed the way they arrived at these grades. There is, however, a reason for this: when the department held group grading sessions, over a decade ago, the disagreements were so violent that the current chair decided to avoid all such meetings in the future. We get some idea about the differing standards from our former Freshman Composition students who tell us how vastly their current teachers' methods and standards differ from those they encountered in our Freshman Composition classes. These are awkward conversations, in which we find ourselves torn by concern for our former students' welfare, doubts about our own methods and standards, and responsibility to respect our colleagues.

The Case of Sherita

Sherita came to John's office about two months into the fall semester, asking, "Why did you give me a B in Freshman Composition?" John assumed she wanted a higher grade, but it turned out she was asking why John hadn't given her a lower one.

Originally from Guyana, Sherita had many of the grammatical and syntactical difficulties common to English as a Second Language students from the West Indies and South America. After the first writing assignment in Freshman Composition, John had asked her to work with a tutor in The Writing Center. A diligent student, Sherita worked hard, both on her own and with her tutor, and produced final drafts that were almost entirely free of grammatical and syntactical errors. In the fall semester after she took John's course, Sherita took Advanced Composition with a different teacher. After the first writing assignment, the instructor told her he thought that she should drop the course, that she did not belong in Advanced Composition. But Sherita had earned a B in Freshman Composition, and she knew she was willing to work hard. Again, she signed on with a Writing Center Tutor, but many of the writing assignments in Advanced Composition were done in class, with no chance for revision, and Sherita's in-class writings were filled with errors.

When it became clear that working with a tutor was not helping, Sherita came to see John. She could not understand how her writing ability had gone from B to F, but, of course, the problem was that her two writing instructors had completely different evaluative approaches. John graded long papers (five to seven typed, double-spaced pages) at midterm and at the end of the course. The midterm and final papers were chosen from previously written papers and revised after the students had had at least one conference with him. When he graded, John placed more emphasis on unity and specificity than on grammar and usage. The Advanced Composition teacher graded short (250–500 word) weekly papers, half of which were written in class. On the annotated papers that Sherita showed John, almost all of the markings and comments were on grammar and usage. At first, John felt that by putting so much weight on in-class writing and on grammar and usage, the Advanced Composition teacher was not being fair to Sherita. Later, John realized that by not grading in-class writing and by placing less emphasis on surface elements, he had not prepared Sherita for this Advanced Composition class. Our concern is not which teacher is at fault; rather, it is that the student suffers by being caught between differing approaches to grading student writing, especially in a department where such differences are never discussed. Instead of speaking to Sherita's Advanced Composition teacher, John advised Sherita to drop the course.

The Case of Jennifer

One of the places in which the differing standards between colleagues became clearest was the Writing Center, which Michael established in 1990 and directed until it was closed at the end of Spring semester, 1994. One day, Jennifer came in with a paper which had been given a D by one of our colleagues. The two-page typed paper was covered in ink, and *all* of the markings and comments focused on grammar, mechanics, and usage. The paper had been assigned and written in the computer lab during an hour-and-fifteen-minute class. Now Jennifer was being given one week to turn in a final revision.

Michael began by asking about the assignment. Jennifer told him that the teacher had not written the assignment out, but had delivered it orally at the beginning of class. Michael had Jennifer double-check the assignment with the instructor. When she returned the next day, all she could tell him was that the assignment was to "write about an issue that had a strong effect on you." Jennifer had written about taking her best friend to get an abortion. The main idea of the paper was that, as a result of this experience, the writer had changed her view on abortion from pro-life to pro-choice. Jennifer had spent several paragraphs recounting her experience and the remainder explaining her change of mind. The main idea and focus seemed clear enough, and since all the comments on the paper were directed at mechanics, usage, and grammar problems, Michael had Jennifer focus mainly on those elements. After he worked hard to get her to correct her own paper, Jennifer turned in the edited version to her teacher. When she got the paper back from the teacher, Jennifer returned to the Writing Center to show it to

Michael. The grade had been raised to D+; there were very few corrections, and this comment: "Your main idea is clearly stated, but you don't support it with enough specific details and evidence." Jennifer was upset, and so was Michael. Minus the vagueness about "details" and "evidence," and in more of a questioning than judgmental mode, this was the kind of comment Michael would have made on her first draft. Michael would have had Jennifer work on generating details and organizing the piece *before* concentrating on grammar and mechanics. If the teacher intended from the first to grade the essay not only for grammar and mechanics, but for "specific details and evidence," why had he not focused first on these things, or at least asked for them when he gave Jennifer the original grade? Michael would give his students extensive feedback on early drafts and a clearly provisional grade, geared to this feedback. And why hadn't the teacher written out the assignment and given his students some idea of his criteria for judging it? Michael would have provided and discussed with his students detailed assignments and his grading criteria for each. How was Michael supposed to help Jennifer with this fellow's assignment when he was not any more sure than she about what the instructor was looking for?

In subsequent sessions with Jennifer, Michael took a more holistic approach; in essence, he took Jennifer through the entire process with each paper. As a result, Jennifer's writing improved, as did her grades. By pointing out the improvement in her in-class writing, Michael was able to convince the teacher that he wasn't writing Jennifer's papers for her, and she passed the course with a B.

In the past two years, because of budget cuts, six full-time English teachers have retired or been laid off, and none have been replaced. The campus Writing Center has been another casualty. The budget cuts and a mixture of indifference and hostility on the part of senior faculty led to elimination of the Writing Center, along with the entire Learning Center. As a result, and despite a unanimous recommendation by the interdepartmental Committee for Hiring, Promotion and Tenure that he be granted tenure, Michael was laid off. He later learned that the Vice President for Academic Affairs had tried to transfer Michael's contract from the Learning Center to the English Department, but the senior English faculty members, including Jennifer's teacher, had rejected this proposal, in large part because they saw Michael as "too liberal" in his teaching methods and grading standards. These faculty members had never visited Michael's classes nor the Writing Center, and none had looked at his assignments nor seen the writing his students had produced.

Getting the Number-Crunchers to Look Beyond the Numbers and Colleagues to Understand What We Are Doing

Department chairs and administrators often base questions of nonstandard grading practices entirely upon the numbers, having little or no idea of what actually went on in the course. How much writing and reading were required? How much and how often did the teacher give students feedback? Did the teacher meet individually with students outside of the classroom, and how often? How well were the teacher's assignments and expectations explained to the students? The best way to defend oneself against grade inflation is to document, as fully as possible, what went into figuring the numbers.

"Why'd I Get a (Fill in the Grade) from Her, When You Gave Me a (Fill in the Grade)?" and "What Did You Teach This Student?"

Preparing students to face the standards and criteria by which their work will be graded in other courses is much more difficult. While one can teach some of the skills one's students will need for later courses, one can also advise students (diplomatically) about other faculty members' assignments and expectations, and advise students to meet with their instructors in subsequent courses to discuss any writing assignments that are unclear to them. Also, invite them to come back to you, after clearing this with these instructors.

Living and Grading in the Pre-Process Department

Many institutions, departments, and teachers have, as yet, refused to bring their philosophies and methods of teaching into anything like accordance with recent (and not-so-recent) developments in composition theory. At the same time, many individual teachers who subscribe to such theories are often too dismissive of more traditional approaches to teaching and grading. The pressures we've described in this article can be seen as symptomatic of a conflict between teachers who see themselves as "student-centered" and colleagues and administrators who see themselves as "protectors of 'standards.'" Students, and their grades, often get caught up in the middle. In such departmental and institutional environments, we have a responsibility to ourselves, our colleagues, our institutions, and above all our students, to establish and maintain an open discussion about grading methods and standards. Until and unless we do this, we cannot even begin to make our grades more fair and equitable.

Notes

1. All of the departmental and institutional examples in this article focus on the pressure to lower grades. We realize, however, that situations exist in which teachers, including writing teachers, face equally troubling pressure to assign higher grades than they believe their students deserve. We have not directly addressed a situation like this, because neither of us has experienced it.

References

Daiker, D. A. 1989. "Learning to Praise." In *Writing and Response: Theory, Practice, and Research,* ed. Chris M. Anson. Urbana, IL: NCTE.

Ekstrom, R. B. and A. M. Villegas. 1994. *College Grades: An Exploratory Study of Policies and Practices*. Princeton, NJ: The College Board.

Tobin, L. 1993. *Writing Relationships: What Really Happens in the Composition Class*. Portsmouth, NH: Boynton/Cook.

Chapter Four

Grading Student Writing
The Dilemma from a Feminist Perspective

Betty Garrison Shiffman

Betty Garrison Shiffman, who has taught in middle school, a small liberal-arts women's college, a large urban community college, and is now teaching in a small urban university, says she has been "most influenced by the needs of those students for whom the system has failed," particularly returning women students. Committed to "inclusive" feminist teaching strategies, she examines, in this article, "the institutionally mandated imperative to rank students against each other in relationship with current composition pedagogy." She offers suggestions about what teachers can do "until the revolution comes."

"We don't like grading. . . . it's the dirty thing we have to do in the dark of our own offices," claimed Pat Belanoff in "The Myths of Assessment" (1991, 61). She dared to speak about a subject few were bold enough to address. Yet, most of us as composition professionals are still stuck with grading as part of our institutions' expectations—indeed, requirements. Nevertheless, a growing minority are rebelling against the time-honored tradition of grading, based on one commonly held conviction: grades get in the way of learning.

For those composition professionals engaged in feminist teaching, the traditional system of grading student text as it has existed for years proves particularly repugnant. Grading, while purporting to be fair and objective, coerces both teacher and student into a hierarchy of power that leaves covert those insidious influences such as gender, ethnicity, economic status, and so on. Rather than promoting conversations, grading stifles the kind of linguistic risk-taking that can lead to creativity of expression. Grading privileges only the final product of writing rather than the enlightening process of creating it.

But even as questions increase regarding the effectiveness and morality of grading, we are frustrated in our attempts to convince the established institutions of higher education that we must do something about it. As we search for theoretically persuasive arguments, we grasp inevitably for strategies that will enable us to work for change while, at the same time, juggling our educational responsibilities to student writers along with institutional requirements for grading. I suggest that feminist pedagogy offers us a powerful platform from which to accomplish both these goals. Feminist teaching urges us toward a position of inclusionary evaluation and away from an isolated, so-called "objective" perspective where we may be called upon to justify what we increasingly recognize are highly subjective judgments. This move, I suggest, allows us to maintain consistency between our composition teaching behaviors and our evaluative stance. Moreover, it opens the door for greater participation, and thus a greater sense of ownership, on the part of our students over their own texts. Specifically, I believe feminist pedagogy pushes us toward alternative methods of grading and evaluation, such as portfolio assessment and contract grading, but moving eventually toward pass/fail courses for all writing instruction.

Feminism and Teaching

In both feminist and radical education theory, the interpersonal relationships between teacher and student and between student and student are of paramount importance; those relationships should constitute a learning dialogue. *Dialogue* has powerful connotations for radical and feminist teachers. The word encompasses a code of behavior, an attitude, a philosophy. Implicit are many meanings. One is the notion of equality. The prefix indicating "two" also implies that the two are of equal status. The root of the word comes from the Greek *logos* having to do with the "word," or message or content, of the dialogue. And with the combination of the word parts comes the notion of a back-and-forth exchange—of words—between equals. It is consequently no surprise that dialogue has become a "god-word" in radical and feminist educational circles. One word sums up the essence of a total philosophy: that there must be a clear exchange of words, of ideas, between two parties who consider themselves equal partners.

Recognizing that education must necessarily be achieved by means of dialogue, Paulo Freire (1990) writes in *Pedagogy of the Oppressed* that "authentic thinking, thinking that is concerned about *reality*, does not take place in ivory tower isolation, but only in communication" (64). In a later chapter, Freire goes on to define dialogue as "the encounter between men [*sic*], mediated by the world, in order to name the world" (76). He insists that one cannot impose such naming on others; it can only be done through mediation. Furthermore, the acts of dialogue have significance for the relationship between those involved. Thus, this dialogue "becomes a horizontal relationship of which mutual trust between the dialoguers is the logical consequence" (80).

But while Freire writes so powerfully and persuasively about the political factors that oppress students, the factor of gender is subsumed under others. What is not revealed in most radical education theories is the degree to which gender, the teacher's or the student's, can perpetuate the same kind of oppression, only more subtly and covertly. Feminist theories seek to take Freire's notion of dialogue further, revealing how the insidious nature of gender-identification serves to perpetuate yet another hierarchical system. Belenky and her colleagues (1986) articulate the need for this effort in their chapter "Connected Teaching," reflecting that what the women in their surveys did *not* want was "a system in which knowledge flowed in only one direction, from teacher to student" (217). Their research indicates that women generally prefer modes of learning that allow them to situate their own experiences in relation to others', and that women also tend to learn better in collaborative settings. Similar investigations, such as that of Myra and David Sadker (1994), conducted within cross-gender classroom settings, raise serious doubts about the likelihood of women becoming involved in educational dialogues.

In contrast, feminist education tries to create a more equitable balance of learning styles and contexts, allowing for gender (and other) differences. Carolyn Shrewsbury (1987) discusses the significance of dialogue and relationships in her article, "What Is Feminist Pedagogy?" In classrooms that apply feminist pedagogy, she writes, "Students integrate the skills of critical thinking with respect for and ability to work with others" (7). In this type of learning environment, Shrewsbury continues, critical thinking "requires continuous questioning and making assumptions explicit, but it does so in a dialogue aimed not at disproving another person's perspective, not destroying the validity of another person's perspective, but at a mutual exploration of explications of diverse experiences" (7). There is an implicit recognition here of mutual respect for those variant perspectives, echoing Freire's call for "mutual trust" among dialoguers. Unfortunately, grading systems now in place in most institutions preclude such mutual trust, often stifling dialogue before it can begin.

Portrait of the Feminist Teacher as Evaluator of Student Text

The feminist teacher engaged in evaluation does not necessarily look so different from many other composition instructors now hard at work trying to help their students become better writers. What is different about them is the feminist's understanding and conscious implementation of the underlying principles guiding her work. She also demonstrates clearly and early to her students those principles, explaining how they guide her teaching and showing how they are fulfilled through specific activities of her classes.

The feminist writing teacher adopts a strategy of evaluation that allows students to continue to write and revise throughout the course in response to collaborative feedback, written and oral, from their teacher and peers. Conversation among students and between the teacher and her students is a constant source of knowledge for both. While the feminist teacher may engage in explanatory lectures as the need arises, that is not her main, and certainly not her only, mode of teaching. Her class resembles to a large extent a busy writing workshop, with students at varying stages of reading, writing, and talking—sometimes working individually, sometimes in small groups, sometimes as a whole group, or combinations of all of the above.

In responding to student text, the feminist evaluator reads with respect for the student's experience and knowledge, commenting orally and in writing as a guide, not as a dictator. Her comments are thoughtfully keyed to the content of the student's text, indicating an engaged and interested reader. She probes with questions to elicit more detail and development in the same way she would if they were involved in an oral conversation. She provides encouragement in the margins, indicating where she is pleased, puzzled, shocked, surprised, or even aghast. Most of all, she maintains through her written and verbal commentary the ethos of the caring, involved teacher, consistent with the persona she has developed throughout the course.

As a reader of student text, the feminist evaluator is highly conscious of her own idiosyncratic filters that color the way she interprets the work of others. This does not necessarily mean that she can escape those filters, but by acknowledging them—even to the students whose papers she is reading— she highlights for herself and her students her role as another reader among many. She reads, as Schweickart (1986) recommends, judiciously and with empathy, trying to read through the author's self, yet recognizing at the same time the impossibility of that task.

With that recognition, she understands the limits of her power as a reader and evaluator of text. And with limited power, she must develop a system of evaluation that does not diminish the student's role. This may mean implementing a subversionary system if the teacher is within an institution that dictates to her how she must evaluate. But she must continue to push at the boundaries that constrain her, for the boundaries that deny her power also deny her students power. Her keen awareness of her responsibility to her students *and* to her discipline allow her to apply the highest ethical principles to her teaching. Given that awareness, she will seek to solve problems, in evaluation and response as well as in other instructional activities, that will further her students' progress as writers and scholars and will avoid those procedures that present obstacles to that progress. This does not necessarily constitute a call to erect barricades of resistance; certainly, resistance may be called for. But the most imperative needs are creativity and ingenuity in achieving those goals while effecting change where change is most desired.

Feminist theory particularly urges us to implement whatever theoretical insight we gain toward improving the human condition. Sometimes we can achieve that in straightforward, overt ways, but sometimes we cannot. Depending upon our respective institutions and departments, or upon our own status within those institutions, we as teachers have varying degrees of freedom in implementing such tactics to evade the constraints of traditional grading practices. The following discussion describes some of those necessarily subversive tactics presently being employed by practitioners within the discipline to circumvent the consequences of grading student text.

Strategies for Subverting the Grading System, or What to Do Until the Revolution Comes

Portfolio Assessment

One of the most revolutionary evaluation practices to emerge in the last twenty years or so is that of portfolio grading. The movement toward portfolio assessment grew out of the apparent recognition that traditional grading and correcting procedures contradict current composition theory and classroom practice. Beginning as a sort of "grass roots movement" (Huot 1994, 325), the method has mushroomed into a national phenomenon largely through the efforts of teachers who were frustrated and sometimes defeated by the demands and limitations of grading. Teachers realized that traditional methods of grading papers, emphasizing finished products, negate the importance of process. The teacher as final and omniscient authority over grades denies the sense of power and control she may have been trying to instill in her developing student writers. Attempting to objectify the characteristics of good writing for the purposes of fair grading defeats the message of the importance of negotiation and collaboration in language, denying as well the realization that writing must be rhetorically contextualized in order to be effective. The list of inconsistencies goes on. But portfolio grading attempts to build on the strengths of composition theory rather than to implicitly deny them as traditional evaluation and grading practices seem to do.

Although they may vary substantially from place to place, classroom to classroom, portfolio methods share many general characteristics, and many of these shared features also reveal their alignment with feminist pedagogy. One common feature is that grades are usually postponed until the end of a designated term as a means of focusing attention on writing instead of on grades. Another characteristic is that students collect multiple drafts in progress, seeking feedback throughout the process, usually from their teachers as well as from other classmates. This aspect of portfolios increases opportunities for multiple *dialogues* between teachers and students, and between students and students. It also obviously indicates a high value placed on the notions of *collaboration* and *negotiation* in the creation of texts. Another characteristic usually shared among portfolio systems is the opportunity for students to cull from among their collected works those that they feel have the greatest potential for excellence, with the opportunity to revise liberally as part of their course grade. This feature offers greater incentives for students to take more responsibility for their own writing and for self-evaluation of that writing, thus providing situations for students to become *empowered* in relation to their own texts and to their own roles as learners in the classroom. The postponement of grades and the emphasis placed on creating multiple drafts and revisions highlights the importance of *process* rather than product. Additionally, the need for frequent conferences over drafts, opportunities for peer revision, and the necessity of student-chosen material for the portfolios theoretically places a clear focus on the student's work as the *subject* of evaluation, rather than as an objectified set of criteria to be measured against others. And all of these characteristics of portfolio evaluation parallel key features of feminist teaching.

In portfolio evaluation, the concepts of dialogue, collaboration, and subjectivity often merge, depending as each does on the other features for success. Collaboration depends on clear and ongoing dialogues among participants; the focus of such collaboration and dialogue is clearly and always the student and his or her work in progress, the subject at hand. In my experience at an urban community college, I've found that this kind of subjective focus and collaborative effort prove especially fruitful among nontraditional students, returning women *and* men who appreciate the greater voice and power over their own work. In end-of-the-semester course evaluations, they write comments that reflect their recognition of the advantages such methods afford them. Moreover, they seem to move more quickly from a dependence upon my comments and feedback to an equal appreciation of the feedback from their peers. They also begin to talk about their own and each other's writing in a mature way. They're very aware of their idiosyncracies as writers but accept at the same time that these differences don't necessarily represent degrees of quality that exist as absolutes, seemingly frozen in time— as a five-point grading scale implies. Rather, they recognize that their idiosyncracies represent just that: that they are different, but valid and valuable nevertheless. They begin more readily to approach each other for advice when they get stuck on a draft, seeking help formulating an introduction when nothing good seems to come forth, quickly identifying especially good readers, or seeking out those individuals who can help them identify and correct their own particular error patterns. Amazingly, their talk begins to sound like those ideal collaborative groups I keep reading about and have struggled so hard to foster. They're responding, I believe, to an evaluation format that accepts their efforts and validates them, urging along the way continued efforts at revising for clearer, more effective expression, and possibly even "timeless prose."

These adults appreciate being treated as adults whose opinions and efforts are valued and encouraged, not judged too early as inadequate or unformed. More like the real life they are accustomed to, ideas are allowed to germinate, shape themselves, evolve, even mutate, until they emerge as part of a collection, not as isolated units. Moreover, expecting students to participate in their own grading and evaluation brings about a more realistic self-portrait for most of them, enabling them to make more informed decisions about their own academic pursuits.

Despite its alignment with feminist teaching, portfolio assessment does not always eliminate those frustrations and preoccupation about grades, even though it may satisfy many of the other tenets of both composition and feminist pedagogy. There are still a number of unresolved issues, too many of them, unfortunately, tied to problems over grading.

In my own community college classrooms, I discovered problems with portfolio assessment that could not be readily resolved to my own or to my students' satisfaction. After employing portfolio grading for several consecutive terms, I was still very dissatisfied with the too-powerful role of judge I had to assume at the end of a course. Even with cover letters and students' written self-assessments, I still sensed a very strong skepticism on the part of students as to how much influence they believed they would actually have on their own grades. In addition, while I had hoped that postponing talk about grades until the end of the semester would relieve students of the burden of grades at least temporarily, I found that it only heightened students' anxiety; in many ways the postponement seemed more like an exercise in cruelty, dragging out their fears throughout the term with no feedback regarding grades. While I used communication as directly and variously as possible— clear (I fervently hoped) and plentiful commentary on drafts, frequent conferences and conversation in and out of class about how they were doing individually—many students simply lacked the self-confidence to judge their own progress by any means of feedback other than grades. I often had to resort to tentative, nonbinding grades on students' papers in order to relieve some of their anxieties about the end of the semester. But I found that this did not live up to my desire to eliminate grades as a guiding factor in students' motivation.

Nor is this preoccupation with grades eliminated when portfolio assessment is employed on a larger scale across a department. Peter Elbow and Pat Belanoff (1991) provide a case study at SUNY Stony Brook that demonstrates administrative problems related to portfolios. Dissatisfied with an institution-mandated writing proficiency exam, the English department turned to portfolio assessment as an alternative (3–4) in their quest for "quality control—not only to avoid inconsistency but to hold up standards" (5).

They report that in their system, portfolios are judged not by the students' own teachers but by others—"outside readers": small informal groups of teachers within the program.

But Stony Brook's pursuit of "programwide consistency" (11) apparently entails "a lot of machinery" (10), despite efforts to keep the process as simple as possible. There seems to be the implicit assumption that, left to their own devices—that is, without the constraints of department-wide guidelines—the teachers would throw caution to the wind and begin to hand out over-inflated and undeserved grades again. Elbow and Belanoff describe the "nervousness" that exists over the possibility that one evaluation group will establish higher grading criteria than another (10). And there is concern that within the small reading groups of teachers, there will be pressure to pass an undeserving student along because of pressure from the student's own teacher.

Thus, despite the implementation of portfolio assessment, many problems still stem from the necessity of grading, of ranking students among others; moreover, much of the anxiety is rooted in teachers' concerns about how they themselves will be judged in terms of their *grading* persona—tough or soft, fair or partial, upholding or letting down standards. What gets lost in this scenario, too, is the focus on student learning. Because of their institutionally mandated quest for consistency, the teachers at Stony Brook are negating the feminist (and compositionist) principles of subjectivity and shared power base. Their preoccupation over department-wide standards reduces students to objects, particularly by presenting their work to panels of readers designed for the express purpose of reading "objectively." Moreover, such practices tend to diminish the collaborative spirit that may have developed throughout the course between students and teachers, students and students, as they must give up their power to the outside panel of readers. Nevertheless, acknowledging the messy and imperfect system that it is, Elbow and Belanoff recommend their system of portfolio grading as an alternative to "what has always been in the closet" (12) in other programs.

Portfolio grading undoubtedly represents a positive move toward more humane and ethically responsible teaching and evaluation of student text. However, grades obviously can still present a major obstacle in the process. Ultimately, at least in most American institutions of higher learning, someone must attach a course grade to student work, and portfolio assessment does not eliminate that disagreeable job; it only postpones it. To some students, insecure and lacking in self-confidence, that grade deferral represents slow torture; used to the old system of grading, they have no adequate frame of reference for measuring their own standing in the class. Even where students may be allowed considerable input into the decision itself, it is usually the teacher who must finally decide what that grade will be. Another option as described at Stony Brook, but often repugnant to many teachers, is to relinquish the chore to a panel of readers who attach the grade based on their communal judgment of the value of each student's collected work. While this may appeal to a sense of impartiality, it cannot atone for the fact that the students and their work have then been further objectified, placed under scrutiny outside the classroom context.

Ultimately, the use of portfolios must be carefully considered within the context and desired goals of a given program or classroom. Any new educational venture runs the risk of ossification if it is adopted too quickly, too broadly, or too rigidly. In his contributing article to *Portfolio Portraits*, Donald Graves (1992) cautions against premature closure, urging teachers to "explore" the use of portfolios while keeping their minds open to possibilities (12).

Contract Grading

Trying to stay open to such possibilities, I discovered a particularly cogent article by Jerry Farber (1990) in *College English* and decided to try contract grading in conjunction with portfolios. Farber describes his frustration when his attempts to empower students to take on more responsibility for decision-making fell flat for the most part. He concluded that the problem was thus: "A major obstacle was clearly the grading system. You can tell students anything you want about 'taking responsibility' and 'thinking for yourself.' The grading system you employ—a middle finger extended before them—is always more eloquent still" (136).

Farber goes on to describe how he managed to circumvent the grading system enough to make it at least palatable for both himself and his students. Like feminist Nel Noddings (1984), Farber believes that there is merit in a system that retains some measure of certification of accomplishment. Unfortunately, most schools have a general and almost universal reluctance to go along with a pass/fail system. Relying on a variation of that system through contract grading, he sets up basic requirements for a C grade, with additional projects required for an A or a B. In this way, students may choose the level they wish to attain, as long as the quality of the work meets passing, or acceptable, standards. Farber describes his motivation:

> What I was after was to de-emphasize grading as much as possible and get it out of our way, while avoiding the unpleasant consequences of a grade give-away; to provide people with as much freedom as could be realized within this institutional setting; and to come up with the kinds of projects that would best help them learn, while reducing the anxiety that some people have about writing and reading literature. (137)

This method of grading achieves the feminist (and radical educators') goal of sharing power while retaining for the teacher the appropriate measure of respect for his or her own knowledge and expertise within the discipline.

Farber has essentially established a pass/fail system within the parameters of a traditional grading program.

Feminist educators such as Nancy Schniedewind (1987) and Noddings (1984) also discuss the concept of contract grading, not necessarily as an ideal solution but perhaps as an interim solution on the way toward the elimination of numerical and letter grades altogether. Schniedewind suggests that, wherever possible, students should participate in the design of such programs, taking part in deciding which activities or assignments should be assigned to each level. By deriving those criteria "communally," Schniedewind believes the learning outcomes will be more effective for students, reflecting students' own standards and input (176). Noddings also describes contract grading as a way to relieve some of the conflict over grades but regrets the emphasis thus placed on quantity, possibly at the risk of quality (194).

The issue of quality and standards is a major stumbling block for many educators who contemplate such an evaluation system. Farber acknowledges the criticism that "a hard-working student might pick up an A without doing what might generally be regarded as A-level work" (138). His response is straightforward: "That's exactly right, and I could care less . . . I would be delighted to see that person working so hard. If 18 out of 25 students in a comp class opt for the A, it's going to make my grade distribution look immoral . . . but, in fact, I'm going to be teaching more to more people than I ever could before. Does this lower standards—or raise them?" (138). One of the axioms of writing instruction is that the more practice and experience students have with writing, the more likely they are to improve. A grading system that asks for more writing is not guaranteed to produce better writers, but it's not likely to hinder their progress either.

For the most part, I would give mixed reviews regarding the results of my own classroom experience with contract grading. On the plus side, I've found that when we decide together at the beginning of the semester the requirements for each grade, students are relieved of the burden of second-guessing the almighty and all-powerful instructor. Their comments have been overwhelmingly supportive and indicate to me that one of my goals is being accomplished: eliminating the fear of grading to concentrate on improving writing. I explain to them in a rather lengthy handout the first day my practices and philosophy, offering them the opportunity to opt out. So far, no one has. I also explain that I reserve for myself the power to judge which papers are acceptable and which are not. Those that I deem unacceptable are returned for revision after one or more conferences with me to discuss the problems. In essence, like Farber, I have created the equivalent of a pass/fail system, while remaining within the standard format of a traditionally graded classroom. Students are pleased because they can readily see what they must do to reach the grade level they wish.

The major drawback for me with this method, however, is that it obviously favors quantity over quality. And a further detraction is that it does not sufficiently reward revision. Students who have submitted satisfactory papers have no further incentive to revise, even for an A, because fulfilling the quantity requirements will be sufficient. I have offered students the option of substantially revising papers already submitted. The drawback with that plan is this: *who* decides what *substantial* revision means? Me, the instructor? That puts me right back into that judgmental and arbitrary seat that I feel is too powerful a role ethically for such subjective determinations.

Theoretically, I can accept that both portfolio grading and contract grading actually can lead to higher standards since the emphasis is on writing well, not on "what must I do to get an A?" I feel less pressure to accept papers that are marginal since ample opportunities exist for revision, and students will not be penalized by a low grade on an early paper or on an anomalous paper. Indeed, I've found that I can sometimes tailor this to the needs of individual students, sometimes asking students who have written "passing" work to revise yet again, knowing that those particular students are capable of better-than-average writing and encouraging them to do better with no penalties involved. The result, I want to believe, is higher standards rather than lower. But, the question remains for me, is this the best way for both my students and me to achieve optimum learning outcomes?

Pass/Fail Systems

Ultimately, the strategies described so far are just that—strategies, or plots, to circumvent for the time being the highly competitive but substantially meaningless system of grading that now exists. In their extensive study of grading practices in higher education, *Making Sense of College Grades*, researchers Ohmer Milton, Howard Pollio, and James Eison (1986) describe the ossification of current grading systems; indeed, their subtitle says it all: *Why the Grading System Does Not Work and What Can Be Done About It*. Decrying the fact that letter grades give students no useful information about their progress toward educational goals, the authors ultimately challenge responsible educators to abandon them in favor of credit/no credit courses (216–17). This starting point would serve to reorient classroom instruction from a focus on ranking to that of learning. Realistically, however, the authors recognize the difficulty of implementing such a conceptual change in perspective. They write: "As a nation, we are just not ready to do that. Another reason militating against acceptance of grade reform is that we are a quantitatively oriented and highly competitive society and the notion of tampering with (abolishing) a well-established metric ranking procedure can be seen only as a type of societal heresy of the first order" (224). And yet it must be done, they argue, to reestablish meaningful learning in the class-room. Laura Bornholdt (1986), author of the foreword to their book, writes: "To reify grades and assume a cross-situational stability is to abuse both the student and the evaluative meaning of the procedure. Grades ought to refer more to the educational process and less to evaluative use by society" (x).

Some feminist teachers, such as Schniedewind (1987, 176), also recommend credit or noncredit courses, wherein teachers either confirm that a student has achieved the goals of the course or not. This does not condone slipshod work in any way; rather, it allows teachers and students to maintain their focus on what is important—the concepts, skills, or knowledge to be gained—rather than to be distracted by other less relevant elements, such as one student's relative ranking to another. Noddings (1984) writes that ideally a teacher should be able to say to a student, "You're ready to move on," or "You're not ready yet." Indeed, she also suggests that teachers may sometimes have to "gently" recommend that students attempt another course of study for which they might be better suited (195). Noddings regards the act of *confirmation* as an integral part of the teaching process, and as such, its importance cannot be minimized nor rationalized away for the purposes of those outside the learning context. And grades, she argues, are not the best method for providing feedback to students about their progress:

> The teacher does not grade to inform the student. She has far better, more personal ways to do this. She grades to inform others about the student's progress. Others establish standards, explicitly or implicitly, and they charge her to report faithfully in observance of these standards. Now the teacher is torn between obligation to the employing community and faithfulness to the student. (194)

This schism places teachers in an awkward ethical position regarding their responsibilities toward students and toward institutions. Pass/fail courses, particularly in areas such as composition instruction where subjective evaluation is impossible to avoid, create an environment more conducive to focusing on achieving mutual learning goals.

Applications for Writing Instruction

An explicit goal of feminist pedagogy, of course, is to change the condition of women students in the classroom. And that context does encompass issues of evaluating student progress and the vagaries of grading. To address the complexities of such matters, feminism advocates contextualizing the strategies intended to resolve them. Most importantly, feminists proffer a multiplicity of approaches rather than one *right* way as a means of solving problems. Marcia Dickson (1991) writes in regard to evaluating student text: "Most of us in the profession have long since accepted that there is no one true way to read a text; why then not admit to the possibility that there is no one true way to grade or approach a student essay?" (276). Huot (1994) strikes a similar chord in a discussion of large-scale assessment systems when he submits this standard:

"Instead of asking which method of assessment is better or best, the question becomes what is it we want to know about a group of students' ability to write?" (332). He goes on to suggest that the most important considerations should be contextual, tied to the needs of a particular institution or learning community (332). And I would extrapolate from that group of contexts to include, on a smaller but no less consequential scale, the needs of individual classrooms as well.

This gets to the essence of the issues at hand: What is the purpose of evaluating student text? Who should benefit from those evaluations? and what strategies exist to achieve the best results? Obviously, a feminist approach to evaluation and grading *should* be expected to benefit women, whose educational needs have too often been subsumed and unrecognized as possibly distinctive from those of men students. But it is not just women students who will benefit by applying feminist theories to evaluation of student text; *all* students stand to gain from a system that urges sensitivity to the individual and to the individual context. And it is not only women who are struggling with such restrictive learning environments; any student who is outside the traditional realm faces obstacles in their paths toward learning. David Bartholomae (1985) in his article "Inventing the University" presents a powerful case to show that basic writers struggle in similar ways, trying to adapt themselves to a new culture. Shaughnessy (1977) initiated an ongoing conversation about the kind of cultural discontinuities basic writers encounter as they enter college classrooms; she describes her early perception of their work as "alien" (vii). But even some students who might be considered well-prepared for higher education still encounter an alien environment when they enter college. Richard Rodriguez (1982) and Mike Rose (1990) both write eloquently about their own struggles to become academically acculturized, coming as they did from backgrounds inconsistent, economically and socially (and in Rodriguez' case, ethnically), with traditional students. All of these students, regardless of gender, race, economic background, or social class, risk being excluded from an educational process that purports to provide equal opportunities for all.

Inclusionary strategies cannot stop short of grading and evaluating student work of any kind; true inclusionary teaching must be aware of the ramifications of every action, of every message sent by the academic establishment. Ultimately, writing instructors must recognize the impossibility of continuing to grade student work as if it were possible to make such discriminating judgments *accurately* on any written text. Refusing to participate in grading does not fail to prepare students to meet standards of excellence; grades do not set or even adequately measure how students meet or fail to meet such standards. Many of the theory and response mechanisms now in place are only band-aid tactics obscuring and even "enabling" (to borrow a term from popular psychology) the detrimental and destructive effects of traditional grading on composition evaluation and theory.

As she describes the issues of grading and moral responsibility, Noddings wonders, "Is this conflict resolvable?" (1984, 193–94). I would have to say that, within the context of most of our tradition-bound institutions, the answer is no. However, the answer could very well be yes, if enough are willing to follow the advice of Nina Baym (1990): "But there is no ground to till except what we stand on; only by learning to apply feminist principles in particular instances does one make change occur" (60). We must begin to bring about change wherever we find ourselves.

References

Baym, N. 1990. "The Feminist Teacher of Literature: Feminist or Teacher?" In *Gender in the Classroom: Power and Pedagogy*, ed. S. Gabriel and I. Smithson, 60–77. Urbana, IL: University of Illinois Press.

Bartholomae, D. 1985. "Inventing the University." In *When a Writer Can't Write: Studies in Writer's Block and Other Composing-Process Problems*, ed. M. Rose, 134–65. New York: Guilford.

Belanoff, P. 1991. "The Myths of Assessment." *Journal of Basic Writing* 10 (1): 54–66.

Belenky, M. F., B. M. Clinchy, N. R. Goldberger, and J. M. Tarule. 1986. *Women's Ways of Knowing: The Development of Self, Voice, and Mind*. New York: Basic Books.

Bornholdt, L. 1986. Foreword to *Making Sense of College Grades: Why the Grading System Does Not Work and What Can Be Done About It*, ed. O. Milton, H. Pollio, and J. A. Eison, ix–xi. San Francisco: Jossey-Bass Publishers.

Dickson, M. 1991. "The WPA, the Portfolio System, and Academic Freedom." In *Portfolios: Process, and Product*, ed. P. Belanoff and M. Dickson, 270–79. Portsmouth, NH: Boynton/Cook.

Elbow, P., and P. Belanoff. 1991. "State University of New York at Stony Brook Portfolio-Based Evaluation Program." In *Portfolios: Process and Product*, ed. P. Belanoff and M. Dickson, 3–16. Portsmouth, NH: Boynton/Cook.

Farber, J. 1990. "Learning How to Teach: A Progress Report." *College English* 52 (February): 135–41.

Freire, P. 1990. *Pedagogy of the Oppressed*. Trans. M. Bergman Ramos. New York: Continuum.

Graves, D. H. 1992. "Portfolios: Keep a Good Idea Growing." In *Portfolio Portraits*, ed. D. H. Graves and B. S. Sunstein, 1–12. Portsmouth, NH: Heinemann.

Huot, B. 1994. "Beyond the Classroom: Using Portfolios to Assess Writing." In *New Directions in Portfolio Assessment: Reflective Practice, Critical Theory, and Large-Scale Scoring*, ed. L. Black et al., 325–33. Portsmouth, NH: Boynton/Cook.

Milton, O., H. R. Pollio, and J. A. Eison. 1986. *Making Sense of College Grades: Why the Grading System Does Not Work and What Can Be Done About It*. San Francisco: Jossey-Bass Publishers.

Noddings, N. 1984. *Caring: A Feminine Approach to Ethics and Moral Education.* Berkeley: University of California Press.

Rodriguez, R. 1982. *Hunger of Memory: The Education of Richard Rodriguez.* Boston: D. R. Godine.

Rose, M. 1990. *Lives on the Boundary: A Moving Account of the Struggles and Achievements of America's Educational Underclass.* New York: Penguin.

Sadker, M., and D. Sadker. 1994. *Failing at Fairness: How America's Schools Cheat Girls.* New York: C. Scribner's Sons.

Schniedewind, N. 1987. "Feminist Values: Guidelines for Teaching Methodology in Women's Studies." In *Freire for the Classroom: A Sourcebook for Liberatory Teaching,* ed. I. Shor, 170–79. Portsmouth, NH: Boynton/Cook.

Schweickart, P. P. 1986. "Reading Ourselves: Toward a Feminist Theory of Reading." In *Gender and Reading: Essays on Readers, Texts, and Contexts,* ed. E. A. Flynn and P. P. Schweickart, 31–62. Baltimore: John Hopkins.

Shaughnessy, M. 1977. *Errors and Expectations: A Guide for the Teacher of Basic Writing.* New York: Oxford University Press.

Shrewsbury, C. 1987. "What Is Feminist Pedagogy?" *Women's Studies Quarterly* XV (Fall/Winter): 6–13.

Part Two

The Post-Process Classroom
Theory into Practice

Chapter Five

Judgment Deferred
Reconsidering Institutional Authority in the Portfolio Writing Classroom

Xin Liu Gale

Xin Liu Gale, who now teaches at Syracuse University, was an in-structor in the University of Arkansas at Little Rock's Depart-ment of Rhetoric and Writing when she composed this piece. UALR is an urban university serving a somewhat diverse population of students: 78 percent white, 17 percent African American, and 5 percent Hispanic, Native American, and Asian combined. Because a great many students combine work with education, nearly half at-tend college part-time. In this chapter, Gale argues that the goals of programmatic portfolio assessment are at odds with the libera-tory goals of a portfolio writing classroom. To create a favorable learning environment in the writing classroom, Gale asserts, the teacher must recognize the incongruity of the goals for which the portfolio is put to use, comprehend how differently institutional au-thority functions in different contexts, and adjust both the class structure and portfolio requirements.

Since the programmatic portfolio assessment was introduced into university writing programs to substitute for the proficiency test and holistic grading about two decades ago (Elbow and Belanoff 1986; Ford and Larkin 1986; Roemer, Schultz, and Durst 1991), portfolios have mushroomed in college composition classrooms. "As the writing process has become the focus of composition classes over the past three decades," Jeffrey Sommers (1991) observes, "it seems an almost natural evolution for portfolio evaluation to have entered the classroom" (153). James Berlin (1994) hailed the portfolio as "a central feature of teaching the process model of composing" and considered it "part of a larger project for reclaiming the classroom for student-centered learning" because the portfolio "will encourage liberatory practices for teachers and students" (61). These general assumptions about portfolios are not unfamiliar to composition teachers: by removing grades from student individual papers during the semester, portfolios help shift students' attention from grades to the teacher's comments and suggestions for revision, thereby ensuring students' genuine interest in learning and writing. Further, by deferring the teacher's judgment to the end of the semester, portfolios encourage students to experiment with writing processes and to develop their writing ability through trial and error without having to worry about grades. Most important, because portfolios are used to assess student effort and improvement over the semester, they foster teacher-student collaboration in the writing class and help create a democratic environment in which the teacher plays the role of a sympathetic reader and "coach" rather than a member of the grammar police or a gatekeeper of the academy (Belanoff and Elbow 1986, 34).

However, despite the theoretically acclaimed merits of the portfolio approach, portfolios in practice have encountered some serious problems: students' procrastination, chaos in the classroom, irresponsibility, an overconcern with the final product rather than the writing process, the overcollaboration between the teacher and the student, problems of revision, dishonesty, and plagiarism, to name but a few (McClelland 1991; Weinbaum 1991; Clark 1993; Cardoni, Fraser, and Starner 1994; Reither and Hunt 1994; Sommers 1991; Schuster 1994). Janet Wright Starner's (Cardoni, Fraser, and Starner 1994) comical description of the chaos in her portfolio class serves to show how much harm portfolios can do when the teacher is unprepared for the changes the new approach may engender in teaching:

> My most vivid memory of that first semester is of a particular afternoon in October. To me, my course seemed to have dropped suddenly into total chaos. I'd had my students generate a fair amount of writing, and I'd responded to it, but I hadn't given them any grades . . . oops . . . because that was the point of the portfolio, wasn't it?—no grades until the end. But then, how could I give them the required midterm evaluation? And anyway, they were becoming more anxious as the days wore on: "Mrs. Starner, what do you want? How will you figure our grade? I want to know how I'm doing!" Yes, well, I could relate to that. I wanted to know how I was doing, too.
>
> Clearly, I had leapt before I looked; with more courage (could that read foolhardiness?) than forethought, I'd jumped into the portfolio boat, but it seemed I'd forgotten some essential equipment, like something to bail with. I could no longer see where we were going; my confidence had been my compass, and that had vanished; my initial flush of good feeling had evaporated. I thought we were all going down together. The only good part

was that my students didn't yet realize how serious the gash in the bottom
of the boat was. But I knew. We were goners. And it was all my fault.
Whose idea was this anyhow? (135)

Starner's class might be an extreme case, but even in some reportedly
more successful portfolio classes, chaos, confusion, procrastination, and frustration are conspicuous phenomena that indicate the teacher's unpreparedness and inability to motivate students when grades are absent. Like Starner,
Kelly Weinbaum (1991) experienced frustration that her portfolio class was,
in the first half of the semester, characterized by a "definite lack of produc-
tivity" for both the teacher and the students (211). Similarly, Kathy McClelland (1991) had to desperately resort to threatening with grades when her
students procrastinated, because in her portfolio class those "who can only
get the work done if they have strict deadlines imposed by teachers often
have a hard time dealing with the freedom and responsibility portfolios
demand of them" (171).

William Thelin's study of Ms. Green, an instructor at a California state
university, further reveals the complexity of using portfolios in teaching
writing. Carefully examining the teacher's comments on three students'
papers and the students' revised final drafts in a first-year portfolio writing
class, Thelin observes that all three students avoided making the difficult
changes their teacher had suggested and that their final drafts included in the
portfolios were not significantly better than the original drafts. Trying to find
out why the students were reluctant to adopt the teacher's suggestions in their
revision, revealing the students' inability to make "mature, independent
choices" in their writing, Thelin suggests several possibilities (121):

First, the students' concerns over the portfolio grade and their increasing anxiety over revising toward the portfolio deadline caused them to opt
for easy solutions; that is, to choose essays easy to revise or requiring the
minimal changes possible.

Second, there was a "basic inconsistency between [the teacher] Ms.
Green's response style, her criteria for evaluation, and her portfolio system"
(Thelin 1994, 121). The teacher's responses to students' writing were often
critical, reflecting her own political and social agenda—primarily feminism
and social responsibility, yet "rarely would she present her opinions as
demands or crucial suggestions for revision" (121). Ms. Green was not clear
about the course goals she and her students were supposed to be working
together to reach; she wanted to teach critical thinking while her students
thought that their major goal was to pass the portfolio assessment in the end
of the semester.

Third, Ms. Green failed to clearly describe her criteria for evaluation to
her students. "Never did she give her students explicit directions about how
or what to revise in an essay," because she "did not want to give the students
orders, so she presented herself as a reader and nothing more" (Thelin 1994,

121). As a result of Ms. Green's ambiguity about what and how to revise and her often explicit criticism of students' values and stances in her responses to their papers, the students became anxious and confused when revising their essays.

As I see it, the reported problems are invariably related to the suspension of institutional authority and to the lack of a structure that will make portfolios work. The teacher's unpreparedness for adopting a new teaching approach; the teacher's ambiguity about the course goals and evaluation criteria; the teacher's unawareness of the demands of portfolios; and the teacher's failure to recognize the lack of motivation created by the deferred institutional authority in the individual portfolio classroom—all these problems occur because we understand little how portfolios change our teaching when they are used by individual teachers. To better understand how portfolios work in the writing classroom, we need to differentiate between the portfolio as a means of assessment and the portfolio as a teaching approach in terms of goal and function. For the portfolio to realize its theoretical promise in teaching, we need to examine the effects of the suspended institutional authority (the absence of grades) on teaching and learning in the portfolio classroom, to describe more fully the mechanism of the portfolio approach in the pedagogic context, and to join William Thelin (1994) in his endeavor to investigate such factors as class structure, evaluation criteria, and response styles to make them consistent with the goals of the portfolio writing class (114).

The Conflicting Goals of Assessment and Teaching

That the portfolio started out as a means to strengthen the authority of the academic institution—to maintain academic standards and integrity of grades in the first-year composition courses—seems to be sharply at odds with its more recent adoption as a liberatory teaching approach, a "postmodern development" whose goal is to nurture "self-reflexiveness about writing" as well as "the identity of writer in the students" (Yancey 1992, 104). Reading the earlier literature on programmatic portfolio assessment, one can not help but notice an almost unified concern for standards and grades in various reports. Portfolio assessment is used to "increase uniformity of standards for 'C' or higher in freshman composition course" (Belanoff and Elbow 1986, 27); to promote "high standards and consistency among teachers" (Roemer, Schultz, and Durst 1991, 467); to maintain the integrity of grades (Ford and Larkin 1978); or to "make our grading more rigorous" (Smit 1990, 51). This concern for standards and grades is consistent with the goal of portfolio assessment, which is, after all, an institutional mandate that serves an institutional purpose: to "objectively" evaluate the effectiveness of the institutional endeavor—teaching—in terms of student achievement. As Charles Schuster (1994) points out, institutionally, first-year composition is a "course that certifies students, an academic version of water dunking, the primary means by which students demonstrate that they are either clean or unclean, deserving of a place within the university or ejected from the land of promise with its allure of economic and social upward mobility" (323). And portfolio assessment, with its requirement that students' "best writing"—the revised final drafts—be presented in the final portfolios for teachers' final judgment, is mainly concerned with the question: Who should be ejected from the land of promise, the university? (Roemer, Schultz, and Durst 1991; Ford and Larkin 1978; Smith 1991). Thus, collaboration among teachers to arrive at more clearly defined standards for the first-year writing courses and more objective criteria for evaluating portfolios serves the institutional goal of assessment. So does collaboration between the teacher and the student, since both have to work together to improve the student's writing so that the student's final portfolio will pass the scrutiny of readers who are not the students' teacher in order to demonstrate both the teacher's professional effectiveness and the student's acceptability in the academic world (Belanoff and Elbow, 1986; Roemer, Schultz, and Durst 1991; Ford and Larkin 1978; Smith 1991). Schuster is right to observe that even though "we intended to honor the entire process of writing, and we are still bathing in the warm glow of our achievements in persuading the University to change from a test-driven composition curriculum to one that is course-driven," the nature of assessment remains the same (322). What serves as the driving force in the collaboration among teachers and between the teacher and the student is ultimately the passing grade, the institutional passport, which is the goal both the teacher and the student strive to reach.

The goals of first-year composition courses, on the other hand, are very different. We composition teachers believe that first-year writing courses should help students to get their foothold in the academic world. We believe that students should not only study the conventions of academic discourse and learn to address the academic audience but also develop critical thinking and critical reading and writing abilities. To attain these goals, we emphasize learning and writing as a process of growth and empowerment; we encourage students to be agents of learning; we use dialogic approach to foster the formation of subject position and critical thinking; and we try to accommodate those students from less privileged communities by embracing the idea of multiple literacies. In Schuster's (1994) words,

> To teach writing, we must work with small numbers of students in interactive, collaborative ways that promote a rhetorical relationship. We must create a context for writing and rewriting; we must offer both the structures and the means by which students learn how to invest themselves in their writing and rewriting. We must, moreover, take a long view, knowing as we do that students learn how to write incrementally, over years and not just semesters, that writing is situational and that writing improvement is alinear at best. (323)

In teaching, evaluation and grades should be the last concerns of both students and the teacher, for both are concerned with "more interesting and useful" questions when reading a piece of writing:

> What is it actually saying? What does it imply? What are the consequences for us and others of what it is saying? How do we feel about what it is saying? What can we learn from it? How would we reply to it? How does it relate to other messages from our culture about this matter? . . . How is it shaped? How do its parts function? What is its relation to its historical and cultural context, and to ours? (Elbow 1994, 52–53)

In other words, writing in first-year composition classes should be an activity of inquiry, interaction, and learning, not just for the purpose of obtaining the certificate but for the development of the mind and the character. If we list the goals of assessment and of first-year composition, we can hardly fail to see the differences:

First-Year Composition	Portfolio Assessment
Inclusion—initiating students into academic world	Exclusion—holding back some students
Utopian—stressing multiple literacies and critical thinking	Meritocratic—stressing academic literacy and academic excellence
Liberatory—teaching as a dialogic and empowering process	Judgmental—teaching to maintain standards
Process—viewing writing as cognitive development and recursive activities	Product—viewing writing as applying skills to produce "best" written work
Agency—seeing students as subjects interacting with texts and one another	Objectivity—seeing evidence of effort as reflected in the final product
Democratic—questioning institutional authority and encouraging autonomy	Authoritative—complying with authority of the institution and strengthening it with certificates

Because of the different goals of assessment and teaching, Schuster (1994) warns us:

> Teaching is hot; assessment is cold. Teaching constructs students; assessment deconstructs student writing. No matter how creatively we fashion our means of assessment, it will remain at odds with our disciplinary and pedagogical principles as long as composition is certification, as long as it is the primary means by which some are chosen—and some are not. (323)

And because of the different goals of assessment and teaching, we need to examine how the portfolio, an institutional instrument of assessment, can be turned into a pedagogical means that encourages liberatory practices.

The Suspension of Institutional Authority and Its Effects on Teaching Writing

While it is institutional authority that girdles the programmatic portfolio assessment and motivates activities in the classroom, it is the suspension of institutional authority—the temporary absence of grades—that supposedly creates a democratic learning environment in the individual portfolio classroom. The major role institutional authority plays in programmatic portfolio assessment is reflected in the general structure of portfolio assessment. (The one that Elbow and Belanoff adopted at the State University of New York at Stony Brook [1986] is representative):

- The portfolio is used as a substitute for the proficiency exam. (Its legitimacy is granted by the institution.)

- The student's final portfolio consists of a) three revised papers: an expressive paper, an academic paper, and an analysis of a prose text; b) a brief informal cover sheet, which explores the student's writing process in the papers and acknowledges the help he or she has received; c) an in-class essay done without the benefit of feedback (Elbow and Belanoff 1986, 336). (The content and emphasis of the portfolio are clearly defined and the portfolio is an institutional mandate.)

- Two readers (one of them is the teacher) will read portfolios to decide pass/fail. (The collectively established standards and evaluation criteria carry with them institutional authority; so does the reading procedure.)

- A midterm "dry-run" is conducted to give students a pass/fail grade. (An institutional measure to motivate students to try harder in the second half of the semester.)

- One-on-one conferences between the teacher and the student are mandated during the semester. (An institutional measure to ensure teacher-student collaboration.)

This structure, centered on assessment, is thought to be responsive to the following six theoretical constructs about language learning, as Sharon Hamilton (1994) summarizes them:

1. There is no single way to define or to assess literacy; teaching and assessment will ideally acknowledge *multiple literacies*. Since student literacy varies by genre and context, assessment should consider a wide range of student writing.

2. Since portfolios contain texts of various genres composed over time
   in a wide range of contexts for a wide range of purposes, they are
   more valid indicators of writing progress than other forms of assessment.

3. Possibly more important than assumptions of greater validity is the
   capability of portfolios to provide congruence among classroom
   instruction, classroom assessment, and large scale assessment.

4. Writers should remain in charge of their writing.

5. Reflection and revision contribute to writing improvement.

6. Reflection and revision are enhanced in a *collaborative learning
   environment.* (160–61)

In comparison, the portfolio adopted by individual teachers usually lacks
the structure of programmatic portfolio assessment and hence its institutional
authority. First, the proficiency exam required of students and the use of
portfolios in the writing class are almost entirely unrelated to each other.
Students, taught how to prewrite, draft, and revise in the writing class, eventually have to demonstrate how well they can write impromptu essays, with
little time to apply what they have learned in class in such a test situation.
For this reason, the incentive for portfolio writing is weakened in the individual portfolio classroom.

Second, in the programmatic portfolio assessment classroom, three best
drafts to be submitted at the end of the semester constitute a goal for students
to strive for. Further, since not only the teacher but another reader will read
the final drafts to decide the grade, the students have to work hard to meet
the standards of passing. In the individual portfolio classroom, on the other
hand, the goal is often less clearly defined and the final portfolios are read
only by the teacher, whose standards are often equivocally implied rather
than clearly written out and therefore less conscientiously followed by the
students. With substantially less pressure from above, it is not hard to understand why not only students but also the teacher can be less motivated to try
their best in the individual portfolio classroom.

Third, the midterm "dry-run" required in programmatic portfolio assessment is an important device to motivate students and the teacher and, according to Elbow and Belanoff (1986) and others, the big percentage of students
who fail at midterm usually serves as a warning that works effectively as an
incentive to increase the quality of writing in the final portfolios and to
reduce the number of failed portfolios (337). In the individual portfolio
classroom, failing as many as more than half of the students (as Elbow and
Belanoff's programmatic portfolio assessment did) at midterm would inevitably cause animosity between the teacher and the students and make teaching and learning difficult, whereas passing those who deserve to fail would

not only affect the rigor of the course but the work ethic that we are responsible for promoting in our teaching. The teacher would be caught in a no-win situation if a majority of the class were not motivated from the beginning, and both students and the teacher would be "goners," as in Starner's class.

Lastly, will the teacher in the individual portfolio class schedule as many one-on-one conferences with her students as in programmatic portfolio assessment? Will the conferences work as effectively in cases of students' procrastination and in cases of the teacher's lack of clearly defined goals and standards? Will the teacher and the students be motivated to work as hard when there is no obvious and immediate pressure from the above? "I allow my students to revise as many times as they want" is an oft-heard remark, but it sounds almost ironical. For we all know that students will not revise "as many times" as we wish unless rewards are made tangible and reachable to them, rewards such as teachers' helpful and encouraging feedback, students' feeling of improvement in writing, and possible better grades toward the end of the semester. We also know that "no study has ever indicated that revising the same paper over and over again is usually of significant benefit for the writer" (Clark 1993, 522). Further, we know that "revision needs to be taught, not assigned" (Hansen 1978, 960). As C. H. Knoblauch and Lil Brannon (1986) explain:

> First, students generally do not comprehend written teacher responses. Second, when students do comprehend the comments, they generally do not know how to use them. And third, when students do use the comments, they do not necessarily produce more effective writing. (qtd. in Burnham 1986, 125)

Given these obstacles to teaching revision effectively, it is all the more important that we address the question: What serves as the incentive for the teaching and learning of revisions in individual portfolio classes? In other words, if we realize that portfolios in individual writing classrooms do not automatically acquire all the characteristics or merits of the programmatic portfolio approach, an urgent and important question then confronts us: How does the absence (albeit temporary) of institutional authority benefit teaching and learning in the individual portfolio classroom? Further, if we intend to shift from the goals of assessment to the goals of teaching writing in the individual portfolio classroom, what changes do we have to make so that the momentum for learning—facilitated by institutional authority in the programmatic portfolio assessment but weakened in individual portfolio classroom—can be refurbished to enable liberatory teaching and learning? How can we shift students' attention from the grade to the meaning or content of their writing when students are fully aware of the importance of grades in their lives? How can we emphasize the writing processes in our teaching when students know what really matters is their written product? How can we convince students of a "genuine" dialogue in the pedagogic context in which communication is first and foremost shaped by an asymmetrical power structure and used to accomplish certain pedagogic tasks? And how can we motivate students to read, write, and communicate more and better in the individual portfolio class, where there is less incentive to do so because of the weakened and often temporarily missing institutional authority? Unless we have tried to answer these questions before we jump onto the portfolio boat, I am afraid we will miss the challenges that portfolios create in our teaching.

Deferred Authority as Space for Innovation and Teacher Responsibility in the Individual Portfolio Classroom

It is true that, as Berlin theorizes (1994), the portfolio "can encourage students to explore in an unthreatening situation the intersections of private behavior and larger economic and social categories in a way that enables both women and men to construct and, in the same moment, critique the spoken subject that is appropriate to discourses of power" (67). Yet the portfolio does not automatically create an unthreatening situation, or enable students to construct and critique the spoken subject, or encourage students to explore the intersections of private behavior and larger economic and social categories in a desirable way. As Hamilton notes (1994), the portfolio is equally responsive to other theoretical assumptions, assumptions that devalue process and discourage students to try and err in their writing:

1. Since portfolios are a compilation of products that form the basis of assessment, the products must be a reliable indicator of human growth and potential.

2. Writing to produce a product to be evaluated doesn't interfere with or shape the process.

3. Everything a student writes should aspire to permanence, and should be read by an authority. (161)

Therefore, Hamilton argues, the portfolio is "no panacea for anything; it can enhance the learning environment in which it is used; it can maintain the learning environment in which it is used; or it can contradict the learning environment. It does not, in itself, *create* a particular learning environment" (162).

Hamilton's observation is an invaluable corrective of our perception of portfolios as an intrinsically liberatory teaching approach. What is important is not the use of portfolios in teaching but a change of our conception of teaching, as Elbow suggests (1994):

> I recommend trying out the following hypothesis in your teaching: assess-
> ment of strengths and weaknesses is really of limited value and what helps
> more is to coax the students into genuine dialogue with us and each other
> about the meaning or content of their writing. (52)

How to do the coaxing and how to create the genuine dialogue are the teach-er's responsibility, not the responsibility of the portfolios. I believe that the creation of a favorable learning environment depends on the teacher's recognition of the incongruity of the goals for which the portfolio is put to use; the teacher's realization of the different functions of institutional authority in different contexts; and the teacher's ingenuity in adjusting the class structure and activities to maximize the benefits that the portfolio has to offer in teaching writing.

I would like to recount an unusual experience with one of my Composition I classes as I attempted to coax students into a genuine dialogue about their writing. This was the second time I experimented with the portfolio, and based on my previous experiences with the individual portfolio, I made some significant changes when beginning this class. First, I changed the class structure from process-centered to text-centered. Instead of using a standard composition textbook such as the *Bedford Guide to College Writing* or the *Heath Guide to College Writing*, I adopted a reader, *Life Studies*, whose sections of readings are thematically arranged and whose focus is on analytical reading and writing. Accordingly, instead of making prewriting, drafting, and revising the major in-class activities, I organized class activities around the four major writing assignments that students were required to complete and the four groups of articles that were related to the topics of the writing assignments. The purpose of the text-oriented class is three-fold: 1. to help students understand in specific terms the overall purpose of the course, i.e. to learn how to read, write, and think analytically; 2. to articulate the course's expectations and prepare students for the tasks they are expected to tackle during the semester; and 3. to create motivation by setting short-term goals for students to reach.

Second, on the first day of class, apart from distributing copies of the syllabus that specified the goals, major requirements, and rules for the course, I handed out the grading criteria that summarized the major characteristics of an A, B, C, or F paper and a tentative schedule, which outlined daily class activities, conference dates, and due dates for the major writing assignments (see Appendix). Acknowledging my reservations about standards and criteria for grading, I made it clear to my students that the standards and criteria were guidelines for them to consider and even critique rather than rules for them to follow blindly. These handouts sketched the major concerns in reading and writing and provided a direction for class activities.

Third, I provided suggested topics for each writing assignment in the form of questions, and I supplied conference questions for each group conference. These handouts serve not only as prompts for prewriting and drafting but as statements of the teacher's as well as of the students' responsibilities. They also provide specific guidance for each writing assignment.

Fourth, for each writing assignment I required that students turn in prewriting, drafts, group comments, and the final, revised draft. I expected students to respond to my comments and revise each writing assignment immediately after I returned them with my responses. This way I made revision an important part of the writing processes, and the immediate revision allowed both me and my students to talk about their writing with reasonable enthusiasm since the memories of the papers were still fresh, and the urge to make them better was still with us.

And last, I did not put a grade on each of the students' papers, but for my own record I did grade each assignment and its revisions to keep track of each student's progress. "I'm not going to put a grade on each of your papers and revisions," I told the class at the very beginning of the semester. "You're responsible for figuring out where you stand in the class by reading my comments on each paper and by measuring up your writing with the descriptions in the Grading Criteria. I will, however, be happy to help you with your writing in all possible ways."

And that was all I had to say about grades in this class. From that day on, I watched with delight how the students actively read and interacted with the texts I had chosen for the course. I marveled at their eagerness to help and get help from each other when revising and editing their drafts. I rejoiced at the choices they made to improve their final drafts when I compared them with their earlier drafts. And I enjoyed the conferences I had with them, when we freely discussed my responses to their papers and why I responded the way I did and how they could improve a certain paper a little more. Never did anyone ask about grades. I could see that reading, writing, learning, discussing (arguing sometimes), and conferencing were all that they were interested in in this class; even the rather laborious tasks, such as answering the questions in my conference sheets and picking out mechanical errors in each other's papers, seemed to have great attraction for them. This group of students amazed me.

At midterm, I told the class that I would like to talk with them about their progress and grades, if that was what they wanted. Puzzled silence was soon followed by heads shaking, and by a unanimous vote my proposal was vetoed. "We're comfortable with portfolio grading," one student representative spoke up after I allowed a few minutes for the class to deliberate among themselves. "We know how we're doing in this class. You have been showing us what is good writing, and we have the grading criteria, your comments, assignment handouts, and conference questions to help us evaluate our own writing. We're doing O.K. and are not worried about grades."

Nodding heads, concurring voices, gleeful smiles, glittering eyes—they made
all the agonies I had had with the portfolio disappear. I asked them what they
liked about portfolios.

"Putting grades on papers will make us defensive and frustrated if they
are poor grades. We like the idea of being able to focus on how to write better without being discouraged by bad grades," one student said.

"It's good to know that you can get so much help from the teacher and
others to improve your papers before they are graded," another said. "We've
learned to criticize each other's papers because we're now more interested in
helping each other to write better rather than to just make each other feel
good," another added. "We're learning, we're learning," another student
smiled, as if to reassure me. "I've revised my two assignments twice now,
and I'll revise them more later for the final portfolio."

The enthusiasm for learning and writing lasted beyond the last day of
class, and the students and I decided that we would continue to read each
other's writing once every month. As I read their final portfolios, I could see
traces of their effort and sweat in the drafts, and I knew that they had learned
to re-see their own words and thoughts from different perspectives and to
revise to make their writing more effective. What worked to have created a
class that is almost a writing teacher's ideal? The portfolio? The special
group of students? The different class structure? The rather clearly articulated goals, standards, and grading criteria? The interesting reading materials? The helpful questions for each writing assignment and group conference? The hope and the possibility of getting a good grade through one's
continuous, persistent effort and with the help from others? All the above?
Or something else?

It is hard to generalize from one successful portfolio class how the portfolio can be used to change our notion of teaching writing and to create an
environment that fosters genuine dialogue about writing. Nevertheless, this
successful portfolio class does tell us something about how motivation must
and can be created in a writing class when institutional authority is temporarily removed. By using texts and assignments as minigoals, by guiding
students through the writing processes repeatedly through the writing assignments and conferences, by spelling out clearly my expectations, by providing students with specific questions, by encouraging students to share with
each other their lived experiences and writing, I was able to motivate the
students to write without having to rely solely on institutional authority.

Would a class like this happen if I were using the traditional grading
method? Perhaps not. In the portfolio classroom, because of the absence of
grades on students' papers, both the teacher and the students feel that they can
afford to ignore the evaluative question, "How good is this paper?" for a while.
Thus, they can focus on questions that are more relevant to students' lived
experiences and feelings, questions that help form students' subject position
and voice as writers. The teacher's attention to students' lived experiences may

well become a motivation for students to write, for, as Jay Robinson (1985) rightly asserts, "even great works of literature, after all, like experiences we comfortably or uncomfortably participate in and remember, are stories that people tell themselves to make sense of their lives" (495). The teacher's ability to ask the right questions at the right time is of vital importance, too. Since "every significant text has been 'written' out of the verbal life of its author," and since writing "is the result of an ongoing conversation or dialectic process, not of a single act of authorship" (Comprone 1992, 217), asking the right questions also helps establish a context in which dialogue is valued and trust is developed between the reader and the writer, a context in which the writer is encouraged to consider all perspectives offered by others to enrich their own thinking and writing.

Joseph Comprone (1992) recapitulates Kenneth Burke's view of writing,

> Burke situates the individual writer within a world of swirling, interactive languages. . . . The job of the writer is to take action within the swirl, employing these different languages as tools in creating new perspectives and eventually new scenes for subsequent symbolic action. (219)

To create a miniature of the "world of swirling, interactive languages" in the writing classroom, to encourage students to take symbolic action within the swirl, the teacher certainly needs to be free from the institutional obligations to judge and to justify every grade. And the students need to be free from the pressure and anxiety that grades tend to cause them, especially when they are new in college, so they can experiment with different ways of writing—to take symbolic action—without having to worry about the consequences, usually reflected in the grade. And here lies the significant contribution of the portfolio to the teaching of writing.

However, we must remember that the freedom created by deferring the grade is after all temporary and illusory, in a sense, since lurking in the back of the "free" classroom is the institution and its constraints, both on the teacher and on the student. As I have confessed, I did grade students' papers and revisions, even though I kept the grades from the students. The students also thought about grades when they read my comments and tried to figure out where they stood in my class. The institutional constraints, or grades, can nevertheless work in our favor if we use them constructively. As Kurt Spellmeyer (1989) interprets Foucault's view of writing, writing happens only through the writer's committing the "knowledge-transforming violence" through trial and error (719). In other words, if writing is the "game of truth," with rules and conventions that exclude and restrain new players, the only way that the new players can join in the game is to learn about the constraints and turn the constraints into enabling power through a strong desire to break into the exclusive practice. The writer's knowledge of the constraints and the writer's desire to join the game, Spellmeyer continues, are two important factors in writing:

Only through a willingness to make room for themselves in the game, only by overcoming their regard for the "rules" and the "truth," can writers undertake the knowledge-transforming violence that distinguishes the empowered from the powerless. (719)

If the portfolio is to have any empowering effects in the writing classroom, if the portfolio is to aid students to commit knowledge-transforming violence in their writing, we must then acknowledge the constraints within and against which the portfolio functions in the classroom and turn the constraints into incentives for writing. We must also find ways to use the portfolio to reach not only our pedagogical goals of empowering students with critical literacy but also to fulfill our institutional obligations to evaluate and judge.

After all, what is the hope the portfolio offers in the writing classroom? I believe the hope is that, rather than *being* a teaching method itself, the portfolio, with its suspension of the teacher's institutional authority, forces the teacher to think of new ways of creating motivations in teaching writing in the pedagogic context. If in the traditional classroom grades constitute the motivation for learning, the absence of grades in the portfolio class will inevitably create inertia and indifference. It is therefore the teachers' responsibility to experiment with new ways to motivate students.

In my most successful portfolio classes, everything had to work together to create new dynamics for learning: from the better-structured classes to the more cooperative students, from the more interesting topics for writing to the better-guided and more productive conferences, from the more explicit standards to the teacher's more sympathetic and constructive comments—all had to work perfectly to help create short-term goals as well as feelings of accomplishment and fulfillment in the teacher and students. In the final analysis, the motivation for a genuine dialogue in the portfolio classroom is generated by the teacher's deferred institutional authority as well as by the ever present institutional constraints, both working together to provide a rhetorical context for the teacher and the student to experiment with written words, not only to satisfy the institutional requirements but to satisfy our deeper needs as human beings to understand ourselves and others better, to comprehend our lives and the world around us better, and to communicate with each other better.

References

Belanoff, P. and M. Dickson, eds. 1991. *Portfolios: Process and Product*. Portsmouth, NH: Boynton/Cook.

Belanoff, P. and P. Elbow. 1986. "Using Portfolios to Increase Collaboration and Community in a Writing Program." *WPA: Writing Program Administration* 9 (3): 27–40.

Berlin, James A. 1994. In "The Subversions of the Portfolio." In *New Directions in Portfolio Assessment: Reflective Practice, Critical Theory, and Large-Scale Scoring*, ed. L. Black et al., 56–67. Urbana, IL: NCTE.

Black, L., D. Daiker, J. Sommers, and G. Stygall, eds. 1994. *New Directions in Portfolio Assessment: Reflective Practice, Critical Theory, and Large-Scale Scoring.* Portsmouth, NH: Boynton/Cook.

Bridges, C., ed. 1986. *Training the New Teacher of College Composition.* Urbana, IL: NCTE.

Burnham, C. 1986. "Portfolio Evaluation: Room to Breathe and Grow." In *Training the New Teacher of College Composition*, ed. C. Bridges, 125–38. Urbana, IL.: NCTE.

Cardoni, A., R. Fraser, and J. W. Starner. 1994. "Collaboration, Collages, and Portfolios: A Workshop." In *New Directions in Portfolio Assessment*, ed. L. Black et al., 129–39. Urbana, IL: NCTE.

Clark, I. 1993. "Portfolio Evaluation, Collaboration, and Writing Centers." *CCC* 44 (4): 515–24.

Comprone, J. 1992. "Dramatism and Dialectic: Kenneth Burke's Philosophy of Discourse." In *The Philosophy of Discourse*, ed. C. Sills and G. H. Jensen. Vol. 1. 205–28. Portsmouth, NH: Boynton/Cook.

Elbow, P. and P. Belanoff. 1986. "Portfolios as a Substitute for Proficiency Examinations." *CCC* 37 (3): 336–39.

————. 1991. "State University of New York at Stony Brook Portfolio-Based Evaluation Program." In *Portfolios: Process and Product*, ed. P. Belanoff and M. Dickson, 3–16. Portsmouth, NH: Boynton/Cook.

Elbow, P. 1994. "Will the Virtues of Portfolios Blind Us to Their Potential Dangers?" In *New Directions in Portfolio Assessment*, ed. L. Black et al., 40–55. Portsmouth, NH: Boynton/Cook.

Ford, J. E. and G. Larkin. 1978. "The Portfolio System: An End to Backsliding Writing Standards." *College English* 39 (8): 950–55.

Hamilton, S. J. 1994. "Portfolio Pedagogy: Is a Theoretical Construct Enough?" In *New Directions in Portfolio Assessment*, ed. L. Black et al., 157–67. Portsmouth, NH: Boynton/Cook.

Hansen, B. 1978. "Rewriting Is a Waste of Time." *College English* 39 (8): 956–60.

McClelland, K. 1991. "Portfolios: Solution to a Problem." In *Portfolios: Process and Product*, ed. P. Belanoff and M. Dickson, 165–73. Portsmouth, NH: Boynton/Cook.

Reither, J. A. and R. A. Hunt. 1994. "Beyond Portfolios: Scenes for Dialogic Reading and Writing." In *New Directions in Portfolio Assessment*, ed. L. Black et al., 168–82. Portsmouth, NH: Boynton/Cook.

Roemer, M., L. M. Schultz, and R. K. Durst. 1991. "Portfolios and the Process of Change." *CCC* 42 (4): 455–69.

Robinson, J. L. 1985. "Literacy in the Department of English." *College English* 47 (5): 482–98.

Schuster, C. I. 1994. "Climbing the Slippery Slope of Assessment: The Programmatic Use of Writing Portfolios." In *New Directions in Portfolio Assessment,* ed. L. Black et al., 314–24. Portsmouth, NH: Boynton/Cook.

Smit, D. W. 1990. "Evaluating a Portfolio System." *WPA: Writing Program Administration* 14 (1–2): 51–62.

Smith, C. A. 1991. "Writing Without Testing." In *Portfolios: Process and Product,* ed. P. Belanoff and M. Dickson, 279–91. Portsmouth, NH: Boynton/Cook.

Sommers, J. 1991. "Bringing Practice in Line with Theory: Using Portfolio Grading in the Composition Classroom." In *Portfolios: Process and Product,* ed. P. Belanoff and M. Dickson, 153–73. Portsmouth, NH: Boynton/Cook.

Spellmeyer, K. 1989. "Foucault and the Freshman Writer: Considering the Self in Discourse." *College English* 51 (7): 715–29.

Thelin, W. H. 1994. "The Connection Between Response Styles and Portfolio Assessment: Three Case Studies of Student Revision." In *New Directions in Portfolio Assessment,* ed. L. Black et al., 113–25. Portsmouth, NH: Boynton/Cook.

Weinbaum, K. 1991. "Portfolios as a Vehicle for Student Empowerment and Teacher Change." In *Portfolios: Process and Product,* ed. P. Belanoff and M. Dickson, 206–14. Portsmouth, NH: Boynton/Cook.

Yancey, K. B. 1992. "Portfolio in the Writing Classroom: A Final Reflection." In *Portfolios in the Writing Classroom: An Introduction,* ed. K. B. Yancey, 102–16. Urbana, IL: NCTE.

Appendix

Tentative Grading Criteria

In this class I will be trying to follow certain principles in evaluating and responding to students' writing: 1. to evaluate how well the student has grasped what has been taught in class; 2. to find out what are the student's main difficulties in writing and in learning in general; and 3. to reinforce what I consider to be important factors in producing good writing, factors that I expect students to experiment with and incorporate in their writing assignments. My criteria of grading are accordingly shaped by this triple purpose.

A "D" Paper

Usually I have assigned a D when 1. the paper indicates the writer's obvious irresponsibility or writing deficiency that results in serious problems such as misspelling, non-standard grammar, erroneous sentence structure, and illogical development of ideas; 2. the paper shows that the writer fails to grasp what I expect my students to learn and demonstrate in a certain writing assignment (e.g., when required to write a persuasive paper, someone turns in an anecdotal story); or 3. the paper fails to convince me that the student is the authentic writer of the piece (the absence of rough drafts that I require to accompany the final draft may well be grounds for such suspicion). Sometimes, it is the combination of all these problems that make me consider a paper a failure. A "D" is a serious message to shock a student into recognition that he or she should either shape up or drop the course.

A "C" Paper

A "C" paper usually presents a main idea and often suggests a plan of development, which is usually weakly carried out. In general, a "C" paper is characterized by general statements or a listing, and the development of ideas is neither sufficient nor clear enough to be convincing. Sentence structure tends to be pedestrian and often repetitious. Errors in sentence structure, usage, and mechanics often interfere with the meaning that the writer intends to put across. The writer, however, does show efforts to grasp what has been taught in class. A "C" sends the message that the writer needs to work hard to improve his or her writing skills and that substantial revision of the piece is absolutely necessary.

A "B" Paper

A paper that deserves a "B" usually presents a thesis and suggests a plan of development, which is usually satisfactorily carried out. The paper usually demonstrates the writer's ability to provide details to support the main idea and to vary sentence structure to achieve certain rhetorical effects. Occasional errors in sentence structure, usage, and mechanics do not interfere with the meaning the writer tries to communicate. A "B" paper usually indicates that the writer knows well what has been taught in class and is able to communicate his or her ideas competently in written symbols. A "B" paper also indicates that the writer has a lot more to learn in order to produce an excellent writing product.

An "A" Paper

A paper that presents or implies a thesis that is developed with noticeable coherence is an "A" paper. The "A" paper usually presents substantive, sophisticated, and carefully elaborated ideas. The writer's language and structure is precise and purposeful, often to the point of being polished. Control of sentence structure, usage, and mechanics, despite an occasional flaw, contributes to the meaning that the writer is trying to communicate. Very often, the "A" paper has an unusually effective opening that catches the reader's interest and makes the reader want to read on, or it has a striking conclusion that drives home the main ideas with convincing finality. It may have an unusually coherent organization that spotlights the main idea and marshals the supporting data so clearly that the reader cannot help but understand what the writer is trying to put across. Or it may use illustrative anecdotes, statistics, quotations, or examples in such a way as to add vigor or convincingness. Or still further, it may here and there use words and phrases so apt and so fresh that the thought seems to fly effortlessly into the mind of the reader and makes a strong impact upon him or her. A writer who produces "A" papers usually not only has a good command of language but an ability and a willingness to experiment with new techniques, new ideas, new modes of thinking in their writing. A truly superior writer shows their open-mindedness and flexibility in his or her papers.

I hope this description will give you a general idea about what I expect in your writing. The criteria perhaps will also help you decide what final grade you want to make in this class and how much effort you need to put into your writing in order to reach your goal. I never doubt that success and victory belong to those who are willing to work hard for them!

Chapter Six

Grading the "Subject"
Questions of Expertise and Evaluation

Tim Peeples and Bill Hart-Davidson

Tim Peeples and Bill Hart-Davidson teach introductory composition and professional writing at Purdue University in West Lafayette, Indiana. A large, state-supported university, Purdue serves about thirty-five thousand undergraduates and is known for its engineering and agriculture programs. Peeples and Hart-Davidson explore how the notion of "expertise" as specialized knowledge located in the written product and in the individual writer is destablized in postmodern theories. They support a move toward "networked expertise" in which the grading process becomes an ongoing process of argument rather than a series of discreet judgments. Thus, grading functions as part of a network that constructs, constrains, and empowers the expert writer.

In "The Idea of Expertise: An Exploration of Cognitive and Social Dimensions of Writing," Michael Carter (1990) testifies to the centrality of the concept of expertise in composition pedagogy. He argues that "the goals of our classes indicate what we think expertise in writing is, and the way we teach indicates how we think writers achieve expertise" (265). In the post-process era, we wish to add to Carter's claims about the importance of expertise; specifically we wish to argue that the debate over what constitutes expertise is also a question of subjectivity and power, of who can be an expert and under what conditions.

Among the many specific practices that make up day-to-day pedagogy in the writing classroom, grading is probably the most heavily influenced by theories of expertise. Our judgments about expert writers—*what* makes them expert and *how* their expertise can be measured—function to direct and constrain our theories of composition, our methods of evaluation, and our grading practices. If theories of composing reflect and constrain conceptions of expertise, it goes without saying that as conceptions of expertise change, so do methods of evaluation and practices of grading.

In this essay, we question how changing theories of expertise affect grading practices in composition. More specifically, we explore how recent developments in theories of expertise suggest changes in the following:

- *how* grading functions in the classroom,
- *who* can be an "expert" and under what conditions,
- and *what* factors should be considered when determining grades.

These three areas of development serve as a broad organizational device; however, they also indicate the way we are shifting the discussion of expertise and evaluation away from previous discussions in two critical ways. First, most previous work in writing expertise uses the theoretical lens of expertise to take a broad look at general theories of writing. A critical shift in our work brings theories of expertise to bear on the more specific concerns of grading as a specific set of practices. In addition to this shift in focus, we approach the practice of grading from a new direction: as a *technology* that teachers employ in the classroom that, like all technologies, enacts the cultural and disciplinary values of its designers and users.

Determining the *How* of Grading: Conceiving of Grading as a Technology

Along with Michael Carter (1990), we agree that theories of expertise are intertwined with classroom practice. As a first step toward an analysis of how grading as a specific classroom and institutional practice is influenced by theories of expertise, we define the relationship between expertise and grading. It is tempting to see this relationship as a theory/practice binary, with expertise as the theory that informs and is enacted in our grading practices. But this kind of relationship is troubling because it presents a misleading view of what grading is from the writing teacher's perspective. The theory/ practice binary tends to privilege theory over practice, suggesting that grading itself is a derivative function, one that has no real intellectual impact on theories of expertise, and by extension, on writing. Obviously, we don't agree. We argue, on the contrary, that grading practices inform theories of expertise; grading necessarily involves theorizing about expertise in the localized context of a particular classroom setting, with particular features and constraints.

Another difficulty with a simple theory/practice split when describing expertise and grading is that it is difficult to narrow the term "grading" down to any one or even a few specific actions. Grading is, instead, a complex set of procedures, policies, and concrete actions involving both advance planning and "real-time" judgment, reflection, and action (Schön 1983). Finally, a theory/practice split doesn't help us address one of the most important functions of grading—its role in creating and maintaining relations of power in classrooms, in institutions, and in our culture at large. Foucault (1984) argues that the kind of multiple, "tiny, everyday, physical mechanisms" that comprise the complex practices of a technology, such as grading, work to mediate relations of power (211). Using Foucault's words, grading can be accurately described as "a type of power, a modality for its exercise, comprising a whole set of instruments, techniques, procedures, levels of application, targets; it is a 'physics' or an 'anatomy' of power, a *technology*" (206) [our emphasis].

Adopting Foucault's view of technology offers a more accurate description of grading as most of us know it. Grading certainly is the web of "instruments, techniques, procedures, levels of application, targets" that Foucault describes, whether we are discussing the intensely regulated procedures of standardized tests, or the more open-ended but no less complicated procedures of localized portfolio assessment. And the consequences of grading practices —i.e., who gets tracked low and who tests out; who gets into school and who doesn't; who gets the job interview and who doesn't—leave no doubt as to the regulatory functions of grading. Foucault's description of this regulatory function once again rings true: grading tends to "characterize, classify, specialize ... distribute along a scale, around a norm, hierarchize individuals in relation to one another and, if necessary, disqualify and invalidate" (212).

Describing grading as a technology in Foucault's terms is a move that greatly enhances our ability to analyze the ways grading functions, but it also leaves us with the problem of how to contend with "a machinery that is both immense and minute, which supports, reinforces, multiplies the asymmetry of power" (212). In casting off the theory/practice binary, we must make sense of a far more complex relationship between the ways our ideas about expertise are involved in the complex practices of grading.

Seeing grading as a kind of technology, we ask the following questions:

- what makes the technology of grading function the way it does?
- and what principles govern its design and use?

Our short answer to the second question is "theories of expertise." The relationship between expertise and grading, then, is similar to the relationship between the values, rules, and habits that determine how technologies are designed and used and the actual technologies themselves. This claim about the relationship between expertise and grading relies on an approach to technology slightly different from that suggested by Foucault, but articulated by Andrew Feenberg in *Critical Theory of Technology* (1991). Feenberg's theory of technology, while complex, provides a helpful basis not only for understanding how grading operates in relation to theories of expertise but also for proposing some concrete strategies for designing more effective grading practices in light of changing notions of expertise. But first, a fuller description of Feenberg's approach is needed.

A Critical Theory of the Technology of Grading

For Feenberg, as for Foucault, technologies are not indifferent to the social systems in which they are developed and operate and for whose ends they serve; they are the mechanisms that maintain these social systems. But unlike Foucault, Feenberg argues that technologies are not *outside* of our control, determining who and how we are. Instead, Feenberg's theory of technology defines technology as an "ambivalent social system suspended between different possibilities" (14). This ambivalence stems from the idea that technology does not consist only of those processes and concrete objects that we normally think of when we discuss "technology"; it also consists of a set of social values and norms—what Feenberg refers to as the "technical code"—that regulates the development and practice of these processes and objects. For the "artifacts" (the sum of technical processes and objects) of any specific technology, there coexists a technical code that influences both the design and use of the technology.

The artifacts of grading include portfolios, essay exams, student-teacher conferences, state proficiency exams, etc. Each of these "grading artifacts" consists of both the material objects needed to implement them (scanners, manila folders, the infamous red pen) as well as the procedures that animate these objects (holistic vs. analytical grading, machine scoring vs. handwritten comments, etc.). But these grading artifacts are only half of the technology of grading, the other half being the network of cultural, institutional, and personal values, rules, and decisions that make up the technical code of grading. Some parts of the technical code, such as published departmental standards for proficiency at a certain level of writing ability, are explicit and their influence on grading artifacts easy to identify. Other parts, such as the idea of grade inflation, are less defined and more difficult to trace in terms of the ways they may influence grading.

What is important to understand about Feenberg's definition is the idea that technologies do not simply develop or emerge by chance or coincidence. Instead, both components—artifacts and technical code—are *designed* to produce some cultural condition. An example from outside the academy clarifies the power of Feenberg's definition. Think of how a familiar but complex technology such as the assembly line fits into Feenberg's definition. The assembly line consists of *artifacts* (both the production *methods* associated with the line and the *machines* that make these processes happen), along with a *technical code* that includes such values as "efficiency" and "division of labor" and makes possible such regulations as around-the-clock shiftwork. In this way, the artifacts and codes associated with the assembly line are easily identified as "technologies," but Feenberg's definition asks us to question an assumption that we make when we think of these artifacts and codes—namely, that they are designed to produce "cars" or some other material product. Feenberg suggests that they are also designed to produce some cultural condition, not merely another set of artifacts. It might be argued, for example, that assembly lines are designed to produce a disempowered yet efficient and complicit workforce. This goal is built into the technology, the technical code, and the artifacts.

This example suggests that technologies are designed to produce individuals; complex technical processes like grading are involved in what Lester Faigley (1992) describes as the process of constructing the subjectivity of student writers, or determining "the selves we want our students to be" (114). We would add that as a high-stakes discourse practice within a web of discourses that constitute writing pedagogies, grading is the means by which student subjectivities are emphatically articulated. To complicate matters, grading is a system whose technical code is written by many hands: teachers and researchers in our field; administrators and institutions that run and fund writing programs; legislatures, workplaces, and other "publics" that shape the cultural goals of literacy education. Seen in this light, the teacher's job of "grading papers" amounts to participating in a number of arguments within and among the institutional frameworks in which she works and with any number of specific subjects: students, writing program administrators, other teachers, parents, etc.

Determining the *Who* of Grading: Connecting Theories of Expertise and Grading Practices

The second question we address in our reconstruction of expertise, specifically in relation to the practices of grading, is *who* can be an "expert" and under what conditions. The way we phrase this question is telling of our own argument. Rather than asking who *is* an expert, which would imply a stable, unified site of expertise, our phrasing destabilizes the site of expertise. Asking who *can be* an expert directs attention to the general conditions that enable experts to arise and be named as such. Following who "can be" an expert with *under what conditions* directs attention to specific conditions of expertise. The argument in this essay focuses on the specific condition that is grading. In other words, we take a closer look at the relationship between grading practices and the possibilities of expertise, beginning with a discussion of four relevant models of expertise.

Traditional Model of Expertise

David Kaufer and Richard Young (1993) identify three models of expertise particularly relevant to composition: the general skills model, the contextualist model, and the interactionist model. To this we add the traditional model of expertise, especially expertise in an art such as writing that considers the expert to be "the genius artisan." Our literatures and histories portray the expert preacher, artist, sculptor, blacksmith, carpenter, etc., as expert because they illustrate their individual genius, their *expertise*, in the products or artifacts that they create. This model argues that the expert preacher or speaker is proven expert by the sermon or speech she leaves for our record on tape, video, or in text. We point to the material record to illustrate the writer/speaker's expertise. In writing classes we play the tapes, show the videos, read the sermons and speeches of expert orators, and then direct students to produce similar expert products. This model of expertise has, of course, found its way into the disciplinary traditions of composition through the pedagogical practices of using model essays to teach writing, placing the focus on final products, which are evaluated against the models produced by expert writers.

The traditional model of expertise answers the question of *who* can be an expert by pointing to the products of experts. In other words, the expertise of the expert is represented in the "textual" product. When asked, *"Who can be an expert?"* the traditional model responds with, "The person who can produce X is an expert." Hidden in this response are the conditions under which X can be produced. The traditional model of expertise "mystifies"— using a composition term from the 70s and 80s—the conditions under which expertise arises.

General Skills Model of Expertise

The general skills model takes the position that "expertise is a matter of controlling general strategies (i.e., making diagrams, analogies, and means-ends analyses) that are useful in any subject area" (Kaufer and Young 1993, 91). This was the central position of the early cognitive rhetoric work done in our field, as exemplified by the early work of Linda Flower. Part of the impetus of this model came from attempts in the late 1950s to develop artificial intelligence (AI). Computer programmers, in an attempt to make "intelligent machines," tried to reproduce the thinking processes of human "experts" in machines. As Kaufer and Young explain, the AI community "developed a computer program called the 'General Problem Solver' that could solve problems in a variety of domains through a common set of general strategies involving the monitoring of goals along with monitoring the extent to which certain actions move toward or away from these goals" (91). This same model of expertise can be seen in cognitive pedagogies that aim at teaching students how to set rhetorical goals and then monitor their progress toward those goals as they write.

Within such a pedagogy, teachers must devise a way to evaluate a writer's ability to use the general writing skills emblematic of experts, such as setting rhetorical goals and evaluating the effectiveness of one's writing against those goals. The portfolio method of grading is one evaluation technology the field of composition has designed to gather together students' plans (where they set their goals), peer feedback (where suggestions could be logged about where the author may have moved away from her goals), and revisions (where an author's attempts to pull herself back to her goals could be documented) in order to "catch" this process conceived to be the writing processes of experts. In other words, the portfolio becomes an artifact of evaluation suitable to the technical codes that arose out of a general skills model of expertise.

Under the general skills model of expertise, *who* can be an expert is the person (or machine) who most consciously sets goals, monitors progress towards those goals, and adjusts writing behavior to meet those goals. The conditions for expertise are primarily cognitive. If the writer is conditioned to "think well" through the writing process, which presumes conditioning the educational context so writers can have access to the techniques and directions for "good thinking," the conditions are better for the development of expertise in writing.

Contextualist Model of Expertise

As discussions of the social nature of writing and literacy developed in the early to mid-eighties, especially in the work of Bizzell (1982), Bruffee (1986), and Odell and Goswami (1985), theories of expertise in writing needed to be reevaluated and revised. Michael Carter's work in 1990 and Cheryl Geisler's work from the late eighties and early nineties, culminating in her recent publication *Academic Literacy and the Nature of Expertise* (1994), mark two of rhetoric and composition's attempts to address the effects of social constructionist thought on our conceptions of expert writers. Responding to the social perspective on writing, Kaufer and Young's "contextualist models" claim that expertise in writing requires one "to learn the local contexts in which discourse communities acquire knowledge" (93). In contrast to a general skills focus, the contextualist model emphasizes the contextual nature of expertise, arguing that expertise is less of a set of general skills one learns once and for all and can "carry" from place to place; rather, the contextualists argue that an expert is an expert because he has learned the local norms of the space in which he is considered an expert.

This move from the general skills model to the contextualist model carries with it a shift in the technologies of evaluation, the technical codes of literacy, and the conditions of expertise. From a Feenbergian perspective, we define what might be called the "literacy code" as the socially negotiated imperatives associated with the teaching of literacy. We argue that as models of expertise change, the literacy code and conditions of expertise change. The socially constructed imperatives of the general skills model direct teachers of writing to identify those basic skills that make for good writing; construct curricula, courses, and activities that teach these general skills to students; and develop evaluative techniques to assess students' fluency in these general skills. However, the socially constructed imperatives—the literacy code—of the contextualist model are different. Rather than searching for general skills associated with expert writing, the contextualist literacy code urges us to identify local discourse norms and create educational spaces in which students can participate in the practice and revision of these local norms. Within the contextualist model, then, *who* can be an expert becomes linked more explicitly to the social, cultural conditions surrounding the writing/writer, and the notion of general expertise is abandoned.

Interactionist Model of Expertise

Kaufer and Young's final model of expertise, the "interactionist model," argues that expertise in writing is neither all general nor all contextual (1993). Rather, the interactionist model argues that "expertise relies on a complex and so far unspecified interaction between context knowledge and general strategies that are in principle articulable and teachable" (94). A key word in this final model of expertise is *unspecified*. Although several theorists may be categorized as interactionists—Michael Carter, David Kaufer, Richard Young, and Cheryl Geisler, for instance—the range for this final model of expertise is so broad and "unspecified" that it is *less a model* and *more a broad category* in which a post-process conception of writing expertise might be situated. Like the recent struggle in theory circles to draw a more helpful and concise line around and within the theoretical space that has been named "postmodernism," there need to be more helpful and concise circles drawn around what is called an "interactionist model of expertise."

Of these four models of expertise, we situate our conceptions of expertise within the interactionist model. There is not space enough to argue our specific conception of expertise, but like the interactionists, we hold that expertise arises out of "a complex and so far unspecified interaction between context knowledge and general strategies" (Kaufer and Young 1993, 94). However, rather than focusing on the *individual* as what might be called the "carrier" of expertise, as if expertise is within the individual subject, we shift grounds and focus on the *network* that constructs, constrains, and empowers the individual subject as an expert. For the sake of brevity, we have named this species of interactionism "network expertise," because our definition of expertise relies on an understanding of the interconnections and networks in which experts are created (Hart-Davidson and Peeples 1995).

We argue here that grading practices are a critical part of the academic conditions for the possibility of expertise. We focus on grading as part of the network that constructs, constrains, and empowers the possibility of the expert writer. Taking this approach, we believe, will draw more helpful and concise circles around and within the broad category of interactionist expert models.

Determining the *What* of Grading: Turning to Our Own Stories of Grading

The "story" really begins when we were collaboratively developing a second semester, first-year composition course, English 102, and came to the joint conclusion that our conception of network expertise called for a new practice of grading. Even though we had between us a combined seventeen years of experience in teaching generally, and composition teaching specifically, we could not put our fingers on discussions of grading that addressed our problem. We were not, however, surprised by this. Our assumption that as theories of expertise change so do technologies of grading prepared us for what was to come: a need to *theorize* a different grading practice.

Rather than turn to some theory of evaluation that we then "applied" to our concrete situation, we participated in the *theorizing* activity argued by Sosnoski (1994): "Theorizing is making explicit in a discourse the conditions of critical reflection . . . making explicit the conditions of practice including its canonical warrants (scholarship) and its regularities (pedagogy)" (192). In our specific context, we tried to map for ourselves the conditions in the field of rhetoric and composition that framed our pedagogical/grading problem and the concrete conditions of our positions as not only writing teachers within a large research university teaching an introductory writing class but also as graduate instructors and graduate students.[1] Mapping the conditions of our problem in terms of the field of rhetoric and composition (as we were able to conceive of them from our contingent subject positions) is what we have represented up to this point. From this point on, we will turn toward the more concrete conditions that we mapped to help us theorize the problem of developing a way to grade our students.

Generating a Heuristic for Determining the Situated What *of Grading*[2]

The following heuristic is designed to respond to our third question concerning grading within the context of changing theories of expertise and changing notions of grading as a technology: *what* factors should be considered when determining grades? Under this broad question, we have identified four more specific questions.

First, What are the features of the "network expert"?

- Expertise is not decontextualized from the context in which it occurs.
- Expertise arises in a social network or context.
- Expertise requires conditions that are fundamentally social/discursive.
- Expertise requires interaction between context knowledge and general strategies.
- Expertise is located in a shifting, social, discursive site rather than within individual subjects.
- Expertise includes procedural as well as productive knowledge.

Second, What grading artifacts are available to you?

- Portfolios
- Holistic grading
- Grade audits
- Conferencing
- Departmental exam(s)
- Grade appeal processes
- State proficiency exam
- Essay exam
- Indirect evaluations (i.e., grammar tests)

Third, What are the context-specific constraints/issues under which you must grade?

Institutional

- Is it expected your grades will represent a standard curve?
- Will your grades/grading be reviewed? If so, by whom and by what criteria?
- To what purposes are your grades put? To determine a student's status? To determine a student's financial position? To establish your effectiveness as a teacher?
- Is your course part of a general core and/or cross-curricular?

Classroom

- In what year are your students?
- Does your class represent divergences/challenges in relation to other courses (i.e., yours is the only computer section, or you are piloting a new pedagogy)?

Fourth, What are your pedagogical goals/objectives?

Programmatic/Curricular

- Writing under pressure
- Rhetorical sensitivity
- Cultural and cross-disciplinary awareness
- Disciplinary proficiency
- Generic accuracy
- Research proficiency
- Situational agency
- Grammatical competency

Classroom

- Audience sensitivity
- Document design
- Computer skills
- Cultural critique
- Ethical positioning
- Metacognition

This heuristic has functioned for us in several different ways and in several different contexts. It has guided the development of syllabi, helping us sequence projects, determine grading policies, and plan specific assignments. For instance, a mandatory essay exam was redesigned to encourage students to explore the disciplinary, discursive network conventions that map the fields of expertise they were working in on a semester-long research project. The heuristic has also aided Bill as a mentor in teaching new instructors ways not only to generate semesterly grading policies and daily grading practices, but also to reflect upon and evaluate past grading policies and practices.

We have divided the heuristic into four sections. In the section listing the features of network expertise, we identify six critical features of our specific species of interactionism, features that address the question of *who* and make explicit features of the technical code of network expertise.

The first feature of network expertise is its contextualized nature. As Geisler (1994) points out, textbooks are examples of decontextualized expertise; the discursive markers of negotiation and debate, of hedging and referencing, are typically erased (19). However, such discursive features are critical to expert practice and participation. Consequently, the social and contextual feature of expertise is erased, or mystified, in the process of decontextualization. Our second feature reasserts the social nature of experts and expertise. The third feature also tries to correct for decontextualizing by emphasizing the social-discursive nature of expertise. This feature argues that experts and expert "sites" are *constructed* socially and discursively (see Lyne and Howe 1990). The fourth feature is simply a reassertion of the basic characteristic of the interactionist model of expertise, within which network expertise falls. The fifth feature is a critical one. Rather than seeing expertise as something that is neural—an ontological reality that is carried within an individual—we emphasize the social, shifting, discursive nature of expertise. And the final feature situates the social nature of expertise epistemologically by reasserting the category of "procedural" knowledge: *how* to get things done.

The grading artifact section addresses the *how* of grading and, thus, heuristically functions to make explicit the technological nature of the practice of grading. This section is but a partial list of some of the grading artifacts that might be used within specific grading contexts.

Through questions, the bottom two sections ask "under what conditions" expertise is constructed, making the contextual, organizational context of grading explicit. To help us make explicit the context-specific conditions of our practice, we referred to Linda Driskill's "Understanding the Writing Context in Organizations" (1989), which illustrates a way to map the organizational context of writing situations. A rough map of the organizational features we made explicit for ourselves includes the course we were teaching, the university, the department, the composition program, our students, and the mentor. The four questions listed on pages 103–104 and Figure 6–1 work in tandem as heuristics for considering the context-specific constraints of the grading situation. The final section encourages making explicit both the larger programmatic and curricular goals and objectives, as well as the goals and objectives of an individual instructor in an individual class.

Our Own Story of Grading in a Post-Process Classroom

While much of our effort has been aimed at complicating the ways grading functions and complicating the responsibilities of the instructor who is engaged in the process of grading, we hope that the heuristic discussed above offers a way to deal with these complications. In this final section, we will use the questions in the heuristic to talk through some of the more provocative claims we have made about expertise and to show how these have come to inform our own grading practices. Specifically, we will discuss how our efforts to make students active participants in the processes of grading led us to conceive of grading as an ongoing institutional argument and to begin assigning value to the metadiscursive activity that signals expertise in writing. For illustration, we will refer to the familiar second semester, first-year writing course, English 102, which has the broad curricular goal of introducing students to formal academic writing and research.

The question that looms largest over the claims we have made can be stated this way: if expertise in writing is not a measurable quality of individual

Figure 6–1

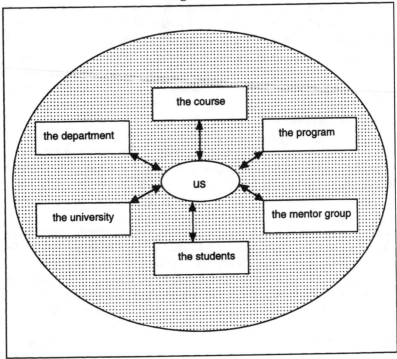

writers, on what basis should we assign grades to students in our writing classes? This question, for us, succinctly characterizes the problem of grading in the post-process era.

A feature of "network expertise" that profoundly influenced our grading practices—both our stated grading policies designed for the writing courses we have taught and the moments of judgment during which a grade is actually assigned—is the idea that expertise arises under conditions that are discursively complex and, quite often, in sites where the most fundamental "truth" claims are under negotiation by the so-called experts. As mentioned earlier, Geisler (1994) argues that expert knowledge is necessarily the result of ongoing argument, not established truths, and that attempts to package expert knowledge in discrete, easy-to-digest forms, such as textbooks, often misrepresent the extent to which expertise is based in invention and argumentation (19).

But what significance does this have for the writing classroom? In the case of our English 102 classes, the social-discursive nature of our conception of network expertise caused us to take a more critical look at the grading artifacts we used. In nearly every case, the kinds of grading artifacts we might have listed in the "grading artifacts" quadrant of our heuristic called for grade judgments to be based on discrete units of carefully packaged discourse. A timed essay examination, a summary of an article from an academic journal, a review essay—all of these left out the kind of messy metadiscourse that, according to Geisler and others, is characteristic of the building of expert knowledge. By looking only at discourse that had been streamlined, in some cases peer-reviewed, commented upon by ourselves, and revised extensively, we would be ignoring a class of discursive activity that is important not only to recognize but to value if our goal is to help writers develop. Put simply, we realized that we needed to make metadiscourse—that messy, unstable written and spoken discourse that surrounds the making of more polished texts—count towards the grades in our courses.

Making metadiscourse count in our writing classes has been a difficult task, a pedagogical goal we still struggle to achieve each time we face a new set of institutional, classroom, and personal constraints. In our English 102 classes, we made progress towards this goal by reconceiving the basic function of the writing portfolio. In Feenberg's terms, we rewrote the technical code underlying portfolios in the context of traditional process pedagogy.

The portfolio, as conceived in process pedagogy, positions the users of that portfolio—both students and teachers—outside the discourse to be evaluated. Further, the portfolio, when seen as a grading technology conceived in the context of process pedagogy, can become a system for the collection and storage of the evaluative material that is meant to represent the writing process of a student. This conception of the portfolio tends to reinforce the idea that expertise in writing can be attributed to an individual, in this case, through the showcasing of multiple samples of that writer's work and/or work in progress. Our problem: as a grading artifact, this portfolio structure eliminates the metadiscursive interaction engaged in by the writer as it isolates an individual's work—the sanctioned "target texts" of the class.

Because we were encouraged to use portfolios, we began to wonder how a portfolio could function differently as a grading artifact if the assumption was made that it should be a site of ongoing negotiation, as opposed to a collection site for completed work. What we developed was a conception of the portfolio as a site where the student and the teacher could engage in an extended, textualized negotiation over grades based on a variety of discursive activities, including the target texts that were the main assignments of the class. Changing the portfolio in our English 102 classrooms involved changing our grading.

When it comes to grading, the idea that an assignment or course grade is, finally, an argument rather than an objective pronouncement of truth is hardly a shocker. While grades, not unlike textbooks, may tend to oversimplify the complexity of the arguments that they seem to stand for or promote, they are certainly not mistaken for absolute truths by the institution. Most universities acknowledge and sanction grades as arguments with elaborate "grade appeal" processes designed to settle differences between students, teachers, parents, and other parties interested in grades. These appeals, treated like lawsuits, usually occur after the semester is over and are nasty, unsatisfying affairs for everyone involved. Our move in rethinking the portfolio for our English 102 classes was to remake the grade appeal process. We decided to make the institution's approach to grades-as-arguments obvious to students, offering them a chance to participate from the beginning in the institutional discussions that shape the way their course grade was to be determined. The process of grading came to be seen, by us as well as our students, as an ongoing process of argument rather than a series of discrete judgments.

One way we found helpful in demystifying this concept of grades-as-arguments was to discuss the "genres," or forms of arguments, surrounding grading (and the certification of experts). We openly discussed the ways grades were supported by claims. Rational, logocentric claims based on fixed standards of proficiency or rates of improvement were discussed along with arguments that questioned these. We encouraged students to identify, critique, and use these kinds of arguments when appropriate. We acknowledged that grade arguments included many voices, not just those in our classrooms but also others representing the university, the State, and a variety of other groups with a stake in the process and/or outcome of grading practices. As instructors, we asked students to articulate their own grade arguments in writing as a way to ensure that they had some measure of control in how their "evidence," that is, their portfolios, were represented. Our responses to these arguments included addressing students' concerns in individual response-memos returned to the students and not simply assigning a letter grade or numerical value to their work. Through the memos, we were able to achieve our goal of continuing and valuing metadiscourse as well as the institution's requirement of "grading" student writers.

The grade argument was one way to capture the metadiscourse we knew surrounded the production of texts in our writing class. It made much of our unspoken (or whispered) expectations about grades, as well as those of our students, explicit. But grade arguments are, themselves, finished documents prepared with a specific purpose in mind, and we noticed that learning to write these arguments was, in our English 102 class, just as important as any of the target texts. We realized that anything prepared for the portfolio (even the ongoing self-analysis tool we called a "process journal," in which students kept track of the types of written and oral interactions which helped to produce their target texts) became "target texts" themselves in the portfolio.

We struggle with the idea that, in shifting the function of the portfolio to a site of negotiation where students represent their efforts in the context of a grade argument, we may simply be asking students to master a more complex genre of writing. What we gain by approaching grading this way, however, is far too valuable to write off that quickly. Before, grading functioned as an extended argument in which students were by and large not involved in critiquing or changing the means by which they were asked to represent themselves. Now, using the portfolio as a site for explicit and direct grade arguments locates students in an active role in the grading process. We could offer many examples of the ways our students were able to make a difference in how we, as teachers, evaluated their work through their grade arguments. The best examples, like the one below, show how students' grade arguments can make a difference not only in their individual grades, but also in how criteria for grades were conceived and enacted in the course.

On an individual level, students were encouraged to engage in a discussion of their grades and the criteria by which they would be determined. When a particular policy or standard appeared to be unfair or, more precisely, insensitive to a particular student's situation, they were able to challenge and change those standards. One student, Jim, a single parent, convincingly argued that the course unfairly privileged students who had access to on-line research resources. Jim's access to the Internet was limited, time and money-wise, by his status as a single parent living off campus. As instructors, we wanted to ensure that students were being introduced to research on the Internet, making it high profile in such assignments as an annotated bibliography. Jim argued that his "research competency"—a curricular goal expressed in the policy statement of the course—was not accurately represented in the document he had produced for the annotated bibliography assignment. Because he had to use a library terminal that had no printer and no access to a word processor, he had not been able to produce a draft of his bibliography according to the standards we had discussed in class. He proposed that his research competency be measured in another way: an oral presentation. He agreed to turn in the original draft of his bibliography and his presentation notes in his portfolio and to reserve a computer that could be brought to our classroom for his presentation. Jim's solution was an effective argument not only because it was part of an extended course argument that earned him an A, but also because it caused us to reexamine the curricular goal of "research competency" and how that could be displayed and/or measured appropriately in a writing course.

As you can see, we still had to deal with the institutional obligation to place grades on students' writing projects. However, putting final grades on individual projects no longer made sense in the context of the grade arguments. If the portfolio were to function as a site where an ongoing grade argument would be carried out, then the meaning of an individual project within that argument could change as the semester progressed. We tried to accommodate this possibility by asking students to write grade arguments in reference to their overall course grade, not an assignment grade. Students turned in the portfolios four times, each time making a case for their overall course grade based on the work they had done. This change allowed a chance to contextualize the discussions of grades by invoking our stated instructional goals for the class, the impact of previous grade arguments on future ones, and the interplay of grade arguments based on progress over time vs. those based on preestablished standards of proficiency.

This contextualization, in our experience, is usually confined to end-of-semester conferences when students are upset about their course grades. Significantly, the process of official grade appeals requires these kinds of grade arguments but only as a result of what is usually tremendous miscommunication and bad feelings between teachers and students. The separation of grades from individual writing assignments, for us, made the grade appeal process up-front—even congenial—and it provided an opportunity for us to actively engage students in expert talk of proficiency standards, evaluation methods, and curricular goals for writing instruction.

Because students turned in portfolios four times, we had a documented grade history to report to our mentor, even though it wasn't based on the assumption that the writing assignments were scored, added together, and computed as a letter or numerical grade. Moreover, our students always knew at any given point in the semester where we, the instructors, stood on their final course grade; they also knew that they could actively influence that grade by engaging in writing and research that would support their case for a better grade. In this way, no single writing performance could be presented as evidence of writing expertise. Instead, students had to show patterns of discursive activity that placed them in the milieu of expert behavior. We found that when they did this, they not only acted like experts, but they produced expert discourse acknowledged by other experts as an important contribution to the knowledge in a particular area of inquiry.

Motivating Expertise Through Grading Practices

Our claim here is not exaggerated for effect. Let us be clear about what we are suggesting. In several cases, our English 102 students came to be seen as experts in the specific areas in which they had been working during the semester. In one case, a group of students researching the effects of political instability on agricultural practices in Haiti participated in an extended debate on this issue over the Internet. After sending email to the list owner, these students were invited to join a scholarly discussion on Haiti. Voluntarily, outside of class, these students dialogued with academic, government, and private sector experts and activists.

As part of their grade arguments, group members included whole threads of conversation in which they had participated and, in several cases, made significant contributions to the knowledge base of the discussion list. For instance, the students' focus on agricultural issues was especially appreciated by the discussion group, which had previously focused almost exclusively on the political activities in Haiti's capital city, Port-Au-Prince. The students' perspectives on Haiti were also influenced by the list participants, and as a result, their final project for the course included a carefully qualified critique of many of the popular media accounts of the political conditions in Haiti. This example demonstrates that concrete results are possible when grading practices position writing as something more complex than discrete units of carefully crafted text and students are invited to participate in the construction of their identities as developing expert writers.

In our focused explorations over the past two years of post-process grading, we have distilled what we see as some of the features of the post-process classroom generally and post-process grading, specifically. First, the post-process classroom lacks foundational theories and a theory/practice relationship that situates practices as the application of theory. Rather, practices within the post-process classroom, including the practice of grading, are characterized by situated, probabilistic reasoning. From this feature of the post-process classroom, we have moved toward using heuristic reasoning to address practices. Second, the post-process classroom is not wholly "other" to the process classroom; process features and practices, including those related to grading, are not eradicated, but revised. We have focused on revising both portfolio assessment as a grading technology and the technical code as it functions within the general skills model of expertise. Third, the post-process classroom pays particular attention to the contextual constructedness of subjectivities, including the construction of teacher and student subjectivities. In relation to grading, this attention to subject construction has led us to conceive of grading as one site where teachers and students construct their subjectivities. This leads to the final feature of the post-process classroom: expertise as a socially, discursively constructed site. Again, this feature directs attention toward grading as one social and discursive site within a network that "maps" expertise. If the teacher/grader begins to conceive of herself as participating in the construction of expertise rather than as an objective evaluator of some individually owned expertise, then the contract between teacher and student changes. The contract requires an engaged and empathic relationship, one that we have concretized in the practice of grade arguments.

Admittedly, the practice of grade arguments can be exhausting. Is this a critique of post-process grading? No. In articles and collegial conversations concerning the topic of grading, we often hear references to "exhaustion." Grading *is* part of the work of teaching, and work *is* often exhausting. However, when our students—even the most resistant to grade arguments—begin to conceive of themselves and participate as "experts," when they leave our classes seeing writing as a social activity worth their energies, the practice of grade arguments is far more invigorating and rewarding than it is exhausting.

Notes

1. Mapping should be considered one of our key strategies for theorizing grading practices within specific contexts. In no way are we implying, though, that we

have included all of the relevant maps for this activity. For instance, we have made institutional structures a focus of our maps. However, we have not considered other crucial maps that can and should be added to our grading practice suggestions. As a crucial example, we have not mapped our racial and gendered positions as white males within the academy. In discussions with other writing teachers, we have seen that the grading practice we developed—grade arguments—assumes a particular positioning within academe. Nevertheless, using mapping to complicate further their own specific social contexts of grading, others have still found our work helpful in reshaping grading for their post-process classrooms.

2. What follows is *not* the heuristic we began with, but rather a broad representation of what we have discovered to be a helpful way to develop, review, and revise our grading practices in both day-to-day situations and in those quarterly/ semesterly situations when we develop grading policies for our classes. More specifically, the heuristic developed out of theorizing our own grading practices as our conceptions of *how* grading functions and *who* can be an expert under what conditions changed. What follows is also *not* an "orthodox theory" to be "applied" situationally. The following works heuristically, to guide situational thinking. Therefore, the impulse to enumerate the heuristic and to follow a regular pattern is highly discouraged. We encourage random, free-floating use of the heuristic, allowing specific conditions to generate various solutions and possibilities.

References

Bizzell, P. 1982. "Cognition, Convention, and Certainty: What We Need to Know About Writing." *Pre/Text* 3 (3): 213–43.

Bruffee, K. 1986. "Social Construction, Language, and the Authority of Knowledge: A Bibliographical Essay." *College English* 48 (8): 773–90.

Carter, M. 1990. "The Idea of Expertise: An Exploration of Cognitive and Social Dimensions of Writing." *CCC* 41 (3): 265–86.

Driskill, L. 1989. "Understanding the Writing Context in Organizations." In *Writing in the Business Professions*, ed. M. Kogen, 125–45. Urbana, IL: NCTE and Association for Business Communications.

Faigley, L. 1992. *Fragments of Rationality: Postmodernity and the Subject of Composition*. Pittsburgh, PA: University of Pittsburgh Press.

Feenberg, A. 1991. *Critical Theory of Technology*. New York: Oxford University Press.

Foucault, M. 1984. "Panopticism." In *The Foucault Reader*, ed. P. Rabinow, 206–13. New York: Pantheon.

Geisler, C. 1994. *Academic Literacy and the Nature of Expertise: Reading, Writing, and Knowing in Academic Philosophy*. Hillsdale, NJ: Lawrence Erlbaum Associates.

Hart-Davidson, B. and T. Peeples. 1995. "Sites of/as Authority: Critique and (Re)Construction of 'Expertise' in First-Year Composition." The Penn State Conference on Rhetoric and Composition (July): University Park, PA.

Kaufer, D. and R. Young. 1993. "Writing in the Content Areas: Some Theoretical Complexities." In *Theory and Practice in the Teaching of Writing: Rethinking the Discipline*, ed. L. Odell, 71–104. Carbondale, IL: Southern Illinois University Press.

Lyne, J. and H. F. Howe. 1990. "The Rhetoric of Expertise: E. O. Wilson and Sociobiology." *Quarterly Journal of Speech* 76: 134–51.

Odell, L. and D. Goswami. 1985. *Writing in Nonacademic Settings*. New York: Guilford Press.

Schön, D. 1983. *The Reflective Practitioner: How Professionals Think in Action*. New York: Basic Books.

Sosnoski, J. 1994. *Token Professionals and Master Critics: A Critique of Orthodoxy in Literary Studies*. Albany, NY: State University of New York Press.

Chapter Seven

Taking Students to Task
Grading as a Collaborative Engine

William Dolphin

Before coming to teaching, William Dolphin spent a decade as a professional writer and editor. This experience has led him to attempt to design classroom experiences that mimic as many aspects of "real-world" writing as possible—which, he is quick to add, is not to say that writing for evaluation by an instructor is not "real." More than 40 percent of the students at San Francisco State come from nonnative-speaking backgrounds; in fact, encountering nineteen-year-old students for whom English is a fifth language is usual, as is facing a class in which no more than two of any ethnicity or national background exist. While most of the students might in some way be identified as marginalized, Dolphin tries instead to make them the center, to convince them that there is work here for them to do and it is work they can, and must, define. He does so because many of them will not survive in the university: only 25 percent of those students in need of remedial writing instruction typically graduate.

From the rush for Sierra gold to the explosion of Silicon Valley, San Francisco has attracted immigrants with the promise of new opportunities. As the city's premier university, San Francisco State has faced the challenge of making good on that promise by developing innovative approaches to the education of a richly diverse population. And with more than 40 percent of the university's students currently coming from nonnative-speaking backgrounds, the English Department is expected to play a key role. It offers a rigorous general writing program for all students, plus two levels of reading and writing remediation and an extensive English-as-a-Second-Language track. Forty-three percent of incoming first-year students are assessed as unprepared to begin college-level English classes—although the vast majority have graduated in the top half of their high school class—and must pass either one or two semesters of basic writing before beginning the two semesters of college composition required for a bachelor's degree. Designing curricula that allow all a chance for success is a particular challenge in such a setting—only 25 percent of those assigned to basic writing courses will graduate—but the rewards are equally great.

While the NCTE's 1993 resolution, which "encourag[es] teachers to refrain as much as possible from using grades to evaluate and respond to student writing," has impacted my approach to grading in the classroom, the "real world" writing class I describe here is primarily an outgrowth of thinking about the roles and relationships of the classroom. Working with social-constructivist accounts of language and empirical research into effective teaching techniques, I became fixated on the problem of student engagement and collaborative construction of knowledge. Particularly influenced by Kenneth Burke's positing that human vocabularies carry with them "terministic screens" that establish the ranges of not just utterable possibility but perceptions themselves (1966), I see special significance in the work of the language arts classroom, for the language practices students learn will affect not just their careers as students, or even writers, but their very sense of the world and their place in it. Influenced as well by the critical pedagogies of Paulo Freire (1970, 1987), H. A. Giroux (1985, 1988, 1991), and bell hooks (1989), who challenge us teachers to truly listen to our students, to engage in a dialogue with them about their lives and ours so that we may together more fully engage the knowledge-making process that defines human progress, I try to enter the classroom eager to learn myself, to be open to the experience, language, and thoughts of my students. In short, I try to arrive ready to communicate, to dialogue, to model the risk-taking we teachers routinely ask of students. Such a vision of teacher-student relations implies that such issues as sentence mechanics and syntactic maturity are subsumed within the communicative process, that there is little point in quibbling over details of usage if students don't have something meaningful to write, and that effective essay-writing requires the genuine desire to argue. For without something meaningful to say and someone real to say it to, few are likely to muster the courage and determination necessary for effective writing, much less the patience for careful editing.

Creating a need to write would seem to be the first step toward a responsive pedagogy for composition. What I initially had in mind was an inquiry-based class with thematically connected writing assignments that were accessible to all and modeled the methodologies of the human sciences. What I struck upon was making the subject of grades—a point of guaranteed commonalty for even highly diverse classes—the initial topic of inquiry, with the goal of arriving at a consensus within the class on a collaboratively written grading policy. In so doing, students analyze personal experience and its relation to institutional issues while working toward consensus on a critical component of the class. Consensus-building entails significant debate predicated on agreement, uniting the class with common purpose, just as purposeful collaborative writing mandates the constructive negotiation of knowledge. But perhaps the most important aspect of this approach is that these are assignments that simply cannot be shirked: writing is students' only way out.

By making grades subject to negotiation—that is, by giving students the authority to negotiate—this curriculum requires students to take responsibility for their part in learning and evaluation. Rather than emphasizing the power of the teacher to fail a student, it demonstrates the student's right to fail—or excel. Instead of lecturing on argument and its possible forms, or theorizing situations that might call for these historical responses, I create a situation that requires clear writing and effective argumentation to resolve.

The first day of class I begin by making clear that this class will be different from most they have had. I hand out the syllabus, asking students to notice that there is no mention of grading on it. I tell them that mine is an inquiry-based classroom, that we will spend the semester inquiring into various topics, and that the first will be their grades. Noting that there is little in the way of consensus within the profession of teaching about how or what to grade, I suggest that they already know that grades can vary widely from class to class, subject to subject, and that there are sometimes good and sometimes bad reasons for those differences. I make clear that as open to negotiation as the grading policy itself is, the basic structure of the class is not. It is also only fair to note that student reaction is, at this initial stage, much as one might expect, ranging from mild incredulity to stunned disbelief. In addition, I tell them that there is no text in this class, that together we will create it, and that their initial assignments are designed to collect the data, which will then be responded to and analyzed. From this they will each present for discussion their recommendations for the class, followed by extensive group discussion, culminating in consensus agreement and the collaborative drafting of the agreed-upon policy. I tell them that we will work through this problem as quickly as is reasonable but that there is no time line for completion. (From my experience, five weeks is about the fastest outcome one might hope for, with six being a reasonable target.)

The first assignment, given the first day and due the next class, is an essay about their best experience with grades, in any class. I return their essays as promptly as possible, without grades but with as many supportive (and sympathetic) comments as I can muster, particularly in the endnotes. The second assignment is the converse of the first: writing about their worst experience with grades. This assignment tends to draw a wider and more interesting range of responses. Much as Tolstoy noted about happy and unhappy families, while good grading experiences tend to be similar, each bad experience seems to be awful in its own special way, ranging from simple lack of fairness (the cheater who prospers) to the most grotesque forms of humiliation and punitive censure. The third assignment requires them to fantasize, to imagine a writing class with no constraints of any kind. How, in a world without restriction, would they ideally be graded and why? I suggest that in considering this question they would do well to consider what they had identified as good and bad in the evaluative experience, that those elements might influence their choices and support them. Importantly, they need to present their positions as clearly as possible, supporting their ideas with evidence from our discussion and their two previous essays. To move from twenty-five separate opinions to a unified one, we identify recurring themes and points of commonalty in their texts. Their subsequent assignment is to categorize the opinions expressed, indicating their own points of agreement and disagreement, and to propose their own whole-class solution. Because this is a new situation for most all of them, my input on both the subject of grading and the process of decision-making tends to carry significant weight. Although I tell them at the onset that one of the outcomes for the process may be that they cannot reach agreement on how they should be graded and subsequently hand the responsibility entirely back to me, many students can be counted on to provide leadership (and I tell them they should), prodding their more recalcitrant classmates to take advantage of what they clearly see as an opportunity. I also enlist the aid of time and impatience, making clear that it is of no real consequence to me if they take all semester to reach agreement, or never do; but that they will miss out on the opportunity to move on to other topics.

When we get to the point of considering what an actual, collaborative statement of a grading policy looks like, I talk a bit about how authority is constituted in texts, considering closely rhetorical situations and the creation of authority, with a focus on texts that play a formative role in self-constituting communities: the mission statement of the university, the constitution of the student government, the city charter, the state constitution, for example. Each group of five or six students is assigned a section of the grading policy to write; when finished, I compile the sections into a neatly typed and formatted document, one copy of which I bring to class. At this point I acknowledge the significance of their accomplishment by having a modest signing ceremony in which they each come to a table to affix their signatures. The historical similarities are lost on no one. As a faculty colleague who observed some of the strenuous student debates on this topic remarked, the U.S. constitutional conference of 1788 must have resembled this class. But as easily as a connection to America's revolutionary past may be drawn, the students' agreed-upon grading policies are surprisingly conservative, focused almost exclusively on the instructor's professional assessment of their written work. One student explains why in the anonymous, semester-end evaluations:

I always thought that if a class was given such an opportunity, they would take advantage of it and say A's for everyone! Our English 114 class, however, reacted quite differently. The sentiment among the class was more like Well, this is a great opportunity for us to express our desires and develop a system that is fair and satisfies everyone.

Devising a grading scheme that is fair tends to be the chief concern of all participants. By and large, they think very carefully about how to provide equal opportunity, given the range of backgrounds and abilities in the class. The issue of native vs. nonnative speakers, for instance, comes to the foreground rather quickly here, with the native speakers protesting that a grading system based solely on an objective evaluation of fluency would make it impossible for those of other backgrounds to achieve a good grade, regardless of effort or improvement. Intriguingly, students, regardless of background or relative strengths as writers, tend to individually ask for grading schemes that are the least skewed toward their strengths. What may be at work is the belief that a good grade is not just high but earned, a genuine measure of effort and accomplishment. Whether the grading policy a class arrives at guarantees that worth or not is, of course, impossible to really say. But the process of arriving at it is indisputably a struggle in its own right, one that gives the class a sense of accomplishment beyond the technical merits of the policy or document itself.

And with everyone invested in the solution, the level of engagement with the class can be startling. While they know that they are only required to produce a limited number of pages to satisfy the basic requirements of the course (the state and university mandate that each student complete eight essays in the course of the sixteen-week semester, for a total of at least 6,000 words), by midpoint in the semester a substantial portion of the class can be counted on to produce papers that consistently exceed the assignment in length and development, a sign that many do in fact come to engage the writing process on its own terms. Likewise, the communicative aspect of this approach works its way into the students' writing processes: even when I no longer require it, many students will ask to distribute their own essays and read their classmates' because, as they say, they want to hear what the others have to say and they want be heard themselves.

This sense of unity the class acquired is all the more noteworthy because the first-year composition class in which this experimental curriculum was first taught, and from which the student comment above was drawn, was comprised of students whose backgrounds included Chinese, Vietnamese, Cambodian, Laotian, Guatemalan, Salvadoran, Honduran, Mexican, Filipino, Farsi, Irish, Italian, and African-American heritages. As one remarked, they could have been a poster for the United Nations. And not surprisingly, many expressed skepticism that they could work together on anything. But together they succeeded: on the last day, all twenty-five of the original twenty-five students in that 8:00 A.M. section were present with completed portfolios in hand. And not only did all complete the class successfully—grappling with their own beliefs and experiences, contributing to the accomplishment of the group objective, and fully meeting the terms agreed to by the class—but the communication they established across cultures, their unity of purpose in the face of disagreement, was an achievement of its own.

References

Burke, K. 1966. *Language as Symbolic Action: Essays on Life, Literature and Method.* Berkeley: University of California Press.

Freire, P. 1970. *Pedagogy of the Oppressed.* New York: Continuum.

Freire, P., with D. Macedo. 1987. *Literacy: Reading the Word and the World.* New York: Bergin & Garvey.

Giroux, H. A. 1988. *Teachers as Intellectuals.* South Hadley, MA: Bergin & Garvey.

—. 1991. "Postmodernism as Border Pedagogy." In *Postmodernism, Feminism, and Cultural Politics*, ed. H. A. Giroux, 217–56. Albany, NY: State University of New York Press.

Giroux, H. A. and S. Arnowitz. 1985. *Education Under Siege.* South Hadley, MA: Bergin & Garvey.

hooks, b. 1989. *Talking Back: Thinking Feminist, Thinking Black.* Boston: South End Press.

NCTE. 1994. "NCTE Members Pass Resolution on Grading and Teaching Tolerance." *The Council Chronicle* 3 February.

Chapter Eight

Grading from a "No Curve" Pedagogy

Juan F. Flores

Juan F. Flores is an assistant professor at Del Mar Community College, a largely Hispanic-serving two-year school in South Texas. In this personal essay, he responds to Peeples and Hart-Davidson's and Dolphin's notion of incorporating context-specific conditions into grading practices. Flores agrees that grading must be context-specific and emphasizes that questions about grading must be couched in consideration of students' culture, class, and gender. He also argues that grading on a bell curve marginalizes students and undermines learning.

In this volume, Peeples and Hart-Davidson and Dolphin (Chapters 6 and 7) suggest that students participate in questions of *how* grading functions in the classroom, *who* can be an expert, and *what* factors should be considered when determining grades. Such a radical position would certainly shake the pillars of the long-established hierarchy at my college and, I am sure, at others. I recall, for example, one colleague who claimed that most of his entering freshman writing students were woefully inadequate to the task of succeeding in college. One hundred and fourteen of them failed or withdrew from his classes that semester, leaving only three who passed with B's or C's. Clearly this teacher, a white upper-class Anglo, had decided the answers to the questions posed in Chapters 6 and 7 before his classes began.

Of the 10,386 students at my community college, 5,359 are Hispanic. Almost four out of five, or 78 percent, have tested below state-mandated standards and require developmental courses. After spending four years at our two-year college, only 10 percent graduate. The typical student is Latina, a single parent, twenty-seven years old, and the first of her family to attend college. At home she speaks the slang mixture of Spanish and English that we in South Texas generally call "Tex-Mex," a kind of spontaneously generated Esperanto sometimes jokingly referred to as "Mocho" by Mexican nationals. As a child, my typical student received no help with the English grammar she brought home from school, nor was she encouraged. Books found about the house generally filled shelves and remained unopened. My typical student is inexperienced in discussions that center on sociopolitical matters, American history, or English literature, or the songs or stories "educated" families use to sharpen their children's minds. Such conversations are as foreign to her as they are to her parents and grandparents, who settled this area long before Texas was divided from Spanish Mexico. The Latina that I teach views herself and others in her cohort as an outcast of mainstream culture. Defeatist images of racial inferiority borrowed from former teachers and other mainstream cultural icons repress her. Stereotypical media images of inescapable third-world poverty, gang affiliation, and assumptions of genetic inferiority are covertly communicated in spite of a mask of "public concern." She diffuses under the assault and borrows elements from the dominant culture in order to survive. Her dark skin, coffee-colored eyes, and high cheek bones, considered "unfortunate" even in her South Texas community, are "infirmities" she cures with bleached-blond hair and blue contact lenses. She has become an American paradox: "You, dear, would be acceptable only if you were completely different than you are." The paradox becomes more distinct set within an academic culture, far removed from her home.

Many teachers within this academic culture customarily grade with a picky-preciseness, as if their students are on trial, guilty before proven innocent. They carefully build their case against them, proving beyond any shadow of doubt that C's, D's, or F's have been objectively assigned and justice dispatched. No matter the color of ink—red for the master, green for the nurturer, blue or black for the color blind—the impact on students is the same. Casualties and fatalities are confirmed when essays are slapped face-down on students' desks. Perhaps learning is demonstrated on the next essay, but the demoralizing consequences of the first disastrous efforts linger and loom larger with time. Even if subsequent essays demonstrate that progress is being made, the consequences of the first failure linger.

Often writing teachers ignore casualties and fatalities by insisting on grading on a bell curve. They do so because they fear their colleagues will disapprove of other ways of grading. Or they believe claims of writers like those of Herrnstein and Murray in *The Bell Curve* about a genetically based cognitive elite. Claims like those bought and sold in *The Bell Curve* degenerate the democratic foundations on which racial and gender cultures can find footing in the educational system.

A frightening outcome of Herrnstein and Murray's correlative studies would be that "the nation would invest society's resources in a few people and forget about the rest. . . . [which is] dangerous, horrible, and horrifying social policy" (Cole 1995, 7). Douglas Massey's (1995) sizzling critique of

Herrnstein and Murray in the *American Journal of Sociology* demonstrates
the methodological foibles of *The Bell Curve*. The inadequacies of the
Herrnstein-Murray hypothesis emerge if we consider the American immigrant history of the shifting "melting pot," including the great migration of
1916. Then we may realize the full-tilt absurdity of a *genetically based* cognitive elite in this country somehow "evolving" in less than two hundred
years. The truth of the matter, one that merits study, is that the roots of the
idea of a cognitive elite are exclusively buried inside "the best money can
buy" educational institutions in our country.

Any basis for *The Bell Curve*'s proposed "cognitive elite" is more fruit-
fully analyzed in terms of socioeconomics, not genetics. The grading factors
that serve my teaching well have nothing to do with I.Q. or genetics but do
consider ethnographics. I find that such subjective measures offer me the
students' past and present: "Where have they been? What do they know, and
where can I help them go?" These are the questions that must be asked concerning how our grading system functions not only in the classroom but also,
ultimately, in their lives. These questions encourage teachers to consider students as an integral part of the answers to such questions as *how* grades
function in the composition classroom, *who* is the expert, and *what* factors
should be considered when determining grades.

In teaching college courses, we should be brave enough to aspire to large
percentages of A's and B's. This can happen only if we are willing and able
to invest the hard work necessary for what I have come to embrace as the
"No Curve" pedagogy. "Your level of excellence is left for you to decide,"
I say to students during my introductions to them. "No Curve" works as a
methodology that liberates our students and encourages dedication and forti-
tude in writing; it creates the possibility that high-quality learning can take
place for a greater quantity of students *qua* individuals.

My work as a South Texas rhetoric and composition teacher involves the
deconstruction of the false images on which minority students have founded
themselves through no choice of their own. They are not genetically predetermined to be working-class fodder; nor are they "dumber" and "lazier" than
whites; nor are they the offspring of an inferior people who seem to have no
place in the world, as the numerous supposed Amerian history and English
literature classes have myopically shown. Therefore, my reading texts are
carefully selected to illustrate issues of culture and class; readings naturally
include historic input from many cultures. I do this not to destroy the Western canon but to enrich it with the souls of women and ethnicities and races
not European who have made contributions worthy of examination. "Inclusion and multiculturalism," writes Barbara Osburg (1995, 14), "have been
the first steps toward a genuine classroom of equity."

An authenticating pedagogy, however, does not stop at mere cultural
inclusion. It also requires the classroom teacher fundamentally to approve of
the student and to allow time for cognitive development for those who need

it most. Though many are aware that the "poison at the center of schooling is the assessment. . . . [of] winners from losers" (Osburg 1995, 14), we too often forget that real teaching goes beyond simple delivery and assessment. It involves give-and-take, what Paulo Freire (1970) calls the liberating pedagogy of dialog.

Evoking students to voice their opinions authenticates their presence and purpose. It includes them in the loci of present events, based on historical threads. As an expression of this philosophy, I incorporate into my classroom curriculum Mary Louise Pratt's (1991) and Patricia Bizzell's (1994) notions of "contact zones," which Bizzell describes as "moments when different groups within society contend for power to interpret what is going on" (167). We discuss and write, for instance, about an eighteenth-century Viceregal painting by José Joaquin Magón depicting racial mixtures. Magón's painting is inscribed, "Spanish father and Mestiza mother produce a Quadroon daughter." In the foreground is a round table between a European husband and his Mestiza wife, who is holding their child. Representations such as this one, lying close to the heart of my students' home culture, inspire students to make thoughtful and provocative written comments like this one:

> Magon purposely divides his painting to show how husband and wife are from different cultures. On the left hand side . . . the man is surrounded by paper, pen, and ink indicating that he was raised to be educated. . . . On the other side, the woman is surrounded by food, flowers, and pottery showing that she was raised in a culture that demands her to be home. . . .

Before any grades are ever given in my writing classroom, though, the student's first lesson is: No piece of writing is ever really finished. Improvement is an ongoing process. I use a simple method that consists of only three marks: C for content, M for mechanics, S for style, along with sweeps of a high-lighter pen and a rubber stamp that reads, "REWRITE." "The student seeking to understand," I say, "like the professional writer, must seek out the problem, not the editor," though I always give some suggestions. Checking the possibilities, considering and reconsidering each suggestion, students revise and submit what has become another "draft." Students are vigorously encouraged to rewrite essays as many times as they can.

Allowing students to rewrite each essay as many times as they choose builds their critical thinking skills. They attempt through trial and error to uncover their own thoughtful meaning, independent of systems that subordinate them with debilitating, codependent directions. This approach to revision through inexplicit directions establishes for my students a sense of being critical contributors. The process of grading multiple revisions is, however, a daunting one for instructors who are teaching five or six classes and likely impossible for those "teaching" casts of thousands.

That students do, in fact, learn from generating multiple revisions should speak eloquently for this approach, since learning, not teaching, is the point of education. Students who want to achieve high grades can work and rewrite until they do. Learning to write well through trial and error is the essential methodology of a process writing course. In the course of learning to succeed, many students are exposed as victims of their own "entity" theories, as paraphrased by Steinberg (1993): "You are born with a certain amount of native ability that determines how smart you are" (52). "I can't write. I can't pass tests; I never could," are the tragic refrains of prisoners of the bell curve. Closed-ended evaluations, defined by time and classification factors either numeric or alphabetic obscure the issue of learning for our writing students. Like Herrnstein and Murray's bell curve, standard closed evaluations are spawned by the perverse politics of administrations that have infected our institutions of higher learning (Wallace and Graves 1995). Meanwhile, as the destructive influences of the bell curve multiply, conscientious teachers, bravely and passionately authenticating human achievement, must steer clear of the carnage of the bell curve and drive learning to the forefront of education.

References

Bizzell, P. 1994. "'Contact Zones' and English Studies." *College English* 56 (2): 163–69.

Cole, N. 1995. "The Herrnstein and Murray Book: A Controversy." *Journal of Teacher Education* 46 (1): 7–9.

Freire, P. 1970. *Pedagogy of the Oppressed.* New York: Seabury Press.

Herrnstein, R. and C. Murray. 1994. *The Bell Curve: Intelligence and Class Structure in American Life.* New York: Free Press.

Massey, D. 1995. "The Bell Curve: Intelligence and Class Structure in American Life." *American Journal of Sociology* 101 (3): 747–53.

Osburg, B. 1995. "Multiple Intelligences: A New Category of Losers." *English Journal* 84 (8): 13–15.

Pratt, M. L. 1991. "Arts of the Contact Zone." *Professions* 91: 33–40.

Steinberg, A. 1993. "When Bright Kids Get Bad Grades." *Education Digest* 58 (8): 51–54.

Wallace, B. and W. Graves. 1995. *Poisoned Apple: The Bell Curve Crisis and How Our Schools Create Mediocrity and Failure.* New York: St. Martin's Press.

Chapter Nine

Dear Teacher
Epistolary Conversations as the Site of Evaluation

Anne Righton Malone and Barbara Tindall

Anne Malone and Barbara Tindall's epistolary conversations on grading began when Malone began research for her dissertation by sitting in on Tindall's first-year writing class at the University of New Hampshire. Although most writing teachers at UNH can trace their teaching commitments back to Don Murray's conference/ process pedagogy, there is no departmentally designed curriculum. Classes are kept to a maximum of twenty-four students, and writing instructors teach two to three courses a semester. UNH students come predominantly from New Hampshire and nearby New England states and represent the top one-third of their high school classes. Approximately 90 percent of the twenty-five hundred first-year students are of traditional age and less than 4 percent are minorities. Malone and Tindall offer epistolary exchanges between student and teacher as a way to bring students into conversations about grading, making grading less an absolute statement of teacher authority and more a socially constructed act of interpretation. This epistolary dialog demands that teachers acknowledge student diversity within the rhetorical act of grading.

Writers do not invent in a vacuum.

Karen Burke LeFevre

Grading essays was easier thirty years ago, or so the story goes. There were scales to follow, criteria to consider, and ultimately grades to give. Recalling the absoluteness of his early grading experiences during the days when no "experienced teacher" had difficulty "slapping an A, B, C, D, or F on a paper," Don Murray (1968) confesses:

> When I first began to teach I was a tough grader, and proud of it. When I had students come before me I slashed red all over the page and was smug about the F's and the D's and the C-'s at the top of the page. I proved to them what they already knew, that I knew a great deal about writing in comparison with them and that I was tough and that they were ignorant. (137)

When the two of us began teaching writing a decade later, it was the notion of grading as a singular moment of teacher-determined fact that we found most problematic. The fault, we argued, lay with an educational system that required us to grade student writing. Working from this stance, we gritted our teeth and reluctantly assigned grades to student papers. Like Peter Elbow (1995), we found that our "first and strongest impulse" was "to be adversarial and fight for the role of the writer against the role of the academic" (73). Thus, when students appeared at our door, paper in hand, to question their grades, we nodded understandingly and cast the ultimate finger of blame at the unfair system of checks and balances that required us to assign grades to often very personal pieces of writing. Although we sought ways to separate the grading and evaluation of student writing from the final products our students created, no matter what direction we turned in this Odyssean search for answers, we were faced with Elbow's warning that as long as we continued to assume the dual role of reader and grader, we would remain sole determiner of "what the student text means" (76).

We explained to anyone who would listen that grades were an inaccurate measure and an unnatural response to student writing. In discussions in staff meetings and at professional conferences, we reiterated our preference for the abolition of grades in English composition courses. Only without the shadow of grades hanging over our shoulders, we contended, would our students be able to write and we be able to respond to their writing. Until such time, however, we conceded that, like taking the spoonful of bitter tasting medicine or like cleaning our office at the end of each semester, IT had to be done. After all, we reminded ourselves, our university required IT, the registrar's office demanded IT, and our students expected IT. Yet, when we turned in our grades at the semester's end, we left the registrar's office feeling that the singularly conceived act of assigning grades left so many things unsaid. As Barbara wrote in a letter at the onset of this epistolary project:

> One of my earliest memories of grading student writing was the day Julie Eastman stormed out of my classroom crying, "But this was the best thing I ever wrote!" I had just handed back Julie's essay with a C+, one of her lowest grades of the semester. Although we had both read the same essay, that day we went away with two very different readings. Furthermore, the

distance between our two readings became the source of pain for Julie and of misinstruction for both of us. Since that time I have learned that grading a student's essay without further understanding that student's reading of that essay can be extraordinarily limiting pedagogically if not downright damaging.

In the past decade, feminist research in composition studies has turned toward finding ways to bridge the gap between things said and unsaid. We authors have followed the lead of Adrienne Rich, Patricia Bizzell, Gesa Kirsch, Joy Ritchie, and others in exploring the implications and limitations of a politics of location. Answering Kirsch and Ritchie's (1995) call "to bring a politics of location to composition research (8)," we have sought to re-vision evaluation and grading in ways that require both teachers and students to "theorize their locations by examining their experiences as reflections of ideology and culture, by reinterpreting their own experiences through the eyes of others, and by recognizing their own split selves, their multiple and often unknowable identities" (8). This essay is the result.

Grading as a Rhetorical Act of Shared Responsibility

As a community, composition teachers have long agreed that student writers need readers; however, we are only beginning to acknowledge C. H. Knoblauch and Lil Brannon's 1984 contention that "responding to student writing is a species of communication, subject, therefore, to the same rhetorical principles that govern other situations" (119). In a similar way, the evaluation and grading of student writing becomes a social (and a rhetorical) act when we invite students to join us in conversations about their writing. As Karen Burke LeFevre (1987) contends in her analysis of invention, writing becomes a social act when writers interact with each other and the texts they read, whether this interaction takes place in the classroom or in the everyday world. When we authors invite students to join us in a semester-long letter-writing exchange about their writing, grading and evaluation become ongoing conversations between teachers and students.

In the rhetorical exchanges this essay describes, students write weekly letters to us and to each other, and we write letters in response. Students write letters to position themselves within the writing community, to accompany their weekly essays, to respond to their conference partners' essays, and to frame their midterm and semester portfolios (see Appendix). Grounded in the belief that grading and evaluating student writing begins the moment students enter the classroom, this semester-long letter-writing project is framed within reader response theory and Ruth Perry's (1984) theory of "mothering the mind." As Knoblauch and Brannon (1984) explain, reader response theory acknowledges that "[r]eadings are always, to a degree, idiosyncratic, dependent on the life-experiences, attitudes, feelings, beliefs, prejudices, which cause individuals to value different things and to construe in different ways" (132). Perry's theory of "mothering the mind" expands on these implications. Emphasizing that there is no singular formula for aiding and abetting another's creation, Perry defines "mothering the mind" as "providing the conditions, both space and support, for explorations that simultaneously take the artist inward and outward" (14).

During the early weeks of the semester, this epistolary exchange provides students with needed support by creating a dialog between writer and reader and linking the act of reading with the act of evaluating and grading student writing. In the same way that these informal letter exchanges can be defined within the framework of Perry's (1984) notion of "mothering the mind," traditional evaluation and grading are defined as "fathering the mind," which Perry defines as "a more insistent, judgmental, and directive exhortation. . . . actually shaping, editing, or directing the composition" (14). She explains this contrast:

> Whereas "fathering" has to do with keeping to the public standard, seeing to it that the rules of a culture are properly internalized, "mothering" probably operates in the early stages of creation, permitting and encouraging the more idiosyncratic tendencies of the art, those aspects done for personal therapeutic reasons, where the purpose is to heal and consolidate the self rather than to do homage to a public tradition. Both functions are necessary, of course: Tradition without private meaning is hollow; and individual expressiveness without a communal context, without an audience, is doomed to extinction. (15)

In addition to providing a framework for our discussions about evaluation and grading, teacher-student exchange adds a third dimension to the process of grading and evaluating student work, combining Perry's theory of "mothering the mind" with the more analytical concept of "fathering the mind," and blending the two so that they are no longer separate, conflictual ways of responding to the same text. Rather than simply requiring that students enter the evaluative conversations in the last weeks of the semester, ongoing student-teacher correspondence requires dialog to begin in the early stages of creation, before students have internalized what they believe to be "the rules of the composition classroom" and before we teachers have assumed our roles as "keepers of the public standard." By asking students to write letters that introduce their essays and by inviting other student readers to give their interpretations of these essays, we are able to begin our own reading through a multidimensional lens. Likewise, as they read our letters to them, students gain a more complete understanding of our response to their writing, both as grader-evaluator and as reader.

What is also significant about the interactive mode of evaluating student writing is that the time we spend writing these narrative responses is comparable to the time we have traditionally spent writing marginal comments on student essays. The introductory letter and several of the others we write during the semester are general letters addressed to the whole class. The move to the personal comes in response to their writing. Although we occasionally write brief marginal comments on their essays, these comments are for the most part incorporated into the narrative of our letters. Thus, these letters mirror conversations we would have with students were they sitting beside us as we read their essays.

In our early letters, we respond to their observations and questions, tell them our own stories of learning to write, give our readings of their essays, and make suggestions for revision. At midterm we return their portfolios with a letter that brings together our mother-teacher and father-teacher voices. Working within Perry's theory of "mothering the mind," we continue to respond to their questions about revision and to tell stories of our own reading and writing experiences. In addition, we also move the conversation to the grading of their work, thus using these epistolary conversations to bridge the gap between the conversations that continue dialog and those that silence. In the midterm letter, we explain the grade we have given their writing, using specific examples from their essays to explain the evaluation, modeling a method of essay evaluation that draws on the text for explanation. These midterm letters allow us to speak both as mother-teacher and as father-teacher, bringing these seemingly conflictual roles together. Not only do these epistolary conversations give us the opportunity to consider the multiplicity of readings for each essay, they also allow our students to more fully understand our multidimensional roles of reader, editor, and grader.

Inviting Students into the Patriarchal Parlor

When we began this epistolary project ten years ago, our first attempt to shift the locus of control was to invite students to share the responsibility of grading by having them include an assessment letter with their final portfolio in which they assessed and graded their work. When we graded their portfolio, we responded by writing customarily marginal comments in epistolary form. In our letter, we commented on their assessment letter and explained their grade as we had determined it. In describing these portfolio exchanges to our colleagues, we acknowledged Knoblauch and Brannon's contention that traditional marginal comments were "essentially a product-centered, evaluative activity resembling literary criticism" designed solely to explain to students why their essays did not "conform to a teacher's Ideal Text" (1984, 123).

Inviting students to join us in grading conversations meant requiring that they become not only "partners in dialog" as James Britton et al. (1975) had urged, but also partners in evaluation. As we read the end-term portfolio letters, we realized students were seldom convinced they had become partners in determining their grades, because they explained in the letters their acceptance of teacher-authority in all grading decisions. As Molly explained in her portfolio letter:

I believe you will grade these essays different from me for one main reason. You are an English teacher and I am not. In other words after reading
hundreds of essays you know what a true A+ is and you know what you
want out of it. Me on the other hand, I graded these by my own progress as
a writer and I did not compare them to anyone else's because I do not think
that is fair or right. I may be wrong but I believe everyone has their own
style of writing and therefore essays cannot be graded with another person's
[essay] in mind.

As we read these letters, we found that students graded their writing very
differently than we did. They often personalized grading, attributing the difference in our assessment of their writing to our stance as teacher and focusing their evaluation not on their written work, but on themselves and what
they had learned from the writing experience. As one student explained, "I
gave myself a B because I have always been a B writer." Other students
defined themselves as "a little below" or "a bit above" average without basing that evaluation on examples from their writing or definitions of what it
meant to be an "average" writer. Still other students based their grades on the
number of hours they had spent writing and rewriting their essays, the care
with which they had followed "the rules," or the fact that they now loved
writing so much that they planned to change their major to English. Reading
these letters, we realized that patriarchal conversations still held sway. If we
planned to invite students to join us in conversations about their writing, we
needed to do more than open the door so they could enter the Burkean par-
lor while their semester grades were being decided.

Parenting the Mind: Wearing Two Hats Comfortably

The impetus for changes in our epistolary exchanges with students was fas-
cination with the stories students told in the letters they wrote to accompany
their portfolios. As we read their letters, we began to understand that there was
much about grading and commenting on student writing that was subjective.
Convinced that students used stories to situate themselves in the writing
classroom, we looked for ways to begin the semester, rather than end it, with
these conversations. Although we initially hoped to discover ways to perma-
nently relegate our grader-evaluator hats to the back shelf, we have discovered
instead that epistolary exchanges allowed us to wear two hats comfortably and
to speak both as mother-teacher and father-teacher. Therefore, by accepting
this multiplicity of roles—roles that from the student's point of view are
always present—we can join the students in conversations about the grading
process. As Barbara explains in her response letter to Molly,

> I'm glad you brought up the idea of comparing yourselves to one another
> when grading. . . . If you knew I gave your conference partner a higher or
> lower grade than I gave you, I'm sure that would have a particular impact

on your work, yourself as a writer, and what you think I thought of you as a person. I agree that it can be very dangerous and perhaps that is what grades do: put all of you on a continuum. People and writing are far too complex to be reduced to a continuum.

By acknowledging in our letters that we understand the difficulty students have in separating themselves from their essay/portfolio grades, we guard not only against reducing grading to a continuum but against leaving students out of the conversation about their writing. Because a letter-writing exchange involves students in a three-way conversation—with their writing teacher, with their writing conference partners, and with themselves—the personal becomes the center point of the evaluation of their writing. This essay discusses the ways that we have sponsored conversations among student writers and between student writers and their writing teachers.

Literacy Letters: Framing Our Conversations

We currently begin each semester by inviting students to join us in conversations about grading. Writing our own introductory letter as a model, we ask students to write a letter in response in which they describe their memories of learning to read and write and explain what they see as their strengths and weaknesses as writers and readers. Students bring these letters to their first writing conference, using them as a way to introduce themselves as writers to us and to their conference partners. These letters shape not only our reading of their essays but also the ways we talk about the essays in subsequent letter conversations, in writing conferences, and in the writing classroom.

Introductory letters also serve as learning experiences for students, many of whom have never before considered what they already know about the grading and evaluation of their writing. Because they create a framework for continuing conversations with students, these letters give us a better understanding of the ways students view themselves as writers and us as evaluators of this writing. In his introductory letter, Joshua compares his fears of writing essays to his fear as a second grader of having to write within the lines. Apparent in Joshua's letter are the standard composition teacher phrases he uses to describe his writing and to define himself as a writer:

> My main weakness is keeping the reader captivated. Most of my writings are personal recollections. They just don't snap readers back and make them say "Whoa." I have a good memory for detail, but my essays need a little more snap, crackle, and pop. I also have an excellent grasp of the English vocabulary which shows in my word choice.

Students tell compelling stories. In their literacy letters students often describe painful experiences of learning to write. A thirty-three-year-old

Inupiaq student who described herself as a C- writer wrote about the Indian boarding school where she was forbidden to speak or write in her native language. Another student described in vivid detail the experience of burning his journals "to keep my father from knowing the truth about me."

Reader-Writer Letters: Discovering the Intersubjective

The process of evaluation begins early in the semester when students write letters to accompany their weekly essays (Appendix). In these letters, written to their conference partners and to us, students communicate what they are attempting to achieve in their essays. They explain any difficulties they may have encountered while drafting the essay, specifying ways they would like their readers to respond. Writing these letters encourages students to apply the skills they are learning in the classroom and to develop the metacognitive skills necessary for assessment. But most importantly, the letters require that writers address readers, that writers acknowledge the possibility that a reader's response can complete the act of writing and give them important feedback for further writing. In requesting and receiving this feedback—and in giving this feedback to their conference partners—students begin to find words to assess and evaluate their own writing.

Prior to the biweekly writing conferences, students exchange essays and letters with their conference partners and write responses. During the early weeks of the semester, these response letters help writers and readers identify the connections and differences in their personal locations. For example, Melinda writes an essay about her acceptance of the practice of arranged marriages in her East Indian heritage and describes her refusal to accept the curfew her mother has placed on her weekend outings; subsequently, she expresses surprise at the contradictory responses she receives in the letters from her two conference partners. Dorie, an eighteen-year-old first-year student from a Boston suburb, tells Melinda she is shocked at the lack of personal freedom afforded Indian women. Sara, twenty-six years old, who emigrated to the United States from Czechoslovakia when she was sixteen, takes a very different position. Sara argues, "I think your parents have every right to be mad at you. They probably were more worried than mad, because it is a crazy world out there. All I know is that this country has *so much* freedom. It is very hard to make the right choices." This discrepancy between the two readings forces Melinda to rethink her position and to come to a more complicated understanding of the impact of a text on its readers.

What Melinda learns about writing is most clearly seen in her comments to the work of another student in the class later in the semester. After reading Edward's essays, she begins to see some of the same problems she has been grappling with in her own writing. In her letter to Edward, she points to this connection in her revision suggestions:

"Now or Never" was a disappointment to me because it didn't have the attention to detail as the other two did. Actually, now that I really had time to think about it, was this particular essay a rush of many feelings you hadn't had a chance to put together before? I ran into that problem in one of my own essays and fixed it by standing back and looking at it objectively. After that I realized the problems I had in the essay. It could be beneficial to you to do the same thing.

As Melinda discovered, ongoing reader-writer conversations provide a written forum for her to return to assessing the development of her writing. For most students, this written commentary offers far more accessible input than verbal conferences. As another student explained, letters are always there to "pour over again and again."

Midterm Letters: Finding Moments of Connection

From this multidialogic letter-writing cycle, we ask students at midterm to compile a portfolio of their work and to write a letter assessing and grading this work. For eight weeks they have participated in discussions about writing and produced the same number of essays and letters. Yet the most fascinating element of teaching writing is the most troubling: No two students have learned the same lessons, and no two students use the same set of standards to grade and evaluate their portfolios. By asking them to write a portfolio letter, we invite them to place their assumptions about grades on the table and to discuss these assumptions with the person who will ultimately be responsible for assigning these grades.

These midterm portfolio letters bring the discussion of grading to the forefront. In contrast to literacy and reader response letters, the midterm portfolio letters require students to describe the writing they have included in their portfolio, state their reasons for making these selections, grade the essay they feel is representative of their best work, and justify that grade. To help them make the transition from reader response letters to evaluative letters, we provide them with questions to consider when writing this letter. We take time during several classes to talk about the purpose these letters will serve.

The letters also allow us to read our curriculum through the eyes of our students. We have learned that for some students, no matter what we do in the classroom, ours is a curriculum of writing rules; for others it is a curriculum of discovery of personal truths; and for others it is a curriculum of pleasing the teacher. Through these letters, we have gained many insights about the various ways students view us and the grading/evaluation process.

Most students use a different set of criteria than we do when grading and evaluating their writing. The justifications students use are often based on the Puritan work ethic and the belief that hard work will bring success. Rather than evaluating their essays, students describe their worthiness to receive a proposed grade. They situate their evaluation within criteria existing outside the text. Students explain their grade using two-part logic: "I should get a good grade on this essay because I worked so hard writing/revising it." As Albert explains in his portfolio letter, "The way I see it, if a student works his heart out trying to get the concept but never does, that to me is worth at least a B." Justifying her contention that she deserves an A-, Bethany explains:

> The whole process I went through to get to the final draft I now have makes me believe that all that work must be worth something, like an A-. . . . I wrote and rewrote the essay four times. . . . The last step I took in trying to perfect my paper was going to the writing center and finding some final assistance there. . . . We spent two hours in total, going over my essays, adding and subtracting different elements of the paper in order to have it reach its final potential.

Students also often base their grade on the response of their peers, justifying their grade by explaining, "Everyone who read it totally related." The difficulty with this argument is that what is being valued is not the text but the experience the text describes. In justifying the grade for her essay, Kate explains, "[My reading partner] could totally relate to my 'plight' and could understand how my relationship with my parents had crumbled just by what I had written. . . . This essay gives a concrete example of how my relations with my Dad (and Mom) have changed since I have been here."

For Fran, response from her peers determines her choice of essays to grade and explains her inability to see the strength in her writing. She includes two essays in her portfolio, one on her attempt to quit smoking, the other on her concerns about her mother's alcoholism. Although from her instructor's perspective, the essay on her mother is more powerful and more complicated in its development, Fran sees it as the weaker of the two essays since "people cannot relate." Therefore, she chooses to evaluate and grade her smoking essay. In her letter she explains, "It's easier to communicate my feelings on [smoking] because everyone can relate one way or another. Not everyone knows what it is like to have an alcoholic mother, and if they do they don't necessarily want to talk about it. I know it's one issue my mother likes to avoid."

Other students evaluate their writing using what one student called "the ten key elements of good writing," thus reducing grading to a checklist of rules. In explaining his choice of essays to grade, Daryl writes, "I have to evaluate 'Remembering McMurphy' over 'The Voice of the Fan' for the simple fact that it sticks to the rules of writing. . . . In my evaluation I believe it is A- work. This is the conclusion I have arrived at after evaluating whether this piece contains certain writing concepts such as focus, lead, idea, interpretation, evidence, flashbacks, and transitional connections to name a few." Using the same argument and the same checklist description, Nicole explains:

> This essay deserves an A because not only is it very powerful but it also catches the reader's attention and it contains all the requirements you gave us. It has a very strong lead, the idea of the relationship with my father is carried throughout the essay, there is a substantial amount of time expansion, there are scenes throughout the entire essay, there are high points where there is a climax followed by reflection and perspective, and there are great flashbacks, good transition, and the ideas of the essay are connected right to the last sentence.

Perhaps the most difficult essay for writing teachers to grade is an essay about an extremely personal experience. Seeing writing as a vehicle for self-discovery, students argue that they have discovered so much about themselves by writing an essay. As Carol writes, "I would give the essays an A and B respectively because they are such strong pieces and are such personal releases from the pain I have encountered in my life. I dove into the essays with an evident idea, then supported each with detail, and eventually I even combated the demon who always looked over my shoulder. I didn't write these essays to hide from my parents. I wrote them for myself as wings to fly away."

These letters offer us ways to step into conversations that begin with students' assessment of their writing. For instance, in Barbara's letter to Fran, she is able to discuss the importance of reader identification and to describe in detail what she sees as the strengths in Fran's essay about her mother. Letters also offer space for moments of connection and encouragement. In the final paragraph of her letter to a student who has struggled with the writing assignments, Barbara writes:

> Telisha, I am pushing you because I want to see you succeed. So often in your writing I see the powerful woman in you, someone who has the courage to take on this frontier, to risk doing the difficult. Other times, I read in your pieces a person who is tired of having to face difficult questions. I would love to see you answer the difficult questions in this piece, for yourself, and for me.

These midterm conversations about grading offer us moments of connection in which we can discuss the writing students included in their portfolios, as well as pieces they have chosen not to include. Because we have their portfolio letter, their literacy letter, and their letters with their conference partner to draw on, we can be specific in our response letters, joining the conversations they have begun, explaining differences and similarities in what we see in their essays, making suggestions for further revision of these essays, and discussing the grade we have given their writing.

Anna: One Student's Navigation
Through Subjective Space

Like many other students in Barbara's first-year writing class, Anna placed highest importance on writing as self-discovery. In her midterm portfolio letter she selected "Ocean View" as her strongest essay, explaining, "[Writing] it helped me so much to accept a situation I was uncomfortable with before." Since emigrating to the United States with her mother and step-father when she was fourteen, Anna had seen her father only during her yearly visits to Germany. The essay explored this long-distance relationship and her anger at her father's apparent indifference. As students often do at midterm, Anna focused her essay evaluation on the extent to which writing the essay has helped her come to terms with her emotions.

From Barbara's perspective, however, Anna's changed perspective was situated less in moments of self-discovery and more in the connections provided by the letter-essay exchange between Anna and her conference partner Natalie. Only a few years younger than Anna's mother, Natalie returned to the university to complete her degree once her two young sons were in school. Barbara read the portfolios of both conference partners before beginning her response, gaining the dual perspective that allowed her to see and to value the conversations in progress. Barbara entered the conversation not by writing traditional marginal comments, but by composing a letter. Barbara wrote to Anna that she was surprised Anna had not mentioned these connections with Natalie in her portfolio letter. Further, Barbara asked Anna to reconsider the impact of the following letter from Natalie:

> Dear Anna
> . . . I am just going to write from my heart about this subject that we have in common. . . . It seems that feelings are universal. Look at how similar the feelings we have are for our fathers. Now looking at that, could it be true of our fathers? Could they also feel cheated and angry because the direction of life's path that caused them the loss of relationship with their daughters? Did they feel afraid to talk to us about their feelings for fear of hurting us or appearing weak? . . . [M]y relationship with my dad actually began when I could understand what parenthood meant . . . and could see that what we think may be the best we can do for our children, may hurt them more than we could know. I saw the reality that my dad was human, not perfect, and I saw the possibility of failing my own children because I, too, am human. I realized that I would hope for understanding and love from my children even if I did fail them. My dad deserved that too. Does yours?

In a move to connect Anna's subjective evaluation of the writing experience with a more objective analysis of the text itself, Barbara encouraged Anna to reconsider the role Natalie (and more specifically Natalie's writing) played in what Anna called "a process of self-discovery." Noting that Anna evaluated only the benefits of self-reflective writing, Barbara asked that she reconsider the impact of text and reader. Urging Anna to revise her essay, Barbara recommended that Anna focus less on listing the litany of reasons for her anger and more on developing a strong text-reader connection. Pointing to the letter exchange between Natalie and Anna, Barbara explained that in the same way that Natalie created an occasion for Anna to respond, Anna needed to create an occasion for her readers to respond. This passion, Barbara explains, needed to be situated not only in Anna's revised understanding of the relationship with her father but also in the essay. Anna's initial response to Barbara's request was anger and disappointment. In her final portfolio, Anna wrote: "When I [handed in the portfolio] I thought I had done a good job. But I was wrong. What seemed like an 'A' essay turned out to be a 'possible A if revised' essay." After her initial negative response to the grade, Anna reread Barbara's letter, first discovering the lens through which Barbara has read and evaluated the essay and then deciding to revise the essay. Explaining this decision in her final portfolio letter, Anna wrote,

> Once again I had to rethink and change things. I agreed and understood most of the comments.... I looked at [the essay] and what was so clear before was now a mess of words, concepts, and ideas.

A central benefit of ongoing letter exchanges between student writers is that it requires students to reconstruct the subjectivity of the writing process. Likewise, the teacher response letters help students and teachers bridge the gap between the private meanings of writing and the public meanings created in the connections between texts and readers. For most students, the strength of the final portfolio is apparent not only in the strategies they have learned for revising their essays, but also in the ways their portfolio letters exemplify their newfound ability to reconceptualize the evaluation process. In her final letter, Anna was able to clearly articulate the ways the letter exchange helped connect her essays with her readers' understandings of these essays. Reflecting on her initial belief that the letter exchange would be "tedious and pointless," Anna explained, "My thoughts were that since the person reading my essay didn't know me and didn't understand me, she probably couldn't give me proper feedback." Anna now acknowledged the role that weekly letters have played in her revised understanding of the relationship not only between herself and her father, but also between a writer and her readers. In her final letter she described this change:

> I had to think about the reader as well [as about myself]. In the beginning of the semester you told us you wanted us to develop a communication system within our group. I believe that system was set up between Natalie and me. It was unbelievable how similar our stories were to each other. The letters showed me a different perspective and a totally different voice. I think writers thrive on variety. Isn't that where the difficulty comes in?

Conclusion and Afterthoughts

Through letter conversations, we have also discovered "a different perspective and a totally different voice" that has allowed us to invite students to join conversations about their grading. From our perspective as teachers, this letter writing exchange has not always made the process of grading easier. It has, however, made the process more honest. For us as writing teachers, such epistolary conversations encourage, in fact, demand, that we be aware of students' diversity and differences and that we acknowledge that grading is a complex, multidimensional rhetorical situation rather than a linear, one-dimensional act of interpretation. Since writing and responding to letters requires that students and teacher work within a socially-constructed framework, space is provided for ongoing dialog between otherwise disparate groups who together inhabit the writing classroom.

Student-teacher epistolary conversations create a powerful dialogic link, clearly acknowledging that the evaluation and grading of student writing is a socially constructed act of interpretation rather than a singularly conceived statement of teacher-fact. As Kirsch and Ritchie (1995) contend, a turn to the personal serves to "challenge and change the conditions that keep oppressive structures in place" (25). With this move to the conversational, evaluation of student writing shifts from its long-held role as an objective, replicable act focused on an authorless, finished product to a process of learning what it means to be citizens in a society of readers and writers. Because a semester of correspondence gives the conversants multidimensional identities, teachers and students alike become multifacted characters in the story that is the writing classroom.

References

Bizzell, P. 1986. "Foundationalism and Anti-Foundationalism in Composition Studies." *Pre/Text* 7: 37–56.

Britton, J., T. Burgess, N. Martin, A. McLeod, and H. Rosen. 1975. *The Development of Writing Abilities*. London: Macmillan.

Elbow, P. 1995. "Being a Writer vs Being an Academic: A Conflict in Goals." *CCC* 46 (1): 72–83.

Kirsch, G. and J. Ritchie. 1995. "Beyond the Personal: Theorizing a Politics of Location in Composition Research." *CCC* 46 (1): 7–29.

Knoblauch, C. H. and L. Brannon. 1984. *Rhetorical Traditions and the Teaching of Writing*. Upper Montclair, NJ: Boynton/Cook.

LeFevre, K. 1987. *Invention as a Social Act.* Carbondale, IL: Southern Illinois University Press.

Murray, D. 1968. *A Writer Teaches Writing: A Practical Method of Teaching Composition*. Boston: Houghton Mifflin.

Perry, R. 1984. "Introduction." In *Mothering the Mind: Twelve Studies of Writers and*

Their Silent Partners, ed. R. Perry and M. Brownley, 3–25. New York: Holmes & Meier.

Rich, A. 1989. "Notes on a Politics of Location." In *Blood, Bread, and Poetry: Selected Prose, 1979–1985*, 210–31. New York: Norton.

Appendix

Dear Folks,

Now that you've finished writing your first draft of an essay, we can begin talking to one another about the ways essays communicate to a reader. For this purpose, you will write two letters each week. The first, a Writer's Letter, will give your conference partners and me your behind-the-scenes thoughts about your essay. The second, a Reader's Letter, written to your conference partner, will explore how reading his or her essay has affected you. More about this in a later handout.

Writing this letter should encourage you to think through what your essay has accomplished and what more you might do with it. And because the commentary will give us, your readers, more insight into you, your topic, and the ways you work, we will be better equipped to give you useful feedback. The thinking required in these letters is probably the most important work you will do all semester: plan to spend a good hour writing them.

The following questions are ones my friends Alice Fogel and Mark Edson ask themselves when they are writing. They are helpful as a springboard to the kinds of thinking I hope to see in your letters. I don't want you to follow them militantly as though they are a checklist for good writing. Apply the questions you feel are most important in your thinking through a draft, those that encourage you to reflect further on your topic and on the quality of your writing.

Questions to Consider for Your Writer's Letter

1. Describe your subject briefly—main points, questions, thoughts you are exploring. Let this conversation with yourself lead you to question #2.

2. What is the main idea, concept, or theme you are exploring? This is not the same as your subject, which is often concrete and easier to say.

3. Where do you state this concept most directly in your essay? Or do you merely suggest this concept? Will you leave the essay this way or will you change it with revision?

4. Describe how your concept expands from specific, personal experience. Is it clear how scenes connect to a more general, less egocentric, insight? Do they create some truth about being human? A good

essay usually gives some kind of instruction for living. How will you refine this in your essay?

5. How do your concrete scenes and examples illustrate your abstract concept? Remember, meaning is an interpretation; scenes don't interpret themselves, unless they are perfectly rendered *and* perfectly read in a perfect world. What changes will you make in your scenes when you revise?

6. How are you turning your experience and insights into literature? Think of specific parts: lead, connections, language, conclusions. The creation of literature from experience is in how the end product differs from reality, not how it reproduces it.

7. What ethical effect does this essay have? How does it affect other people and the way you see the world?

8. How has writing this piece changed you? What new questions might you ask to break through old ways of seeing into something that would surprise even you?

9. What thoughts do you have on how to strengthen this essay? What feedback would you like from us?

Remember, evaluating a piece of writing is an interpretive process. An essay cannot merely be cross-checked with a list of criteria to determine its strengths and weaknesses. Instead, as we evaluate an essay, we are interpreting the complex values we hold about quality writing; we are interpreting the complex ways a reading works on us, the reader; and we are interpreting the ways complex *ideas* work throughout a piece. For this reason, I don't want to hand you a checklist of qualities (e.g., a good essay has focus, makes an insightful point, uses specific detail). We cannot go to an essay and point to *focus* in the same way we can open the refrigerator and pull out a carton of milk. Instead, I am giving you a set of questions that do not yield simple answers but encourage you to interpret the ways you see quality working (or not working) in a piece of writing. The difference between the checklist approach and the Writer's Letter is this: the first leads to "Yes" or "No" answers, and the second leads to essayistic thinking, thinking that attempts to investigate and explore its own assumptions.

Chapter Ten

Demystifying Grading
Creating Student-Owned Evaluation Instruments

Kathleen and James Strickland

James and Kathleen Strickland both teach at Slippery Rock University, located in western Pennsylvania. James teaches first-year writing courses and graduate courses in the teaching of writing and literature; Kathleen teaches Language Arts methods in the College of Education. In order to demystify the grading process for their students, the Stricklands and their colleagues at Slippery Rock involve students in the creation of generative and inductive grading schemes, thereby encouraging self-evaluation and growth as readers and writers.

Let's face it—grades are a flawed creation. From the college student suing a university because he earned all As while studying little (May 1996, A29) to the student threatening to sue "because a professor had chosen not to give grades and she had not dropped a course in which she was a making a grade that would not help her get into medical school" (Driskill 1996), evidence of students' dissatisfaction with grades appears regularly in newspapers, on the nightly news, and, increasingly, in cyberspace. That teachers are dissatisfied with grades is shown by how often we try to fix the design. The faculty at our university, for example, recently debated the virtues of modifying our grading system to include plus and minus grades, one more attempt at fixing a problem that apparently cannot be reasonably repaired. If our faculty actually believed students would be better served by more grades, we could revert to the percentage system—that way they could distribute one hundred of them. Obviously, we don't need more grades; we need to learn how to use evaluation techniques so they are valuable to students and to teachers (and parents and administrators).

We need to admit, finally, how little grades actually tell us. For example, a teacher at a nearby high school had to take an extended sick leave. The substitute followed the teacher's lesson plans and assignments, including homework, papers, and tests. The classroom teacher was out so long that the substitute had to assign grades for the nine-week marking period. When the grades were released, the students and their parents noticed that on-average grades were nearly ten points higher than the previous marking period. Some students and their parents attributed the higher grades to a new-found seriousness on the part of the students. Some believed that the students might have been more motivated and subsequently tried harder, but most suspected that the substitute was either a better teacher or an easier grader. The cynics felt vindicated when in the next marking period, with grades assigned by the classroom teacher, the students returned to their original grade levels. Was it simply a matter of harder grading or tougher standards? No. The classroom teacher graded on a weighted point system: completed homework assignments were each worth five points, papers were worth thirty-five points, and the test accounted for forty-five points. The substitute teacher had graded each task on a 100 percent basis. Homework assignments were each worth 100 (most students did well on the "questions at the end of the reading" type problems), papers were worth 100, and so forth. When the substitute averaged the grades, the students did better. While this particular instance occurred in a high school, its lesson is especially relevant to postsecondary writing courses as well. Many a college writing instructor has experienced colleagues' questioning looks and mild reproach when students who have earned high grades in one writing context earn failing grades in another. (See Agnew and Sandman and Weiser, this collection.)

Traditionally, grades are more a form of reward and punishment than a true evaluation. When asked, many teachers are hard pressed to distinguish evaluation from grading. Evaluation and assessment, terms defined by one's philosophy of learning and teaching, are not interchangeable. Assessment is data; it can come in many forms (checklists of behaviors and evidence of growth; anecdotal notes that help define and describe student performance and attitudes; rubrics; conferences). Yetta Goodman (1996) calls this "kidwatching"; qualitative researchers call it field observation. No matter the form of assessment, its purpose is to collect data or evidence, not to make judgments.

Assessment is an integral part of a constructivist teacher's normal day. Teachers put together assessments gathered during student observation and analyze these data, much the way qualitative researchers do. In doing so, teachers evaluate: that is, they make informed judgments about learning. Evaluation, judgment based on assessments, can be made by the teacher, the student, peers, or a combination of interested involved parties. Evaluation can depend partly on artifacts and products, but the bigger picture, which seeks to describe the learning that has taken place, includes process, effort, etc.

Evaluation is most useful if it is *for* the student, if it helps the student along a path to further learning. One way to share evaluation is through reporting (report cards, student-teacher conferences, parent-teacher conferences). Teachers evaluate student performance based on extensive data. The student looks to a teacher to explain what all the data mean—Where do I go from here; What are my strengths; How can I make it better? Responding to these and other questions posed by students is the responsibility of the teacher. As professionals, teachers arrive at a judgment based on research they've conducted in their classrooms while collecting data. Traditionally, reporting has been done through assigning a letter grade, but a grade can be much more meaningful if the criteria used to make that judgment are clearly understood.

We would like to help teachers demystify the grading process and allow students to understand and to participate in the assessment and evaluation of their progress. As this chapter progresses, we will describe how teachers in a post-process, constructivist classroom can achieve that goal. We will describe how teachers can bring to their classrooms a new understanding of grading and the reciprocal roles of assessment and evaluation. We believe that assessment not only drives instruction, but has as its goal helping students recognize their strengths and needs (Tierney et al. 1991). The purpose of evaluation as an end product of assessment is to assist students in setting attainable goals as determined by their own interests and by the purposes of each course.

What Grades Measure

Grades measure many things and are often more a reflection of a teacher's marking system than a true evaluation of learning. Sometimes a marking system is nothing more than a pragmatic pattern, an objective, organized standard, applied to all students in the class. In a post-process classroom with a constructivist approach to learning, teachers are often frustrated by the attempt to make a system of grading that is based on a behaviorist orientation conform to their belief that grades should demonstrate what learning has taken place.

Grades are often seen as a measure of ability; in fact, grades become ersatz identity markers. Who hasn't heard of people referred to as A students or C students, as if the grade defines for the world who these people are not only in terms of accomplishment but as a definition of their ability for the remainder of their academic lives? Consider, for example, a sophomore student named Renee, who received grades of D's and F's in chemistry. After the first chemistry test, the teacher told the class, "Even a monkey could get 25." Renee got 24. Does this grade help Renee in her growth as a scientist? Does such a grade reflect the teacher's perception of Renee and ultimately

Renee's perception of herself? Obviously, Renee learned to hate chemistry and learned she couldn't do it, being no smarter than a monkey.

Many look to grades as a report of achievement, a finite measurement. Regardless of whether letters or percentages are used, grades measure achievement as a final product, not progress and certainly not process. Students and teachers see each grade as final and regard the next assignment, course, or semester as a new beginning. When viewing grades this way, there is no room for goal-setting or growth. "The sequence of grades a student receives through a semester represents nothing more than a locus of points suggestive of his or her competence at a certain stage of personal development. . . . [Fluctuations] typically result from the crudeness of evaluation, the degrees of student effort on different occasions, the differences of writing task, good or bad luck, and unconscious or intentional shifts in the grader's standards or perceptions of different students" (Knoblauch and Brannon 1984, 165).

Grades also reflect teachers' perceptions of themselves, since they are perceived as "strict" or "easy" in comparison with those with whom they work. Grades can serve as a measure of who a teacher is rather than as an accurate descriptor of a student's accomplishments, achievements, or abilities. Teachers know their A is not the same as an A from someone down the hall or in another department.

Grades are not objective; they reflect a pedagogical stance or philosophy and depend on the teacher's understanding and definition of teaching and learning. No matter the teacher's pedagogical orientation, grading also depends, to some degree, on professional judgment—what used to be called "teacher's intuition." A teacher's judgment is not unlike a medical doctor's. When doctors make professional judgments, they weigh evidence. They look at data and begin putting together pieces of a puzzle, creating a complete picture of a person's health. A teacher's professional judgment, although arguably more subjective than a doctor's, is not arbitrary; it is based on observation, conferences, and artifacts, the research tools that inform judgments about the content area as well as the learning process. Teachers use these assessment tools to get to know their students: their interests and motivations, their strengths and needs. This kind of data gathering drives instruction, allowing teachers to use what students tell them to plan their instruction so that it becomes authentic and purposeful instead of merely satisfying prescribed curricula. If teachers understand what they are trying to evaluate, it will be easier to determine the criteria required to make those judgments. Although we would choose to demystify grading by involving students and others in the process, in the end a teacher's professional judgment is required to make evaluative decisions.

What Are the Alternatives?

When required to assign traditional letter or number grades, post-process teachers must devise systems that do the least harm and help students view grades as part of the learning process. Some teachers employ a contract type of grading system that takes into account effort and accomplishment. Other teachers use checklists, which are discussed and made clear early in the course, that can be checked off by students after they provide evidence of accomplishment. If expectations are shared, then students will be aware of what an A requires. However, no matter what type of assessment and evaluation system is used, post-process teachers encourage students, support them, help them to set personal goals, and provide opportunities for growth.

Generative Evaluation

One way to involve students in their own evaluation is to include them in the process of drawing up the criteria by which the assignment will be evaluated. Over the past few years, we have included students in our college classes in their own evaluation because we believe the primary purpose of evaluation is to help learners perceive strengths and areas of need, regardless of course or grade level. For each assignment, students help to draw up the evaluation instrument, basing it on what they have read and discussed in class. It may take several class periods to help the students develop appropriate rubrics or checklists for their assignments. Even when assignments are open-ended, each product is judged by the criteria developed in common for that assignment. Frequently we include a self-evaluation component with assignments, asking students to complete the evaluation rubric the class developed and turn it in with their assignment. As teachers, we are ultimately responsible for assigning the grade, based on evidence of each element in the rubric. We award points according to whether there was much evidence, some evidence, or no evidence of the predetermined criteria and translate the total into a grade, according to a point spread previously decided by the class as a whole (see Figure 10–1).

As a result of student-owned evaluation, the work turned in is, for the most part, very good and, as best we can tell, a reflection of time spent contemplating the assignment itself without wondering "what the teacher wants." Students worry less about the grade and more about producing something that reflects what they know. Students own their work; they make decisions about topics, purposes, and components of the assignment, based on what they have learned in class. Instead of directing and making all the decisions, we have been able to facilitate student ownership, as post-process teachers do. Although we grade these assignments, we no longer lose sleep wondering if we've been fair.

While we are happy with our experiences with student-generated rubrics, one of our colleagues at Slippery Rock University, Diana Dreyer, was unhappy with the results in her college writing classes. Many of her students came from traditional educational backgrounds where they had "learned" through traditional evaluation that writing is more a matter of "correct" presentation than the communication of thoughts and ideas. Surface features are

Figure 10–1

EVIDENCE

Much	Some	None	
			A. This autobiographical memoir tells a story.
			It has a good opening.
			It has a good middle.
			It has a good ending.
			It flows so it's not choppy.
			It is focused and to the point.
			It has cohesion (holds together well).
			It makes a point.
			It's a story worth telling in the first place.
			It is mostly about the writer.
			B. It is well-written and interesting.
			It has details.
			It has visual description.
			It is imaginative and not boring.
			It is free from grammar/mechanical problems.
			It follows a logical time frame.
			It has character development.
			C. It appeals to me as a reader.
			It is something I can relate to.
			It touched my emotions.
			It seems organized.
			It does not leave out important information.
			It sticks to the point.

the most important aspect of writing for these students. Dreyer has found this attention to presentation to be especially true among her international students who write in English as a second language. (William Dolphin, in this collection, writes of a similar experience with international students.)

To demystify the grading process, Dreyer gave her students topic choice and used rubrics and analytic scales to remind them that content, development, organization, voice, syntax, word choice, and print-code conventions are all important in conveying ideas in written form. At midterm, she used a reflective questionnaire as part of her evaluation to encourage students to consider audience, purpose, invention, and revision, and to become aware of themselves as writers. Among the questions she asked students to respond to are these:

1. Who's your audience for this paper? (No somebodies, anybodies, people who are interested in family, etc.; be precise.)

2. What was the hardest thing for you to do as you drafted and revised this paper?

3. What did you learn from writing this paper—about your writing process and/or your topic?

The questionnaire is one piece of assessment data, collected but ungraded. The reflective nature of the questionnaire prepares the students for an essay Dreyer asks them to write for their final portfolio, one giving specific rationale for the writings chosen to include in their portfolios. She feels pleased, if, by the end of the course, her first-year college writers have learned to value writing for its content and begin paying attention to higher order concerns rather than focusing only on spelling and punctuation.

Inductive Rubrics

Inductive rubrics are another way to involve students in their own evaluation. Neil Cosgrove, a colleague in our English department who teaches first-year writers, asks his students to bring in examples of what they consider good writing. He tells them that this sample can be from their own writing or someone else's, including published writing. The samples are selections taken from a variety of sources: traditional classics ("The Tell-Tale Heart" by Edgar Allan Poe and *The Grapes of Wrath* by John Steinbeck); newspaper stories; advertising copy (the ad for a new Chevy Lumina); popular writers (from Dean Koontz to Maya Angelou); famous speeches (Martin Luther King, Jr.'s "I Have a Dream"); less well know works ("Body Ritual Among the Nacirema" by Horace Miner, *The Ruby Knight: Book Two of the Elenium* by David Eddings, *Emigre #25* by Erik van Blokand, *A Distant Mirror: The Calamitous 14th Century* by Barbara Tuchman, and "Manzanar, U.S.A." by Jeanne Wakatuski Houston). In groups, the students try to articulate what writing traits made each piece of writing "good." As is evident in the students' responses, the groups identify a variety of traits from focus to word choice, from ideas to beginnings, from a variety of sources: anthologies of readings for writers, advertisements, the newspaper, even their own essays (see Appendix). Cosgrove then collects the individual groups' contributions, copies them, and distributes them to the class. Once more in groups, the students formulate a description of the traits of good writing, an inductive rubric, from which Cosgrove develops a class checklist that is used for the grading of their papers:

Characteristics of an A Paper

- The focus of the paper remains clear throughout; moreover, the writer maintains a consistent tone or "voice."
- The writer uses ample details, examples, or other kinds of supporting information that make the paper's ideas persuasive while holding the reader's interest.
- The paper's ideas are connected in a way that makes sense to the reader; paragraphs flow smoothly into each other, in part because clear transitions are employed.
- The style fits the purposes and audiences for the paper, with appropriate word choices and carefully constructed sentences.
- The writer demonstrates a knowledge of standard usage and of the conventions for punctuation and spelling and employs that knowledge to serve the purposes of the paper.

Characteristics of a B Paper

- The writer maintains a consistent tone; some of the reasons for writing are momentarily lost.
- The writing holds interest, but supporting information is somewhat less ample, less relevant, and therefore less persuasive.
- The reader can easily follow the logic that holds the material together; nevertheless, the organization may be commonplace, and it does not propel the reader forward in a seemingly inevitable direction.
- Sentences are structured in a clear but also predictable manner; word choices may be repetitive or not quite the right fit for the purposes or audiences.
- There are a few inadvertent deviations from standard usage or punctuation and spelling conventions, but none that seriously distract the reader from the content.

Characteristics of a C Paper

- The writer loses track of his overall intent and/or his "voice" on occasion.

- Some ideas are supported by adequate examples of other kinds of detail; others are not, and the writer seems unconcerned that the reader will be dissatisfied.

- The governing trait is inconsistency; some ideas are clearly connected, others might be if transitions were employed, while still others may seem "tossed in" to "flesh out" the paper.

- Sentences may be awkwardly or confusingly structured; word choice is characterized by repetitiveness and/or imprecision; clarity has become more of a concern than appropriateness.

- Deviations from standard usage and/or punctuation and spelling conventions are commonplace; a few may distract the reader from the meaning the writing seeks to convey.

Characteristics of a D Paper

- The paper lacks any kind of "hook."
- The paper lacks a clear set of purposes or an identifiable personality or voice.
- There are few supporting details or examples that will serve to make the writer's assertions believable.
- An organizational scheme is not discernible; ideas are tossed on the page in no apparent order, often in one long paragraph.
- The meaning of some sentences is lost, perhaps because of poor grammar or excess verbiage; the writer is struggling to discover meaning, rather than to communicate meaning to a reader.
- Deviations from common usage and accepted conventions are so frequent they are annoying; a reader may be tempted to give up wading through them all.

Because Cosgrove develops a different checklist for each class using his students' actual words and expressions, they understand that they are a part of the evaluation process. Cosgrove's exercise helps the class develop a vocabulary for talking about writing and traits of good writing. Cosgrove believes that through this process his students discover what "good" writing is, and he bases their grade, in part, on those understandings of writing.

Journals

Journals can provide another occasion to involve students in their own evaluation. Since students spend a great deal of time writing journals in language and literature courses, evaluating them is important. Twice a semester, Jim collects his students' journals, reads and comments, and gives the students credit for completing the minimum number of entries and for the length of entries (see Figure 10–2). Counting pages is admittedly the least reflective way to handle journals, and he found that his students were slacking off on the third entry of the week, the one that required them to reflect on the dialog created by the first two entries, until they realized that it "counted." Such thinking is learned from years of school that teach students if it isn't graded, it isn't "serious" work.

Kathleen, however, felt uneasy about grading journal entries; it went against what she believed about writing to learn. Yet the semester she didn't grade them, her students failed to put much effort or thought into that part of the course. Dissatisfied with Jim's number-crunching approach, Kathleen asked her students to design an evaluative system for journals, thinking about the purpose of journals in the course. They decided that points should be given for completion, since the actual commitment to writing is beneficial in and of itself. The students also felt that content should be evaluated, but they were concerned because not all of the readings that they responded to (sometimes as many as forty) were equally interesting and stimulating. Kathleen agreed, partly because she knew she couldn't read, respond to, and evaluate forty responses from every one of her students. The students decided that they would xerox what they believed were their three best entries to be evaluated according to the criteria that defined content—evidence of understanding and theory, and connections to actual experiences (see Figure 10–3). Because students chose what they feel reflects their "best work," they are part of the process of evaluation; they understand that everything "counts" towards their grade, still an important consideration when students decide the relative worth of an assignment. When it comes to deciding whether the criteria have been met, the teacher must still depend on professional judgment, but terms are defined and discussed ahead of time so such judgments are not a mystery.

Conclusion

Teachers will always be required to evaluate student performance, but we continue to believe that "more honest, worthwhile, and humane ways exist to assess than have been employed in traditional classrooms" (Strickland and Strickland 1993, 135). Grading is subjective; it still comes down to a teacher's professional judgement, an evaluation based on continuous and multiple assessments. Teachers in post-process classrooms are not abdicating or abandoning evaluation; they are seeking to demystify it by involving students in the process.

As Elliot Eisner (1992) says, "We need . . . to approach educational evaluation not simply as a way of scoring students, but as a way in which to

Figure 10–2

Journals are to be kept as a matter of routine. Each entry is to be dated and titled. The minimum entry length will be two pages (8.5 x 11 inch looseleaf paper). Anything less will be given partial credit at the instructor's discretio Late work will not be accepted since the purpose of the logs is to track your growth as a learner, and the first two entries are somewhat timely.

Pages	Date	Chapter Assignment from *Subject Is Writing*
	Aug 18	response to 3: Changing as a Writer
	entry #2	response from a classmate
	entry #3	your reflection
	Sept 4	response to 4: That Isn't What We Did
	entry #2	response from a classmate
	entry #3	your reflection
	Sept 11	response to 2: Struggle for Clear Voice
	entry #2	response from a classmate
	entry #3	your reflection
	Sept 18	response to 7: The Computer Changes . . .
	entry #2	response from a classmate
	entry #3	your reflection
	Sept 25	response to 8: Writing as a Tool
	entry #2	response from a classmate
	entry #3	your reflection
	Oct 2	response to 20: How to Get Writing Done
	entry #2	response from a classmate
	entry #3	your reflection
	Oct 9	response to 16: Journeys . . . Journaling
	entry #2	response from a classmate
	entry #3	your reflection
	Each entry dated (4 pts. max)	
	Each entry titled (4 pts. max)	

_____ Total points (50 pts. possible; 2 pts. per entry)
47-50 = A   44-46 = A-   41-43 = B
38-40 = B-   35-37 = C   30-34 = C-

Figure 10-3

A. Credit for completing response to the assigned readings:
   (2 pts possible)
   [18-20] of 20 readings responded to = 2 pts
   [15-17] of 20 readings responded to = 1 pt.
   [fewer than 15] of 20 readings   = 0 pts   _____ pts

B. Consideration of content in the responses:
   (2 pts each; 6 pts possible)

   B1. Evidence of Theory   _____ pts
   B2. Connected to Actual Experience   _____ pts
   B3. Depth of Understanding   _____ pts

                     Total (8 pts possible)   _____ pts

Scale	
Points	Grade
8	A
7	A-
6	B
5	B-
4	C
3	C-

find out how well we and our students are doing in order to do better what we do" (5). Each year post-process teachers continue to help our students to reflect on their learning and their own development as learners. Each year our students help us become better teachers.

References

Beach, R. 1993. *A Teacher's Introduction to Reader-Response Theories.* Urbana, IL: NCTE.

Driskill, L. 1996. "Grades." rhetnt-l@mizzou1.missouri.edu (22 Aug 1996).

Eisner, E. 1992. "The Reality of Reform." *English Leadership Quarterly* (October): 2–5.

Goodman, Y. 1996. *Notes from a Kidwatcher.* Ed. S. Wilde. Portsmouth, NH: Heinemann.

Knoblauch, C. H. and L. Brannon 1984. *Rhetorical Traditions and the Teaching of Writing.* Portsmouth, NH: Boynton/Cook.

May, H. 1996. "Ex-Students Sue Universities over the Quality of Education," *The Chronicle of Higher Education*, 16 August: A29, 32.

Purvis, A., T. Rogers, and A. Soter. 1990. *How Porcupines Make Love II: Teaching a Response-Centered Literature Curriculum*. New York: Longman.

Strickland, K. and J. Strickland. 1993. *Un-covering the Curriculum: Whole language in Secondary and Postsecondary Classrooms*. Portsmouth, NH: Boynton/Cook.

Tierney, R. et al. 1991. *Portfolio Assessment in the Reading-Writing Curriculum*. Norwood, MA: Christopher-Gordon.

Appendix: Traits of "Good Writing" with Examples Offered by Neil Cosgrove's Students

A. Eliciting Emotions—Sarcasm

The whites were going to have a chance to become Galileos and Madame Curies and Edisons and Gauguins, and our boys (girls weren't even in on it) would try to be Jesse Owens and Joe Louises. (from "Graduation" by Maya Angelou)

B. Imagery or Word Pictures—Personification

The man's dead words fell like bricks around the auditorium and too many settled in my belly. (from "Graduation" by Maya Angelou)

C. Maintaining Focus

"I Have a Dream" by Martin Luther King, Jr. In each paragraph from 11 to 18 King makes it evident that he is striving for equality. We are never allowed to forget that is his goal.

D. Style and Content

"Body Ritual Among the Nacirema" by Horace Miner. It has effective style and content. The style reflects a different view of our culture. The content is interesting, in that our culture is depicted as an outsider might perceive it.

E. Word Choice and Sentence Formation

It was awful to be a Negro and have no control over my life. It was brutal to be young and already trained to sit quietly and listen to charges brought against my color with no chance of defense. We should all be dead. I thought I should like to see us all dead, one on top of the other. A pyramid of flesh with the white folks on the bottom, as the broad base, then the Indians with their silly tomahawks and teepees and wigwams and treaties, the Negroes with their mops and recipes and cotton sacks and spirituals sticking out of the mouths. The Dutch children should stumble in their wooden shoes and break their necks. The French should choke to death on the Louisiana Purchase (1803) while silkworms ate all the Chinese with their stupid pigtails. As a species, we were an abomination. All of us. (from "Graduation" by Maya Angelou)

F. Description That Pulls You into a Scene

The tavern was a fairly typical workingman's place with a low beamed ceiling smudged with smoke and with a utilitarian counter across the back. The chairs and benches were scarred, and the sawdust on the floor had not been swept up and replaced for months. (From *The Ruby Knight: Book Two of the Elenium* by David Eddings)

G. Clear Explanation of Unusual, Interesting Idea

Design can be described as the process of traveling around in design space, from controllable into the unexpected and maybe even the uncontrollable. Good design is a clear route out of the expected area of design space. (from *Emigre #25* by Erik van Blokand)

H. Strong, Evocative Opening

Turku, Finland—There was panic. Blood. And then Hannu Seppanen was in the water. He couldn't see anything in the frigid blackness. But he could hear. (from Wire Reports, *Harrisburg Patriot,* October 1, 1994)

I. Suspense and Identification

The "Tell-Tale Heart" by Edgar Allan Poe. Poe keeps you in suspense the whole way through this story. Poe also made you feel like you were the one going through the guilt and he made you remember how it feels when someone is suspicious of you. He makes you feel almost like you are the character in the story.

J. Descriptive Writing

The Grapes of Wrath by John Steinbeck. The author makes use of colorful adjectives and uses some artistic license to hold reader's attention.

K. Ability to Maintain the Element of Surprise

Advertisement for Chevrolet Lumina

L. A Particular Writing Style That the Reader is Partial to; i.e., Fact-Based Novel, Abstract

14,000 Things to Be Happy About. I like it because sometimes I get so sick of my hometown and the little book makes me feel better.

M. Author Is Able to Hold Reader's Attention Because Piece Is Interesting and Informative

Unbelievable rumors trickled into Paris in the first week of December. That the infidel could have crushed the elite of France and Burgundy seemed unimaginable; nevertheless, anxiety mounted. In the absence of official news, the rumor-mongers were imprisoned in the Chatelet and, if convicted of lying, were to be condemned to death by drowning. The King, the Duke of Burgundy, Louis d'Orleans, and Duc de Bar each sent separate envoys speeding to Venice and Hungary to learn news of the crusaders, to find them, deliver letters, and bring back replies. On December 16 trading ships brought news into Venice of the disaster at Nicopolis and of Sigismund's escape, but by Christmas Paris was still without official word. (from *A Distant Mirror: The Calamitous 14th Century* by Barbara Tuchman, excerpt from Chapter 27)

N. Suspense—"Edge of Your Seat" Action

Roy was searching the cars.
Colin sat up, cocked his head.
Another corroded door opened with noisy protest.
Colin could not see anything important through the missing windshield.
He felt caged.
Trapped.
The third door slammed. (from *The Voice of the Night* by Dean R. Koontz)

O. Exact Tone (Despairing)

Dad took us back, staggering, tripping, his head bowed, as if the sadness in his mind weighed more than the monstrous loads he carried at work. When we got near our place dad put me down, saying he could no longer bear my weight. The dust of the world rushed into my eyes. The bad smells of the streets, more intense at my height, crowded my nostrils. Everything I saw drew my spirit away from the world: the poverty and the cracked huts, the naked children with sores and the young women who had accelerated in aging, the men with raw faces and angry eyes. Dad, with his head bowed, like a giant destroyed by the sun, released a profound sigh. (from an African story)

P. Facts—Dates, Historical Moments Recreated

Martin Luther King, Jr. was born on January 15, 1929 in Atlanta, Georgia. He went to Morehouse College and became a Baptist minister in 1948. On August 28, 1963 King gave a speech to approximately 250,000 Americans on the steps of the Lincoln Memorial in Washington, D.C. He was named "Man of the Year" by *Time* in 1964 and in December he won the Nobel Peace Prize.

Q. Details

You see pretty girls on bicycles, chicken yards full of fat pullets, patients back-tilted in dental chairs, lines of laundry, and finally two large blow-ups, the first of a high tower with a search light, against a Sierra backdrop, the next a two-page endsheet showing a wide path that curves among rows of elm trees. White stones border the path, two dogs are following an old woman in gardening clothes as she strolls along. She is in the middle distance, small beneath the trees, beneath the snowy peaks. It is winter. All the elms are bare. The scene is both stark and comforting. This path leads toward one edge of camp, but the wire is out of sight, or out of focus. The tiny woman seems very much at ease. She and her tiny dogs seem almost swallowed by the landscape, or floating in it. (from "Manzanar, U.S.A." by Jeanne Wakatuski Houston)

Chapter Eleven

Grades for Work
Giving Value for Value

James J. Sosnoski

James J. Sosnoski is a professor of English at the University of Illinois at Chicago. At present, he is the Director of eworks, an emerging virtual department, and its Cycles and TicToc projects. Like Peebles and Hart-Davidson, Sosnoski finds the master/ apprentice model of education and the mode of evaluation we have inherited from the nineteenth century obsolete, especially in electronic educational environments. Proposing that we evaluate writing instruction as work, he describes an alternative model of collaborative work and a concomitant mode of evaluation better suited to cyberspace. Students are graded on a pass/fail basis but may petition the faculty to grant them an A on the basis of "real" audience responses to their writing—or work.

In *Contending with Words* (Harkin and Schilb 1991), a collection of postmodern essays on the teaching of writing, I noted that the contributors to the volume had little to say about grades. No surprise that, since grading establishes hierarchies and postmodern thinkers customarily critique hierarchical structures. Though the practice of grading is required, postmodern writing teachers are reluctant to speak about their grading practices lest they seem to contradict themselves. Postmodern thinkers, however, need not be singled out on this account; many teachers avoid talking about grading except to complain about how difficult it is to do. It is probably the least enjoyable task a teacher undertakes, partly because it is so time consuming and partly because it is so perplexing.[1] In addition to the tortures of determining a grade in the face of self-doubt galvanized by the subjective, arbitrary, and imprecise character of the practice, teachers worry that their grading practices might reward compliance over commitment, thereby undermining the enthusiasm for writing they are trying to inspire in their students. Yet as hazardous as grading in print environments is to the psyche of teachers, how much more perplexing it becomes in electronic environments where teacher/student roles characteristically shift. In computer-oriented classrooms, students often teach their teachers. When boundaries of authority blur, grading can become an arbitrary use of power.

Many teachers believe that grading should be a value-for-value tradeoff. Yet as we know from our experiences as teachers, what we value about reading and writing is not necessarily what our students value. Nonetheless, if grades are to be more than measures of compliance, then grading should presuppose a shared set of values. In order to acquire self-understanding as a result of evaluation of their performance, students must first respect the criteria underlying that evaluation. This is not possible unless students and teachers agree upon the values underlying the evaluation—*to some degree*.

If we assume that our students' evaluative values *should* match ours, how do we establish a learning situation in which both parties achieve an exchange of value for value? I believe that such an exchange is possible if we regard reading and writing as work, the work of culture building. In a culture where jobs are scarce, students value learning that prepares them for the job market. Though this motive does not fit well with a nineteenth century rationale for humanistic study that presumes that knowledge is its own reward, a work ethos fits postmodern classrooms, especially virtual classrooms, surprisingly well.

I propose that we evaluate writing instruction as work.[2] In the next section, I indicate how a new teaching situation (educational electronic environments—henceforth EEEs) is making obsolete the master/apprentice model we have inherited. Then I describe an alternative model of collaborative work and a concomitant mode of evaluation better suited to cyberspace. I conclude with a description of the TIES (code name for "*T*eaching in *E*lectronic *S*chools") project to provide an example of evaluating work in EEEs.

EEEs Present a New Evaluation Situation

Since the 1880s teachers have been regarded as specialists in reading and writing, masters or doctors in possession of highly developed skills.[3] Students take courses of instruction to learn how to acquire the skills their teachers possess, and they learn largely by imitating their teachers' writing and reading. Accordingly, the test of students' success is their ability to perform in a manner similar to their teachers'. The heart of this learning system is schooling; that is, placing students in a "preparatory" environment where they practice the skills their teachers model, doing exercises designed to simulate the tasks required in actual work environments.

The "master-apprentice" learning system has a long history. In its earliest form, apprentices imitated their masters' craft on the job in the workplace. As the economy shifted, apprentices were trained in schools, ersatz workplaces conducive to simulating tasks required in the real workplace. In the nineteenth century the rationale for schooling shifted toward the pursuit of knowledge for its own sake. But as professionalization spread, specialists in the branches of knowledge acquired a different social status from workers. As a consequence, for many professionals today knowledge production and work seem to take place in separate spheres. We have inherited an educational system in which students apprentice themselves to masters at sites of schooling and learn their skills through a series of well-planned exercises intended to transmit requisite skill by enforced imitation.

In the last decade of the twentieth century we can anticipate a radical departure from this historical learning system due to the advent of the classrooms without walls we know as cyberspace. As distance learning spreads, classrooms are being virtualized, and this change in site radically changes teaching and learning, as becomes apparent when comparing a virtual classroom whose site is the Internet to a walled classroom on a university campus. If a classroom has a website, anything a teacher or student says is available to anyone on the Internet who visits the site. In such a classroom student writing is automatically published. Unlike print classrooms, virtual ones are constructed during the course of study, creating a public record in the process. The teacher may create a template for the site, but students do the construction. Because constructing sentences (variously encoded) is the work of writing, and writing in hypertexts radically alters the writing situation, EEEs present a new situation to the writing teacher.[4] Let me illustrate this point with two examples.

That the master apprentice relationship is radically altered in virtual classrooms became clear when I taught the teleseminar, "Cultural Turns," with David Downing in 1992. I had to contend with a complex and variegated set of relations with students. Not only did I have to direct students from another university who were not constrained by membership in "my" class, but I had to deal with students who knew more about technology than I did. One student, Michael Wojick, was intimately familiar with VAX and UNIX machines, which were both new to me. From the first day he appeared in my office to the end of the course, he taught me more than I taught him about the technology we were using. It was, from the beginning, a tradeoff. Whereas I introduced him to cultural studies, he introduced me to the intricacies of the VAX mainframe. The master/apprentice model could not be applied to our relationship.

A second aspect of the new learning—collaboration—was brought home to me in "Rhetoric and Cyberspace," another on-line course I taught just as the World Wide Web was exploding on the scene. Two of my students had already become experts in HTML code and hypertext authoring on the web; the rest did not even know how to access the Internet. One of the savvy students, Keith Dorwick, taught us how to compose using HTML code. The learning situation demanded collaboration. The other savvy student, Niki Agurrie, agreed to assist Keith and me in helping the class begin the construction of English department web pages as the course project. Such project-orientations are quite common in computer classrooms and, I would argue, an outgrowth of the ways in which web technology lends itself to collaborative work.

The two teaching scenarios I describe above prompt me to ask the following question: how do I evaluate persons who know more about an aspect of a complex subject than I do? If I evaluate their work solely on the basis of their acquisition of the techniques at *my* command, I discount their valuable expertise, even though it is critical to the tasks we undertake. At the heart of the shift from print environments to EEEs is a shift in the role of the teacher from a master lording it over apprentices to a project director working with collaborators. The tendency toward project-orientation in EEEs presupposes shared commitments and the need to rethink student/teacher relations. Because the collaborative aspect of this new learning situation makes students more than apprentices, traditional ways of evaluating students are less and less adequate to the task. Teachers who continue to think of themselves as masters of a discipline in these complex electronic environments may well place their students in limiting "subject positions." As writing shifts from print to electronic environments, the days when student essays had no consequences (except as confirmations of students' ability to simulate their teachers' practices) may well become a thing of the past. Writing in electronic environments is, after all, work.

EEEs as Public Writing Workplaces

The work of the writing classroom is writing. The moment that writing affects an audience beyond the classroom, it becomes "work" in the same sense that constructing a house is work. On the Internet, as I have earlier suggested, the work accomplished is a publication. If we imagine on-line writing classrooms as publications, then teaching writing takes place in a workplace, a virtual publishing house. But a virtual writing workroom functions somewhat differently from the classrooms to which we are accustomed. In this environment, students are less likely to mimic their teachers. Most importantly, they do not learn by exercises; rather, they learn by publishing their work. As I've implied, the key difference between writing as work and writing as an exercise depends upon the audience. If the audience is the teacher or other students, writing is an exercise, its primary purpose to demonstrate how well students can mimic their teachers' writing skill. When students write to mimic their teachers' skill, they write to obtain a grade, thereby limiting themselves to the position of student.[5]

Furthermore, print-oriented classrooms structured by exercises decontextualize writing. Writing an essay for a class assignment rarely matches the experience of writing an article for publication in a widely read periodical. Writing a memo to other students never quite matches the importance of writing a memo to one's employer. Submitting one's research to a teacher doesn't have the impact of submitting a proposal to a board of directors who have the power to implement it. The examples multiply as quickly as the exercises are named. When you are concerned about the real effects your writing may have, you work harder at it.

Writing needs its workplaces. Like most work, it requires a special kind of space and specific tools. Professionals write on desks, usually sitting, in rooms often designated for that purpose: teachers have studies in their homes; lawyers have offices; researchers write in libraries. Writers use many different tools: pencils, pens, typewriters, pads, notebooks, scrap-paper, computers, terminals, hard drives. Habits of writing are formed in these workplaces. Such writing spaces are habitats; that is, environments where habits of writing are engendered.[6] Though often neglected in the teaching of writing, environments are as crucial to the work of writing as a garage is to the work of repairing a car. Most persons who enjoy their work enjoy their workplace. Many students enjoy their web pages more than their classrooms. Their web spaces are the virtual workplaces where they write in multimedia for the world. One of the advantages of virtual writing spaces is that they are often created by the writers. Making one's workplace comfortable and familiar is something most writers find necessary to their work, and the viability of a workplace often depends upon a commitment to a project.

Web pages are publications. They can and often are read by persons from all over the world. They are the zines—electronic magazines on the Internet—of the postmodern world. And it is not uncommon for web pages to also serve as virtual classrooms. Once educational MOOs (interactive writing sites on the Internet) become WOOs (websites with graphics and audio), virtual classrooms may outnumber physical classrooms. Virtual writing habitats will, like all other sites on the WWW, become publications. Web pages are read and looked at like magazines. That a web site might also be a classroom (a place where "students" meet their "teachers") does not change this fact. And such virtual classrooms can also serve as workplaces. Let me first describe the courses I have taught that lead me to this conclusion.

Courses as Work Projects

I first began thinking about courses as projects in the 70s when I taught a course on "Structuralism and Its Critics" and published several essays co-authored with the seminar participants.[7] This experience led me to structure my courses as projects whenever feasible. My computer-oriented courses, for example, often culminate in a hypertext project, intended to function somewhat like the research paper assignment that caps traditional writing courses. Once I invited students in a first-year class to coauthor a textbook on writing

("Compwrit") that would explain to students who followed how to cope with the course. That course led me to structure an advanced writing course around the production of a booklet, an attractive volume of essays, cartoons, poems, and graphics on Generation X from the perspective of Gen-X students.

In these courses, I organized students as an editorial staff of which I was the Editor-in-Chief. Each student assumed an appropriate role. I felt that this was an appropriate way to conduct the business of the class since all of the tasks of writing are represented by an editorial staff. Our classroom felt like a work environment. Classes often served as staff meetings; group activities formed around staff functions. My experiences in both the seminar and writing courses were positive and encouraged me to continue developing my courses as projects.

Labor Intensive Times: The Work of Writing Cultures

Whatever we might say to administrators to justify our programs, at the most basic level the value of writing is building culture. Texts make up our cultural texture. The WWW is a storehouse of cultural materials. As teachers, we should recognize the excitement students have for writing their cultures in cyberspace, and we should recognize how much writing and reading are valued in the virtual world. Students seem to enjoy building microcultures on the Net. As I argued in "Students as Theorists: Collaborative Hypertextbooks" (1991), I would argue even more forcefully now that we should give our students the opportunity to build the cultures *they value* collaboratively. If we did so, many of our fears about student values would prove groundless. For instance, I believe we would discover that the classics would survive; they have many student advocates. With the WWW as publisher, students will be given the opportunity to be the intellectuals they are capable of being, as they comment on-line on our cultures, including business, sports, and science.

But if this sort of collaborative work is to be made possible, we need to change our ideas about grading. The master/apprentice system of grading makes the master the arbiter of value. In EEEs this system does not work well because often the alleged apprentice is the master. The source of value might be better located as the *culture* the collaborators wish to build. Thereby values are not identified with any one collaborator. In this scheme, cultural value is not an objective property of any set of cultural artifacts but a negotiated goal of a common project to which collaborators contract themselves. The "teacher" is really a "director," since all collaborations require direction but not a "master." From this perspective, work is evaluated on the basis of contributions to building the cultural texture the collaborators agreed to construct, whether it is a zine or a database or a manual.

When collaborators are evaluated in terms of their contribution to a project, grades are in effect a reward for contributing to an overall effort; that is, grades are payment for work. In this model the work is the value being exchanged and the collaborators are the persons who exchange their labor in the construction of a text, a symbolic action, for a symbol of achievement they can parlay into jobs. In this system, as in life, job satisfaction is a personal matter. The exchange of value depends upon a contract to do a specific amount of work for a specific payment of a grade.

The idea of giving a grade as a form of payment does not correspond to the traditional roles we assign to teachers and students. However, as Patricia Harkin (1992) has argued, many contemporary students conceive of grades as commodities they have purchased by paying tuition. We can add that students often perceive their teachers as "salespersons"; that is, as the persons from whom they obtain (purchase by paying for admittance to classes) not only information but also a certificate that they now have that information at their disposal. As Evan Watkins (1989) points out, grades are a form of currency in the sense that they are exchanged for jobs, whether we attribute that value to them or not.

In the culture we inhabit, it is dangerous to romanticize student/teacher relations. Universities have been modeled on corporations since the late nineteenth century and they currently operate on business principles in their hiring and firing and funding policies. (See Bleich, this collection, for further discussion of this issue.) Teachers cannot afford to disregard the corporate climate in which they work. Nonetheless, work is a positive phenomenon. To reconsider what we do as teachers with respect to the work that can be accomplished is not a betrayal of our ideals, unless those ideals involve the pursuit of knowledge for its own sake, which is, to my mind, a dubious educational goal, one that we have inherited from nineteenth century rationales for universities and one that is now outmoded.

Work is a cultural value and working on building culture is the value teachers have espoused for centuries. But rather than discuss this issue in abstractions, let's take a concrete and practical look at the consequences of the proposal that we construe grades as payment for the work of making the cultural texture that surrounds us richer by building web sites and similar learning environments.

TIES Projects

In this section I describe an ideal, project-oriented course network, in which several writing courses are joined in the common endeavor to construct an on-line almanac on the Internet that features writing about the locale of the school. "Teaching in Electronic Schools" is the prototype for a curriculum we are developing at University of Illinois, Chicago. What follows is a version of a proposal used in designing UIC's "Reading, Writing, and Enacting Cultures" entry level writing course.[8] After a description of a typical TIES project, I discuss how a work contract can be designed in relation to such a project to provide the basis for the evaluation of student work.

The TIES project I propose links students and faculty from university campuses, as well as persons in the communities neighboring the campuses, to an on-line network.[9] It is designed to improve college-level writing and reading skills through involvement in editorial processes, culminating in the publication on the Internet of an "almanac" written for the benefit of persons living and studying in the area.[10] The fundamental idea of the project is to tie writing instruction at separate university campuses together on-line and link this instruction to the local communities. The instructional problem that TIES addresses is that introductory writing courses are based on artificial exercises directed at imaginary audiences, and, therefore, students tend to write only for their teachers, abandoning what they learn as soon as they are no longer required to write in such "hothouse" environments. The underlying premise in TIES is that students learn and retain more about writing and reading when they write for an identifiable audience and publish what they produce in a habitat conducive to the rituals of writing. With respect to work, TIES resembles programs like Miami University of Ohio's "Laws Hall Associates," where students from the School of Business work on tasks related to local businesses; for example, developing a marketing campaign for a campus restaurant. As an on-line environment (assuming M/WOO technology), TIES is a virtual district in a city where editorial offices, restaurants, and cafes provide an environment that gives flesh and bones to the work of writing.

The publication produced by the TIES project is an on-line almanac devoted to a university community and its neighborhoods.[11] An almanac is an annual reference work on the sites, sports, entertainment, etc. in a given region organized as a calendar of events and featuring "forecasts" or trends. This format provides an opportunity for students to publish an unusual variety of information and forecasts important to persons living in a locale. It can contain any number of entries on trends and tendencies in business, science, and culture, as well as facts relevant to a community. Since its genre is an annotated "calendar," it must be updated at regular intervals, a feature that fits nicely into a semester format. That it is produced on-line makes it, in principle, accessible to anyone and yet quite inexpensive.

The model for the TIES On-line Almanac (henceforth TOA) is the *Chicago Sun-Times Metro Chicago Almanac: Fascinating Facts and Offbeat Offerings About the Windy City* by Don Hasner and Tom McNamee (1993). This volume contains information about everything in Chicago: geography, disasters, weather, sports, movies, music, art, parks, cemeteries, ghosts, famous citizens, pizza parlors, and so on. A similar volume could be done for any university locale and provide an opportunity for students to investigate on-line trends in fashion, music, film, business, science, and so on.

As in the case of the Gen-X project I mentioned earlier, TIES would be organized as the editorial house for TOA.[12] TIES recasts staff members of a composition program presently housed in an English department as the staff of a virtual editorial house whose work it is to publish the almanac. It would be situated in an on-line environment parallel to LinguaMOO at the University of Texas-Dallas. In this virtual set of rooms, staff, including students, would have their offices and decorate them to suit their personalities, freeing students from the regimentation of the conventional classroom. Rather than arrive in a walled room of an on-campus building, students would log on from their homes or dorms and work on TOA. This would require some rather unusual changes in the ways one might think of a composition program. The design of a TIES project presupposes that:

- The traditional classroom arrangements will *not* be used. In the TIES project, students follow a set of tasks, which they do outside of the traditional classroom walls. Further, the arrangement used in the traditional classroom (one teacher in front of twenty-three to twenty-five students two or three times a week for fifty to seventy minutes) gives way in the TIES project to a teacher/student ratio of one to twenty-three in an arrangement in which the teachers function *as a staff* parallel with other technical support and editorial staff.

- The project will be an alternative to the traditional class, permitting students to earn credit hours for freshman writing outside of the traditional classroom.[13] In many respects, TIES might be considered a "proficiency exam" that allows students to bypass the traditional classroom.

- Student admission to the writing staff of TOA parallels admission to a special section of a writing course, such as an honor's section. However, the requirement for admission is not a grade point average but signing a contract to do the work.

- Students and faculty will meet off-line as well as on-line. However, instead of meeting in a traditional classroom, students will have face-to-face encounters via faculty interviews, conferences, editorial meetings, presentations, and so forth in any number of locations.

- TIES staff members are not assigned to a particular group of students but will have contact with virtually all the student "associates" at some time during the semester.

- The grade for successfully publishing essays in TOA is "pass," but can be "upgraded" to an "A" on the basis of client reviews, if the student so petitions the staff.

- Faculty will not have the same functions and responsibilities. For example, some staff will do the technical work so that others who are not knowledgeable about technology will do editorial and support work. In sum, the staff will focus on those aspects of the program that best suit their abilities.

TIES would acquaint students not only with the techniques of writing but also with various on-line programs and facilities. TOA itself would be published on the World Wide Web; communications concerning editing, for instance, would be transmitted via email. In addition, students would post drafts of their work on in-house mail and use Internet search engines, USENET as well as LEXIS/NEXIS, to do research on trends and tendencies. TIES would also acquaint students with various MOOs, library sites, electronic text sources, and bulletin boards and their services.

The TIES project improves writing instruction by giving students hands-on experience with the technologies of writing and reading in a "real world" context. It can also tie into other programs within the university, especially journalism. TIES staff might engage members of their journalism program to publish a print version of TOA. They might also coordinate with their technical writing staff when they work out formats, protocols, and guides to procedures, etc. Further, they can coordinate help files with Computer Services. The forecasting dimension of TOA ties in nicely with other disciplinary programs within universities. TOA reporters might take courses in which their contributions would satisfy the requirements of a sociology, economics, or even chemistry course. Of course, one of the most important ties would be to businesses and services within the local communities. Any number of ties could be established—e.g., with a travel agency on trends in vacationing, with a local pharmacy on trends in the prescription of various medications for lowering cholesterol, and so on. Another important tie in would be with the Alumni and Recruitment offices at universities housing TIES On-line Almanacs. If done well, the Almanac could be an excellent public relations source and recruitment tool for any university (note the advocacy of the Windy City in the *Metro Chicago Almanac,* 1993), since it could be accessed by high school students, their parents, and alumni interested in host campuses.[14]

Most of all, TIES would provide a rich realistic environment for writing so that its habitués might acquire the habit of self-motivated writing as an intellectual passion. One of the benefits of TIES is that it frees teachers from having to be all things to all students. It also frees students from having always to be students.

TIES Course Requirements

Traditional grading practices are not well-suited to the curriculum described above that features a collaborative project-oriented writing program. To establish such a collaborative and cooperative atmosphere in the learning situation, several protocols need to be stipulated. Since the work to be done is collaborative, these protocols state the course requirements. As friendly as they may seem at first, they are very difficult to foster. Yet it is part of the requirement of the course that contributors to TOA cooperate rather than compete. Also, to foster collaboration, teachers need to learn from their students even though many students expect teachers to be "masters." Here is a typical list of protocols, which I describe on the first day of class in my "Introductory Remarks":

- Since electronic environments, especially those in cyberspace, are quite different from our habitual and familiar ones, try not to bring your usual expectations about course work. Rather, think of yourselves as joining the staff of a magazine where you and a group of other people are working together to publish an issue. In the workplace, there are many tools and devices; some of the staff have used them before and others have not, but everyone is friendly and willing to share what they know.

- Do not think of me as a traditional teacher. Rather consider me a person who has been on the staff for a long time and has published many issues similar to those you are interested in creating. However, try not to assume that I know everything, especially about the technology we will employ to make this issue. I have used many of the technical tools but not all, and some more than others.

- Think of this as a collaborative project, not a competitive nightmare. Everyone benefits by the work of the others in the group.

- Try not to believe that this course is located in Chicago. It is not. It will take place in cyberspace, which is worldwide and virtual.

- Keep in mind that persons in this locale must find what you write helpful. In short, your articles should be publishable. Working together, our group can produce an entire issue.

- Since we are learning about what's on-line, much of the course will be on-line. It's like taking a course in French in which everything is said in French.

- This course is designed as a "collective tutorial." Everyone can take it at his or her own pace. Go as fast or as slow as is comfortable for you. Once you have a beta version of your HTML hypertext, you have finished.

- A semester (14 weeks plus) is more than sufficient time to do everything in the course. Since you can work at your own pace, you should be able to finish this course well before the last week of the semester. Keep in mind that you do not have to keep pace with anyone else. However, also keep in mind that the early tasks are likely to be the most frustrating and time-consuming. As you become more familiar with the environment, the pace picks up dramatically. As a rule of thumb, you should be starting work on your hypertexts by midterm. If you are not, then your pace will not permit you to finish before the semester is over.

Notice that the conventional classroom tends to disappear in TIES. The time it may take students to do the work might not coincide with the beginning and ending dates of the semester, and students might not come to the classroom at a scheduled time. Allowing students and faculty to work in terms of issues rather than dates and being quite flexible about the time it takes to earn credit yields many advantages. But these differences from conventional classrooms raise many questions, too; principal among them are the following three: What is the role of the teacher in TIES? What kind of writing assignments are given? How can students be evaluated in such a "loose" structure?

Let me answer these questions in the order I've enumerated them.

1. What Is the Role of Teachers in TIES?

As I have suggested above, the faculty who comprise the staff of TIES in any given semester would function much as an editorial staff of a major periodical. From a practical point of view, this means that each faculty member works in ways that complement rather than duplicate the work of other teachers. For example, whereas one staff member might act as a support person in technical matters, another might act as an advisor, another as the general editor of TOA, another as copyeditor, and so on. In addition, students would be able to achieve certain ranks within the editorial staff. These achievements could be related to merit (performance specifications) and rewarded in the form of a "promotion." Various positions might be sequenced: a noncontributing reporter whose work went only into the TOA archives, a contributing reporter whose work was published, research staff, copyediting staff, editing staff.[15] TIES relies heavily on sharing skills. Everyone in TIES is designated as teacher because everyone in the project will teach someone. As the semester progresses, students experienced in TIES will instruct less experienced students in the use of writing and reading technologies. Everyone involved functions at some junctures as teacher and at others as student. Thus, the traditional boundaries of teacher/student relations are abandoned in this project because the traditional roles are exchanged.[16]

One of the main concerns about on-line works is that if the staff do not teach in conventional classrooms, they will have much less contact with students. In TIES, the staff will have a range of different relations with all of the students in the program, relations that mirror encounters between a recently hired reporter and the long-established editorial staff of a major periodical. The staff and student reporters will have much contact: in interviews, presentation meetings, conferences on assignments, editorial meetings, and so on. Much of the teacher/student contact would be on-line. Given this combination of off- and on-line contact, teachers in this program will typically have *more* person-to-person contact with students than in conventional classrooms.

2. How Many and What Kinds of Writing Assignments Are Given in TIES?

The number of essays published in TOA has to be calculated based on a teacher/student ratio equivalent to the conventional ratio and the requirements of a given writing program. If the ratio is one teacher to twenty-three to twenty-six students, then two teachers to forty-six students and so on applies in TIES. If 115 students produce three final drafts, then 345 entries in TOA will be required, assuming one entry equals one credit hour. Keeping in mind that some entries are less than a page, this figure easily correlates to the number of separate entries in the *Metropolitan Chicago Almanac,* though the WWW can accommodate many more entries.[17] If three assignments were first submitted as drafts and then revised, then six papers per student would be evaluated.

The editorial staff would assign topics to contributors on the basis of an autobiographical, essay-style résumé, which students would be asked to submit on acceptance to the contributor's staff of TOA. Interviews would follow, during which students would be assigned specific topics. On certain questions, several student contributors might collaborate.

Alternately, a query-line could be set up so that members of the local communities could ask the TOA staff to answer specific questions such as "What is Gopher?" or "Are there any Indian restaurants in the area?" A query-line would be consistent with the dialogical character of Internet discourse and would make TOA interactive with the community it served as well as give it a very personal touch. In many instances, answers to the questions could be addressed to the questioners by name or pseudonym. In such instances, TOA would have the character of a highly personal help column.

3. How Will Grades Be Assigned?

This question has to be answered at each site. The basic grade in TIES should be pass/fail, but this is not always feasible. In principle, grades in TIES are given on the basis of a contract to complete a set of tasks in a specified manner. Even students whose work is not published will receive a passing grade since the course operates in general as a credit/no credit one. If students did not complete the work, they would fail. However, in cases where a client-oriented review process was adopted, in which the readers or users of TOA evaluated the publications, then, upon petition, students might have a "pass" reviewed and instead receive an "A" for their work.

Task-Oriented Assignments

TIES projects have a task-oriented syllabus, unlike a conventional syllabus that lays out a series of assignments that are determined prior to the arrival of students in the classroom. In contrast, a task-oriented curriculum tracks the tasks that lead to the completion of a specific project. For example, log on to a mainframe or UNIX machine, telnet to another university, access a library catalogue, determine if a library holds "X" book. If followed, this sequence of events results in the fulfillment of an assigned task. Such tasks can be sequenced as a series of performances leading up to the publication of an article. In a task-oriented syllabus, each student is assigned specific tasks on a personal syllabus. (See the Appendix for a sample task-oriented syllabus that culminates in a hypertext draft of an article that could be published in TOA). It is possible to ascertain whether or not a given student is doing the work by on-the-spot requests to perform tasks assigned (uploading or downloading files, for instance) or by periodic quizzes if problems of cheating arise. Generally, however, students want to learn how to accomplish these tasks and, if given time and support, will learn to do so.

After students have submitted their articles for publication in TOA, the staff decides which essays are to be published and informs the students of their decision. If a student whose article was not selected feels that it should be published, the article might be circulated to participating subscribers in the local community for their judgment. If they suggested that it would be valuable, then that student would receive an A. Students who did not submit essays on time because they failed to meet the deadlines could receive a C, upgradable to a B if their work got published. Students who did not get the work done would fail the course.

In effect, students would be paid for their work. If they did the work competently and punctually, they would be paid a B. If their work was published, they would receive a bonus, a B+ or, under certain review conditions, an A. If they didn't do the work, they would not be paid.

A Final Anecdote

TIES in not yet fully realized. Whether or not this particular type of course is the wave of the future, many of its features will be. And those features, as I've remarked at length, require us to rethink our evaluation procedures. If my remarks are not convincing, let me offer this final anecdote as evidence:

Recently, I asked a student who was failing one of my courses why he did not hand in his assignments. "I'm too busy learning how to design web

pages," he explained. "There are many jobs advertised for web page designers, and none of them requires a university degree." Though this student was
flunking out of the university, he was using the technology in its computer
labs to learn HTML code so that he could get a better job than English
majors with four-year degrees. While this student's disdain for a university
education might seem short-sighted, he cared less about grades than he did
about being paid for work.

Notes

1. In *Token Professionals* (1994), "Examining Exams" (1993), and "Multivalent Pedagogy" (with David Downing) (1993), I comment extensively on the contra-
dictions inherent in our current grading practices.

2. In numerous ways, literature teachers seem to take a knowledge-for-its-own-
sake attitude toward teaching reading and writing rather than a pragmatic one. Historically, this has disposed members of English department to devalue a work ethos.

3. Clark Kerr (1991), David Russell (1991), James Berlin (1984), and Lau-
rence Veysey (1965) have each made this point in their historical studies of the profession. Russell speaks of changes in education—students were no longer being prepared for only the pulpit or the bar—but in writing instruction (emphasizing writing
as transcribed speech) did not change nor did instruction in writing. Hourigan (1994)
notes that, "From 1969 to 1976 alone, enrollment in the preprofessional programs
grew from 38 to 58 percent. In the words of Clark Kerr, Chairman of the Carnegie
Commission on Higher Education from 1967 to 1980, 'This was the last and conclu-
sive triumph of the Sophists over the Philosophers, of the proponents of the commer-
cial over the defenders of the intellectually essential'" (xiii).

4. The situation is new because of a change in the ratio between articulation
skills and technical skills. In the traditional classroom, articulation skills dominate,
technical aspects of writing are often regarded as relatively trivial matters. In the last
half century, the ratio between articulation and technology has changed dramatically.
At the beginning of the century, pens and pencils constituted writing technology;
through the 60s and 70s, typewriters constituted writing technology; and in the 90s,
computers do (Bolter 1991). The introduction of computer technology into the writing classroom has forever changed the learning situation. Though at first computer-
assisted writing classrooms were laboratories, now in many instances they are virtual
classrooms. Recently, the availability of multimedia computers has shifted our attention from techniques suited to typewritten essays to those suited to the multimedia
hypertexts now proliferating in the cultural scene we call the Internet. These dramatic
changes have altered our teaching situations and call for more complex, more collaborative, and more project-oriented practices.

5. Getting a grade is not the best motivation for learning to write. Retention
becomes a problem. As soon as the reward of a grade is removed, the motive to write
is severely diminished. Unless writing becomes habitual, it fades into the past. Yet,
habits are rarely formed outside of a desire to act that is so strong that the act is
repeated over and over for months. Few writing habits get formed during a semester

or a quarter. After final grades are in, students' personal writing habits tend to reassert themselves. With luck, an improvement or two survive.

6. By a writing habitat I mean the place where a particular kind of writing is typically done. Calling it a "habitat" underscores the fact that writing practices must become habits and that practices are more likely to become habitual when they are situated.

7. "Analyzing 'Araby' as Story and Discourse: A Summary of the MURGE Project (with Rick Barney, James Flavin, Lois Hinrichs, Rachel Kelly, Ruth McMaken, Paul Olubas, Tim Russell, and Diana Uhlman, members of the Miami University Research Group Experiment): *James Joyce Quarterly,* Spring 1981, 237–54.

8. Because we are still in the experimental stage, UIC's "Reading, Writing, and Enacting Cultures" entry level writing course does not implement all of the TIES features in the proposal; e.g., the final product is not an almanac. But student essays will be published in eworks. Also, though the two experimental courses to be offered next fall are coordinated with each other, we are not presently functioning as a staff.

9. I originally drafted the TIES project at Miami University in Ohio. John Heyda, who was the director of Freshman English at the time, strongly supported it, and a group of teachers had agreed to work as a TIES staff. It would have linked Miami's Hamilton and Middletown campuses to the main campus in Oxford. However, the project was not funded. We had requested release time for all the staff because of the time-consuming work of setting up the project. The funding source was largely intended for hardware purchases and our request for release time and no hardware (we purposely wanted to use existing resources) was not looked upon favorably by the awarding committee.

10. The TIES approach to writing/reading has been under development for four years and several "precursor" projects have been written up in professional journals. In "Students as Theorists: Collaborative Hypertext Books" (1991), I describe an experiment undertaken in English 112 in the winter of 1990 in which students created their own textbook. In "A Multivalent Pedagogy for a Multicultural Time" (1993), David Downing and I describe another experiment in the fall of 1992 in which students in English 111 developed their own guide to writing, COMPWRIT, a hypertext help manual published on USENET. COMPWRIT has subsequently been used and imitated at Indiana University of Pennsylvania by David Downing and his colleagues. In "Professing Literature in 2001" (1994), I argued that the problem Gerald Graff identifies as "the lack of connectivity" in university curricula can be reduced by utilizing on-line technologies. Through these pedagogical experiments and others at IUP, especially those in connection with the Cycles project (see "The Protocol of Care in the Cycles Project" [1994] with David Downing), nearly every aspect of the TIES project has already been classroom-tested and theorized. The exception is the "tie in" with a local community.

11. The almanac is a convenient type of publication. The TIES project could be developed with other types.

12. The editorial house would be located in cyberspace. At UIC, it will eventually be an aspect of eworks. In our present plans the essays developed in our experimental courses will be published in a special section of eworks. We also hope to create a WOO; students will be invited to establish their editorial offices there.

13. Since many of the functions a composition teacher performs in the traditional classroom parallel the functions of an editor of a major periodical, students in TIES will experience the same benefits nonetheless.

14. TIES might become a model for other on-line courses in which persons from the community register for courses and interact with their teachers without ever leaving home. On-line courses in Best Sellers or Romance Novels in which a network was established through which members of the local community might share ideas and get professional opinions about the value of the readings as literature might be a fallout of the project.

15. The analogy here is to obtaining a promotion rather than earning a grade. This might add a dimension to student evaluation that corresponds to the "real world."

16. Note: the editorial decision process is separated from the teaching process in TIES as much as possible. Teachers are support personnel who help others learn the technologies of writing and reading.

17. Even paragraphs can be excellent writing assignments if a premium is placed on the quality of the writing. But in the last analysis, such decisions must be made at the discretion of the teacher involved.

18. Up to this point, students can easily be asked to produce textual evidence of their work. For example, if the email message required by the first task does not arrive in the TOA staff mailbox, no questionnaire would be sent to the student and the second task cannot be completed.

19. This sequence of assignments (12–14) is easy to confirm and parallels the traditional submission of a typed and formated essay in response to a given deadline.

References

Berlin, J. A. 1984. *Writing Instruction in Nineteenth-Century American Colleges.* Carbondale, IL: Southern Illinois University Press.

Bolter, D. 1991. *Writing Space: The Computer, Hypertext, and the History of Writing.* Hillsdale, NJ: Lawrence Erlbaum.

Chatman, S. 1978. *Story and Discourse: Narrative Structure in Fiction and Film.* Ithaca, NY: University of Cornell Press.

Harkin, P. 1992. "The Case for Hyper-Gradesheets: A Modest Proposal," with J. Sosnoski. *College English* 54 (1): 22–30.

Hasner, D. and T. McNamee. 1993. *Chicago Sun-Times Metro Chicago Almanac: Fascinating Facts and Offbeat Offerings About the Windy City.* Chicago: Chicago Sun-Times.

Hourigan, M. 1994. *Literacy as Social Exchange.* Albany, NY: State University of New York Press.

Kerr, C. 1991. *The Great Transformation in Higher Education, 1960–1980.* Frontiers in Education Series. Albany, NY: State University of New York Press.

Nelson, T. 1987. *Computer Lib/Dream Machine.* Seattle, WA: Microsoft Press.

Russell, D. 1991. *Writing in the Academic Disciplines, 1870–1990: A Curricular History.* Carbondale, IL: Southern Illinois University Press.

Sosnoski, J. 1981. "Analyzing 'Araby' as Story and Discourse: A Summary of the MURGE Project," with R. Barney, J. Flavin, L. Hinrichs, R. Kelly, R. McMaken, P. Olubas, T. Russell, and D. Uhlman, members of the Miami University Research Group Experiment. *James Joyce Quarterly* (Spring): 237–54.

————. 1991. "Students as Theorists: Collaborative Hypertextbooks." In *Practicing Theory in Introductory College Literature Courses,* ed. J. Calahan and D. Downing. 271–90. Urbana, IL: NCTE.

————. 1993. "Examining Exams." In *Knowledges: Historical and Critical Studies in Disciplinarity,* ed. D. Shumway, D. Sylvan, and E. Messed-Davidow, 305–326. Charlottesville, VA: The University of Virginia Press.

————. 1993. "A Multivalent Pedagogy for a Multicultural Time," with David Downing. *Pre/Text* 14: 307–40.

————. 1994. "Professing Literature in 2001." In *Teaching the Conflicts: Gerald Graff, Curricular Reform, and the Culture Wars.* New York: Garland Publishing.

————. 1994. "The Protocol of Care in the Cycles Project," with David Downing. *Journal of the Midwest Modern Language Association.*

————. 1994. *Token Professionals and Master Critics: A Critique of Orthodoxy in Literary Studies.* Albany, NY: State University of New York Press.

————. 1995. *Modern Skeletons in Postmodern Closets: A Cultural Studies Alternative.* Charlottesville, VA: The University of Virginia Press.

Veysey, L. R. 1965. *The Emergence of the American University.* Chicago: University of Chicago Press.

Watkins, E. 1989. *Work Time: English Departments and the Circulation of Cultural Value.* Stanford, CA: Stanford University Press.

Appendix

1. GET ON-LINE

   First, it is necessary to get "on-line" (obtain an Internet email address). After you have obtained an address, send an email message to the staff indicating that you are on-line and have learned how to send an email message.

2. UPLOAD AND DOWNLOAD A FILE

   Unless you can upload and download files that you create, revise, and proof on your own word processor, your use of email will be severely limited, since on-line editors are gruesome to use. When we receive your first message, we will send you a form to fill out. You will need to download it to disk, respond appropriately, upload it to the mainframe and send it back to us.

3. USE THE TAO LISTSERV
   To communicate among collaborators (the other members of the
   project), we will use a listserv. As soon as you return our questionnaire, we will send you instructions about how to use our listserv
   and a second questionnaire concerning your project, which will ask
   you about the hypertext you wish to author.

4. DECIDE ON YOUR TOPIC AND BEGIN RESEARCHING IT
   Once you have determined what topic you wish to use for your
   hypertext in consultation with the TOA editors, begin your research
   process by submitting the "topic form" you received through the
   listserv to the TOA staff.

5. CREATE A PERSONAL NOTE-TAKING SYSTEM
   Before you begin collecting data for your project, you should give
   careful thought to computerizing your note-taking system. A discussion of how to design note-taking systems will be the inaugural discussion on the listserv. Note: you are required to describe your
   note-taking system on the listserv.

6. USE ON-LINE LIBRARIES
   Once you know your topic/query, you should begin a bibliographic
   search for materials and references suitable to your project in various libraries around the world. (Please include in the first draft of
   your alpha version the text file you captured from your screen or
   downloaded with each search result.)

7. USE INTERNET SEARCH ENGINES
   In addition to library searches, you should use the search engines
   accessible through Web browsers such as Netscape, Internet
   Explorer, Mosaic, and others. (Please include in the first draft of
   your alpha version the text file you captured from your screen or
   downloaded with each search result.)

8. USE THE MLA BIBLIOGRAPHY
   Access the MLA Bibliography either on-line or in the library.
   (Please include in the first draft of your alpha version the text file
   you captured from your screen or downloaded with each search
   result.)

9. USE LEXIS/NEXIS
   LEXIS/NEXIS is an on-line information retrieval service that contains millions of full-text articles and thousands of resource files,
   including newspapers and magazines. It is difficult to use. However,
   there is a tutorial program showing how to use this software. (Please
   include in the first draft of your alpha version the text file you captured from your screen or downloaded with each search result.)

10. USE USENET AND OTHER LISTSERVS
    After your have completed your bibliographic search, you should check the various discussion groups on the Internet to see if any of these discussions might be relevant to your project. (Please include in the first draft of your alpha version the text file you captured from your screen or downloaded with each search result.)

11. COMPILE A BIBLIOGRAPHY FOR YOUR PROJECT[18]

12. LEARN TO CREATE WEB PAGES [OR A HYPERTEXT][19]
    After the workshops on formatting web pages, you will be asked to create a web page specific to your TOA assignment.

13. MAKE AN ALPHA VERSION OF YOUR HYPERTEXT
    Next you will be asked to develop a hypertext version of your article in HTML code.

14. MAKE A BETA VERSION OF YOUR HYPERTEXT
    After you have designed a basic version of your hypertext, you will need to test it on a control group. So, once you have a version that works, you need to submit the beta version to the TOA staff. Once your essay has been reviewed and you have revised it accordingly, then it should be submitted to the Editor-in-Chief and you should begin work on your second article and so on. Submitting three articles concludes your obligation to the working group of TAO.

Afterword
Bearing Repetition: Some Assumptions

It's all true. Grades are the tools of bureaucrats who, even when well intended, cannot help but be servants of the State. Grading undermines the very work we do: the encouragement to suspend completion, to be always open to revision, to see the acquisition of abilities with writing as slow and long-term.

It's all true. We're in a post-writing process, techno-comp classroom where collaboration is key, where what constitutes discourse is being challenged, where students often carry more authority than teachers. Student authority must be recognized, be brought into the construction of assignments, be brought into the construction of assessment criteria, have that assessment, in terms of letter grades, suspended until the end of the semester (or maybe midsemester). It's all true.

I am fortunate. I have worked with people like William Condon and Richard Haswell and Susan Wyche at Washington State University who dedicate themselves to assessment considerations. I work with talented instructors like Anne Maxham-Kastrinos and Michael Delahoyde who carry students to new ways of viewing themselves as writers. But I'm also always working with teachers who are learning to become literary critics of various sorts, who look at their students' papers with eyes trained to trick out Chaucer or Milton (even if with culturally studious, postcolonial lenses)—good folks, loving folks, yet folks who "know" (raising my brows here) an F paper, "know" a plagiarized paper, who wonder why their students "can't read," who figure that exposure to the *Decameron* or *Macbeth* will make them better writers. I am always exposed to teachers of writing who are like dentists who have never had a cavity—oblivious to the pain some (maybe even most) students experience in coming to the new writing environment that is the university.

There are assumptions made in this collection that maybe ought to be spelled out for those new teachers of writing. So let me take these last few pages to explain how the contributors have arrived at their arguments and recommendations. These are the things all of the contributors believe, I believe:[1]

1. Language is ontological and epistemological

The ways in which humans conduct any business—from the most mundane to the most esoteric, scientific, or technological—are founded on our unique ways with language. Other creatures might have and use language, but no other creature has done with language what humans have done with it. The manipulation of symbol systems—language, broadly defined—is uniquely and inherently human. It is ontological. The technology that renders language an artifact to be studied, analyzed, criticized is writing—a precise way (though no science) of ordering thought, of bringing to light muddied emotions and fragments of ideas, maybe even the means to produce ideas. Writing is epistemological, in other words. Here's Aristotle on the matter (forgiving his sexism): "It is absurd to hold that a man ought to be ashamed of being unable to defend himself with his limbs, but not of being unable to defend himself with speech and reason, when the use of rational speech is more distinctive of a human being the use of his limbs" (*Rhetoric* I.i.1355b.1–5).

2. Rhetoric is the root and the business of academic discourse

The admonition that learning to be conscious of our use of language is more our duty than learning to fight physically can be found in Aristotle's *Rhetoric*. That's our business—the uniquely human literary art, rhetoric. This is not to denigrate the study of literature. But literature is specialized (for which Aristotle wrote *Poetics*). Our business as first-year composition teachers must embrace the entire academic discourse community. Rhetoric is founded on Aristotle's notion (and similar notions from others before him and since) that writing is at least epistemological—a way of discovering what goes on within our minds, a way of learning what we think we know and what we're trying to know. Rhetoric is also a way of communicating those discoveries to ourselves and to others. And rhetoric is a means of engaging in the dialectical process—meaning that rhetoric becomes a way of engaging in a two-way (at least) communicative process, an exchange that will further learning. In short, writing is a means of discovery, a means of learning, and a means of communicating something to someone.

3. The dialectic process is basic to academic discourse and thereby basic to a first-year writing course

Writing is considerably more than just a requirement of a university system. But from a most pragmatic position, it is surely that—an academic requirement and an ability required to manipulate complex sets of cognitive and manipulative skills necessary to arrive at products that contain certain characteristics—the voice of objectivity or reasonableness, a clear line of argument, substantiation from prior scholarship or research—following relatively predictable patterns and conventions. Our immediate responsibility is to provide an environment, a set of circumstances, that will encourage students to incorporate new information into existing frameworks of knowledge, to look beyond immediate causes to less apparent antecedents, to communicate these discoveries to others in writing, within the conventions that this institution—the university—finds meaningful and valuable. The means to that end is to discover writing processes and to enter into dialectical exchanges, pressing issues to the point of questioning, not converting students from what we may believe to be wrongheaded, but to provide an environment that will foster critical reconsiderations of the familiar.

The method whereby students might be brought to consider the possibility of changing their minds about "accepted wisdom" is the dialectic. In teaching circles, the best known is Plato's dialectic: the question and answer method known as the Socratic method. Within the academic community, the most revered (apart from the scientific method) is Aristotle's dialectic: disputation, where the aim is to win. But an approach better suited to the aims of first-year composition—foregrounding, questioning, coming, maybe, to the point where teacher and student alike begin to question the familiar, begin to consider the possibility of changing perspectives or of knowing the reasons for maintaining long-held beliefs—results from a careful coupling of several sources that come under the umbrellas of hermeneutics, cultural studies, and critical pedagogy. The approach begins with discovering students' prejudices (as in preconceived notions more than bigotries) and having students discuss the sources of those beliefs within them—discussing them, then researching them, then discussing them (best in writing) yet again. The idea is to look to initial sources of ideas, to question them, to see the political or cultural assumptions present in all things, then to write a critical-documented essay—an opinion, backed by research, presented in a relatively conventional format.

4. Reading is necessary to writing

One way to meet the goals implicit in learning that writing is a process, a process of discovery and learning, assisted by a dialectical classroom dynamic, is through readings. Readings provide students with challenges that heighten their awareness of questions of culture while enriching their academic experience. Although readings should not be intended as models for students to follow, students should be exposed to the conventions they will be required to mimic in some sense.

5. Writing is a process

Ultimately, first-year composition emphasizes awareness of writing as a process—from a process of jotting meaningful marks on a page (even if through a computer monitor), to a process of discovery, to a potential process of change (of the self and of others). All of this adds up to first-year composition as a means of introducing students to ways in which writing is an integral—a crucial—element in their achieving individual educational goals and larger social needs.

4934

6. Responding to student papers is not grading

Immediate feedback to student submissions is critical. That feedback should be judicious. Rules of grammar and correctness are many, so that an inordinate attention to such matters becomes the principal cause of writer's block. Confine marking of errors to about three per paper. Otherwise, responses to student papers should be generative and never abusive. By "generative," I mean the kind of response that might prompt revision: paraphrases of what the student wrote ("Are you saying . . . ?") or alternatives ("Couldn't someone argue . . . ?"). Whatever the tack, the emphasis should be on stimulating revision, not on justifying a grade.

I believe this is what all the contributors to this collection are about: making explicit what is grading and what is responding, reacting to institutional pressures (especially when the reaction is resistance) while remaining faithful to our felt need to have students discover the ways in which writing is itself discovery—the discovery of things felt, experienced, known. We have to remember both our assumptions and our now decades-old and often replicated research about writing as recursive so as to apply recursion to response; or better, to remember that responding to writing is best when the responses take students back to their writing processes. And that means beginning with the things we soon take for granted: that writing is an epistemological process, that the classroom is a political site—and often not the same site that bureaucrats see. The essays in this collection enjoin us to recognize that we are as subject to ideological revision as our students, insofar as the essays remind us of the work grading is supposed to do and the work that responding to student writing is supposed to do. We are enjoined to become part of dialectical enterprises ourselves: with our institutions, with our students' texts, with our students, with our Selves.

Or maybe all I'm trying to say is that we should remain conscious of our relation to and within bureaucratic State apparatuses while going about our responsibility to foster an awareness of writing as individual awareness and as social action.

Victor Villanueva, Jr.
Washington State University

Notes

1. The sources for these assumptions are many and varied—figures from classical rhetoric to Kenneth Burke and Paulo Freire and so much of composition studies for the last thirty years. Beyond those, there is the work of members of the composition staff at Washington State University who helped to compile the document from which the following borrows: Michael Delahoyde, Sue Hallett, Anne Maxham-Kastrinos, Eric Miraglia, and Mada Morgan.